Airshipmen, Businessmen, and Politics

Smithsonian History of Aviation Series

Von Hardesty, Series Editor

On December 17, 1903, on a windy beach in North Carolina, aviation became a reality. The development of aviation over the course of little more than three-quarters of a century stands as an awe-inspiring accomplishment in both a civilian and a military context. The airplane has brought whole continents closer together: at the same time it has been a lethal instrument of war.

This series of books is intended to contribute to the overall understanding of the history of aviation—its science and technology as well as the social, cultural, and political environment in which it developed and matured. Some publications help fill the many gaps that still exist in the literature of flight; others add new information and interpretation to current knowledge. While the series appeals to a broad audience of general readers and specialists in the field, its hallmark is strong scholarly content.

The series is international in scope and includes works in three major categories:

SMITHSONIAN STUDIES IN AVIATION HISTORY: *works that provide new and original knowledge.*

CLASSICS OF AVIATION HISTORY: *carefully selected out-of-print works that are considered essential scholarship.*

CONTRIBUTIONS TO AVIATION HISTORY: *previously unpublished documents, reports, symposia, and other materials.*

Henry Cord Meyer

AIRSHIPMEN
BUSINESSMEN
AND POLITICS
1890–1940

SMITHSONIAN INSTITUTION PRESS

Washington and London

© 1991 by the Smithsonian
Institution
All rights reserved

Editor: Martha J. King
Production Editor: Duke Johns
Designer: Alan Carter

Library of Congress Cataloging-in-
Publication Data

Meyer, Henry Cord, 1913–
    Airshipmen, businessmen, and
politics, 1890–1940 / Henry Cord
Meyer.
        p.   cm.—(Smithsonian history
of aviation series)
    Includes bibliographical
references and index.
    ISBN 1-56098-031-1 (alk. paper)
    1. Airships—History.
    I. Title.   II. Series.
TL657.M39   1991
387.7′325′09—dc20   90-22345

British Library Cataloguing-in-
Publication Data is available

Manufactured in the United States of
America

98 97 96 95 94 93 92 91   5 4 3 2 1

∞ The paper used in this publication
meets the minimum requirements of
the American National Standard for
Permanence of Paper for Printed
Library Materials Z39.48-1984.

For permission to reproduce
illustrations appearing in this book,
please correspond directly with the
owners of the works, as listed in the
individual captions. The Smithsonian
Institution Press does not retain
reproduction rights for these
illustrations individually, or maintain
a file of addresses for photo sources.

To the memory of my mother,

Sophie Ahlemann Meyer,

at whose knee I first

learned of Count Zeppelin

and his wondrous airship.

Contents

Foreword

In the small world of airship historians, everyone knows everyone else. I have known for some years that Henry Cord Meyer has been at work on the political history of the rigid airship. Herewith appears an initial installment in his scholarly enterprise: various profiles and vignettes of the airshipmen and businessmen who were engaged in building and flying these airships.

There are many standard works dealing with the sky giants, their design, their technology, their construction, and their accomplishments in the period when the airplane was only a short-range craft carrying no more than two dozen passengers. We also have the accounts of personnel who piloted the rigids, first in bombing operations during World War I, then flying them in peacetime across continents and oceans.

Meyer is the first to research the hidden story of how the giant airships—prohibitively expensive by the standards of the early twentieth century—were financed. He documents the persistence of technological visionaries in their dealings with officials and governments, for only governments could under-write vehicles so experimental and so costly. He charts all the significant airship successes and failures, based on two decades of foraging in public and private archives in Germany, England, and the United States. Further, he has interviewed all the major participants in the airship drama, together with their assistants and disciples, preserving the reminiscences of key figures who no longer survive.

The first profile illuminates the achievement of Count Ferdinand von Zeppelin, the genius who created the giant rigids' essential features—enormous size, light metal frameworks, and gas-filled interiors free to expand or contract inside the fabric-covered hulls. Meyer stresses three aspects of the Count's career hitherto obscured. First was the role of the rigid airship as Zeppelin's vigorous psychological compensation for the terrible blow he suffered at age fifty-two, when Prussian intrigues forced him to abandon his cherished profession as a soldier. Second was his idealistic tenacity and adroit management of his advantageous aristocratic status, through many years of technological frustration and financial hardship, to achieve belated public and official recognition of his airship achievements. And third was his steadfast endeavor to enhance German military power and assure the nation's political preeminence in early twentieth-century Europe.

The author draws an extended vignette in further essays on Alfred Colsman, the Count's astute business manager, who gave the military airship a civilian career and then led the Zeppelin Company to wealth during World War I. In the postwar decade, however, when Colsman tried to redirect the Zeppelin Company as a viable diversified industrial complex, he clashed tragically with the Count's spiritual descendant, Hugo Eckener.

Almost every page of this book testifies to the high technological competence, operational skill, and psychological felicity of Dr. Eckener, who dedicated himself to resurrecting the zeppelin for peaceful commerce. He combated the vindictive prohibitions of the Treaty of Versailles. He saved the Zeppelin Company by securing a contract to build an airship for the U.S. Navy, and he gained worldwide attention by flying the ZR 3 (later the *Los Angeles*) across the stormy Atlantic to America. Through a variety of subsequent maneuvers, virtually blackmailing the Weimar Republic, he completed the famous *Graf Zeppelin* and flew it to America, around the world, and to the edge of the Arctic Circle. Together with the Goodyear Company, he wrestled with American investors in an attempt to finance airship services to the New World and across the Pacific. Failing in these efforts, Eckener was finally helped by the Nazi government, whose support permitted him to plan four giant craft to assure his North and South American routes. Soon the essentially anti-Nazi Eckener was cut off from these politically manipulated airship operations and left only with the Zeppelin Company. The destruction of the *Hindenburg* at Lakehurst effectively ended transoceanic airship travel, but Eckener remained steadfast in his endeavor to carry on the work of Count Zeppelin. The United States' unwillingness to give him helium ultimately led him to design the *Graf Zeppelin II*, buoyed with hydrogen, and available for Nazi electronic espionage along Germany's frontiers in the summer of 1939. Meyer sympathetically illuminates the tragic career of this greatest of the modern airshipmen.

Johann Schütte, virtually unknown today, also receives his due in new and original research. Considering himself superior in technological competence to Count Zeppelin, and seeking the same public acclaim, Dr. Schütte associated with Mannheim industrial leaders to create a rival construction firm. While basically these Schütte-Lanz airships were superior to the zeppelins by virtue of their aerodynamics and other design features, there were fatal flaws in materials and production schedules. After Schütte fell victim to the Versailles Treaty prohibitions in Germany, he briefly established a design and capitalization beachhead on the American shore, enticing (among other prominent Americans) the ex-Navy Secretary, Franklin D. Roosevelt. Ultimately, however, Schütte was undone by the resolute opposition of Eckener and by his own problematic personality traits.

Another illuminating profile is that of Lord Thomson of Cardington, whose story contrasts tellingly with that of Dr. Eckener. Idealistically enthusiastic but without comparable technological skill or operational experience, the Briton presided over a program of airship development involving great expenditures and inviting political manipulation. In the ultimate disaster of airship R 101, Lord Thomson was both product and victim of the bureaucratic meshes he had helped to create. Here Meyer implies the larger question: to what extent were the technological and financial requirements of these airships, together with all the accompanying bureaucratic and political baggage, themselves responsible for their failure?

The author presents an engaging portrait of German-American "facilitator" F. W. von Meister. He shows him interacting with Dr. Eckener, with Paul W. Litchfield of the Goodyear Company, with American naval experts, and with officials on both sides of the Atlantic. Indeed, so much does Meyer tie American airship activities with German origins, German commitments, and German continuities that an essentially original American airship identification (except for the unique Navy involvement) seems hard to find. Other American authors might dispute this presentation.

Be that as it may, Meyer has compressed a great deal of relevant, and often hitherto unknown, information into these ten topical essays. His scholarship is of the highest order and his information authoritative. The men he portrays are the outstanding figures in the history of the rigid airship. The problems he raises are those at the very heart of the brief developmental life of the great sky ships. Withal this book is a valuable, indeed unparalleled, contribution to the literature of the rigid airship.

Douglas H. Robinson

Acknowledgments

After fifteen years of research it is a pleasure at last to express my appreciation and thanks for all the assistance and enlightenment I have received from half a hundred individuals scattered over four continents that were touched by the actualities or promise of rigid airship operations. On eight occasions my travels have carried me to the eastern United States, to Britain, to Germany, to Australia, and to Brazil. In all these areas I have enjoyed friendly reception, generous hospitality, and liberal cooperation—for all these gifts and aid I am deeply grateful.

Since historians usually rely on documents, let me begin by listing these bedrock institutions to which I am indebted, together with particularly helpful individuals: the National Archives, Washington, D.C. (Drs. Fishbein, Wolff, and Mendelsohn); the National Air and Space Museum, Washington, D.C. (Ms. Catherine D. Scott); the Public Record Office, London, Chancery Lane, and Kew; the Bundesarchiv, Koblenz (Drs. Vogel and Montfort); the Political Archives, German Foreign Office, Bonn (Drs. Weinandy and Keipert). Equally significant are the archives of several business firms: the Goodyear Tire and Rubber Co., Akron, Ohio (Mmes. Marjory Garman, Cecil R. Norman, and Mary E. Manley); much airship documentation from Goodyear deposited with the archives of the University of Akron (Dr. John V. Miller); the Henry Ford Museum and Greenfield Village, Dearborn, Mich. (David R. Crippen); Luftschiffbau Zeppelin Archives, Friedrichshafen (German Zettel and Manfred A. Sauter); HAPAG-LLOYD Archives, Hamburg (Rolf Fink); Lufthansa Archives, Köln-Deutz (Dr. Werner E. Bittner and Mrs. Hünebach).

Personal archives and collections of papers constitute the next stratum of documentation: Papers of Garland Fulton, Naval Historical Foundation, Washington Navy Yard, Washington, D.C. (H. A. Vadnais, Jr.); Scott E. Peck Papers, Chula Vista, Calif.; Douglas H. Robinson Collection, Pennington, N.J.; Hallett Everett Cole Airship Collection, University of Oregon,

Eugene, Oreg., (Walter J. Wentz and Patrick Parson); Papers of F. W. (Willy) von Meister, Peapack, N.J.; Barnes Wallis Papers, the Science Libary, London; Eckener Papers with Mrs. Lotte Simon-Eckener, Konstanz; Dr. Uwe Eckener Archives, Konstanz; Johann Schütte Papers, Oldenburg (J. Friedrich Jahn) and Mannheim-Rheinau (Dr. Dorothea Haaland and Andrea Schulz); Capt. Hans von Schiller Archives, Tübingen (Mrs. Elisabeth Pletsch); Friedrichshafen Rathaus Archives (Messers. Scharpf and Buhl); Airship History Collection of Max Schorn, Friedrichshafen; and the two very important private airship history archives of the late Alfred F. Weber, Karlsruhe, and Werner Strumann, Münster/Westfalen.

I have enjoyed the resources and services of the Library of Congress, the New York Public Library, the National Air and Space Museum, the British Museum, the Royal Aeronautical Society (A.W.L. Nayler), the Imperial War Museum, the Royal Swedish Academy of Sciences (E. Ljungdahl and Ante Strand), the Deutsches Museum, and the Hoover Institution (Agnes F. Peterson).

Without the interviews that I was privileged to have with a number of survivors of the airship era between 1972 and 1985, significant data and insights simply would not have been available for posterity. I am thus particularly indebted to Capt. Garland Fulton, U.S.N.; Vice Adm. Charles E. Rosendahl, U.S.N.; Vice Adm. Thomas (Tex) G. W. Settle, U.S.N; Rear Adm. Scott E. Peck, U.S.N.; F. W. (Willy) von Meister; Thomas A. Knowles; George H. Lewis; Capt. Clarence (Dutch) Schildhauer (DO-X and PanAm); Lord Kings Norton; Sir Barnes Wallis; Capt. George F. Meager; Crispin Rope; Mrs. Lotte Simon-Eckener; Capt. Heinrich Bauer; Capt. Albert Sammt; Capt. Hans von Schiller; Erich Hilligardt; German Zettel; Klaus F. Pruss.

For further documentation and data, and especially for illustrations, I am greatly indebted to Peter W. Brooks, Geoffrey A. Chamberlain, Barry Countryman, Harold G. Dick, Stephen V. Gallup and Mlle. Marie Montlaur, Hans G. Knäusel, Sir Peter G. Masefield, Peter and Rudi von Meister, Lee Payne, John Provan, Werner Rau, K. H. Royter, H. Jo. Scheer, Richard K. Smith, Heinz Steude, Rolf Striedacher, Dr. A. D. Topping and officers of the Lighter-Than-Air Society, Heinz M. Wronsky, and John D. Archbold.

I am grateful to each of the following individuals for a particular contribution to my work over the years: Col. Günter Baum (ret.), D. W. Brown, Zenon Hansen, Guy Hartcup, Prof. Robin Higham, Rolf Italiaander, Mr. and Mrs. Frank Kiernan, Prof. E. J. Morpurgo, Francisco Pfalzgraff and Francisco Lago of Rio de Janeiro, Prof. Jürgen Schläger, Prof. Franklin D. Scott, J. Gordon Vaeth, Lord Ventry, and Hepburn Walker, Jr.

Financial support for my venture over the years is gratefully acknowledged from the Research-Travel Committee, School of Humanities, University of California, Irvine and for a travel grant from the American Philosophical Society in 1975.

Finally, there are words of very special acknowledgment in recognition of: Dr. Hans-Robert Ahlemann, host, driver, and data procurer in the Friedrichshafen area; Werner Strumann, equally attentive in northern Germany; the late Paul Max Weber in Bonn; and last, but not least, Manfred A. Sauter, archive director, Luftschiffbau Zeppelin G.m.b.H. in Friedrichshafen. For the preparation of my text I enjoyed the unfailing scrutiny and assistance of Dr. Douglas H. Robinson, Prof. Theodore F. Brunner (UC Irvine), and Prof. Hans-Adolf Jacobsen (Bonn University). My special thanks to my colleagues, Prof. Roland Schinzinger for help in understanding the electronics of the LZ 130 spy flights and Prof. Robert M. Saunders for preparation of the map on the flight of Aug. 2–4, 1939. My thanks also to Ms. Linda M. Weinberger, head of the interlibrary loan section of the UCI Library, and her staff for the procurement of dozens of books from all over the United States. I am indebted to my publisher, the Smithsonian Institution Press, and to my editors, Director Felix C. Lowe, Duke Johns, and Martha J. King, for their patience and unfailing assistance. All these institutions and individuals have given me the benefits of their assistance and knowledge; any errors that occur are obviously my own responsibility.

Acknowledgment is given to the following periodicals for allowing articles to be republished here: *Aerospace Historian, Bouyant Flight* (The Lighter-Than-Air Society, Akron, Ohio), *South Atlantic Quarterly*.

These publishers have granted permission for direct quotation from their books: Alfred A. Knopf, Inc., New York, N.Y.; Droste Verlag, G.m.b.H., Düsseldorf, Ger.; Crown Publishers, Inc., New York, N.Y.; Little, Brown, and Co., Boston, Mass.; the MIT Press, Cambridge, Mass.; Schirmer-Mosel Verlag, München, Ger.; University of Washington Press, Seattle, Wash.; Verlag Pestalozzi-Kinderdorf Wahlwies, Stockach, Ger.; Verlag Stadler, Konstanz, Ger.; Methuen and Co., London.

Finally, I gratefully acknowledge permission to publish illustrations from the following individuals and organizations: Luftschiffbau Zeppelin Archives, G.m.b.H., Friedrichshafen, Ger.; Barry Countryman Collection, Toronto, Canada; Bildarchiv Preussischer Kulturbesitz, Berlin, Ger.; Henry Ford Museum and Greenfield Village, Dearborn, Mich.; Goodyear Archives, Akron, Ohio; HAPAG-LLOYD Archives, Hamburg, Ger.; Landesmuseum für Technik und Arbeit, Mannheim, Ger.; Lee Payne Collection, Newport Beach, Calif.; Lighter-Than-Air Society, Akron, Ohio (especially James E. Hill); Lufthansa Archives, Köln-Deutz, Ger.; Naval Historical Foundation, Washington Navy Yard, Washington, D.C.; Quadrant Picture Library, Sutton, Surrey, Eng.; Universitetsbibliotek, Stockholm, Sweden; Uwe Eckener Collection, Konstanz, Ger.; von Meister Family, ex-Peapack, N.J.; von Schiller Archives, ex-Tübingen, Ger.; Werner Strumann Archives, Münster/Westf., Ger.; the G. A. Chamberlain Collection, Ashford, Eng.; Verlag Pestalozzi-Kinderdorf Wahlwies, Stockach, Ger.; and John D. Archbold. And last, but certainly not least, I am particularly indebted to Sanders Associates,

Inc. of Nashua, N.H. for their gracious provision of a photograph of the painting by Alfred "Chief" Johnson of that company, showing a realistic conception of LZ 130 in flight over the countryside with the spy basket fully lowered. It is reproduced with their permission.

Three proofreaders, Mrs. Helen G. Meyer, Prof. Gustave Bording-Mathieu, and Dr. William F. Gross have saved me from errors that my own bleary eyes missed. And John Miller produced all the word processing expertly and betimes.

Introduction

The study of the rigid airship has long had a band of devoted enthusiasts. They have admired the inventive and courageous genius of Count Ferdinand von Zeppelin and appreciated the daring of the fliers that followed him. Their interest is nourished by a number of first-rate professional works about the intricacies of design, construction, and powering of airships in Germany, England, and the United States. These enthusiasts participate vicariously in accounts of hazardous experimental flights, in the strikes of German zeppelins during World War I, and in the peacetime commercial voyaging between 1928 and 1937. The record of all these events is periodically punctuated by the spectacular crashes of the sky giants that have a morbid fascination all their own. Some works, particularly those published in Germany, delight their readers with a broad variety of illustrations about design, flight, and disaster. Quite understandably, most of all these books focus on technical specifications and performance data, and on the drama of technology wrestling with its own imperfections or in contest with the dynamic forces of nature.

The group of essays which follows touches on all these aspects in the half century that saw the birth, development, and destruction of the rigid airship. It places these events in a different context, however. It explores some of the psychological, social, and political dimensions of the earthbound world from which the airship ascended and to which it always returned, safely or not. How did the emerging technology of the rigid airship encompass or reflect the inner drives and conflicts of its designers and operators? What was the impact of airship building and flying upon the three societies intimately involved in realizing and operating their sky ships? How did their home communities react to their emerging presence and their fate? Given the powerful popular attraction of the rigid airships, how did outside forces seek to affect and manipulate them politically?

These ten essays are spin-offs from a larger continuing study of the political history of the airship. Three have been published previously. Each is topically self-contained. Cumulatively they seek to illuminate the sociopsychological world in which the airship developed. Most of the essays probe more intimately into the human dimensions of six airship, or airship-related, personalities. Count Zeppelin and Dr. Hugo Eckener have each enjoyed a flood of laudatory notices—often patriotically cloying in the case of the Count, always respectfully admiring of Eckener's high professional standards. It should not demean either of these pioneers for a later generation to seek to understand their motivations and attitudes in terms of a spectrum of more generally perceived human emotions and reactions. The activities of Dr. Johann Schütte and Director Alfred Colsman have not so far had the recognition that each in his way deserves. For each of these men, his involvement with the rigid airship venture was a personal disaster, yet each one made an indispensable contribution—Schütte to airship design, Colsman to the Zeppelin Company and the wider Friedrichshafen community. Both Colsman and Eckener had brief contacts with Henry Ford. Even if the relationships were ultimately unproductive, they demonstrated the intersection of an attractive technology with dynamic businessmen under unique political circumstances. The career of Lord Thomson of Cardington has had mixed and unfair reviews; he can most reasonably be understood in context of the larger sociopolitical forces of his time. Finally, F. W. (Willy) von Meister was a most attractive personality and an indispensable facilitator for the airship cause among builders, fliers, businessmen, and governments—notably in the milieu of broader German-American relationships. His career mirrored the rewards of interaction between two cultures, as well as the illusions of dealing with one of the two when its basic political drives became malevolent. These various dimensions of the human drama often have been hitherto obscured by all the technical and operational data about airships.

A second major theme of these essays explores the socioeconomic environment of airship construction and flying. The financial trials of Count Zeppelin, and the miraculous economic improvement after the airship disaster at Echterdingen in 1908, are well known; but that was only the first chapter. How were construction and operation financed thereafter in Germany and abroad? Who were the men and women who built the airships? How did employer, employee, and community interact? Where and how did Britons and Americans subsequently finance and establish their airship industries, and with what relations to government? Business history of the airship is almost nonexistent. Perhaps these essays can stimulate further interest in that field before the records of these activities, already badly mutilated by war and neglect, are entirely lost.

A third theme constantly appearing throughout the essays is that of political behavior—from the personal political maneuvering of individuals to the more general party or government behavior. Such politicking was essential to Count Zeppelin between 1890 and 1909, when (after the shattering political blow of his enemies to end his military career) he chose to manipulate his protective social network in efforts to restore his honor and to maintain his dedicated service to the *Vaterland*. Similarly, astute personal political strategy was central to the career of Dr. Hugo Eckener in the 1920s in his efforts for the zeppelin cause. The lack of such personal political shrewdness in the struggles of Johann Schütte and Alfred Colsman no doubt affected the negative outcome of their careers. Lord Thomson and F. W. (Willy) von Meister were each less involved in the politics of personal survival than in the higher and more sophisticated areas of relating the airship to the political programs of their respective nations. Each one of these men was manipulating the technology of the airship in his own personal context, or was being more or less voluntarily caught up in the larger governmental processes of using the popular attractive qualities of airship technology for purposes beyond its immediate intent.

All three governments of the airship building nations were at one time or another intimately involved in construction and flying of their sky ships. Pre–World War I Berlin had a schizoid relationship with Count Zeppelin's invention; wartime Germany used it as long as it was militarily effective, and even beyond that. Weimar Berlin was reluctantly unsupportive, whereas Nazi propaganda seized upon the airship and turned it to very different political ends. In Britain and the United States, government participation in airship building and flying was crucially fundamental—an imperial political and commercial ambition in the former, a combined naval and commercial motivation in the latter. Whether as unwilling and skeptical semipartners (Weimar German cabinets), interim handmaiden (British Air Ministry), forthright advocate (United States Navy), or cynical manipulator (Nazi Air Ministry)—each of these governmental agencies dealt with the airship in a larger political perspective.

The men who built and flew the airships in each of these nations had their own unique group relationship with the technology. Flying an airship required such a large crew, and demanded such an unusual combination of intense cooperation and concentration of experience and psychological energy, that it produced its own rare qualities of comradeship and commitment to the enterprise. This singular and powerful camaraderie readily communicated itself to the larger citizenry of builders and maintenance personnel of the airship community, especially in Germany. The very complexity—indeed, the sense of inherent risk—of the undertaking gave all the participants in the venture a special fervor of expertise and accomplishment. Building and operating the technology could become an end in itself, concealing from its eager participants the dangers of some ulterior political manipulation of their enterprise. In this way the German zeppeliners were caught up in their Faustian relationship with the Nazis. Only in this context can one understand the jubilation of the zeppelin crews in 1938–39, that they were at last once again out and up with their sky ships—even though they were now on military missions in direct contradiction to the peaceful commercial purposes avowed time and again by Dr. Hugo Eckener.

The photographic illustrations in this book were, in many instances, selected as sources of information in themselves. They portray the zeppelin as a social catalyst in Germany before World War I. They show various airships and various individuals in interrelated political context. They illustrate the airship as an embodiment of national pride and prowess in Britain and America. They demonstrate the Nazi exploitation of the zeppelin in service of National Socialist racial imperialism. In various ways they seek to give a third and visual dimension to text and judgment.

All in all, the character studies, the quotations, the documentation, the events and circumstances in airship history hitherto obscured, and the illustrations—all serve to illuminate remarkable individuals, dedicated builders and fliers, and powerful political forces. These interacted with an ingenious technology of compelling attractiveness in circumstances that the world is not likely to see again.

CHAPTER I   In Search of the Real Count Zeppelin

In sparkling Lake Constance sunshine, on June 16, 1985, the city of Fried-richshafen at long last dedicated an impressive memorial to Ferdinand Count Zeppelin. After many false starts over decades of war, revolution, and changing economic fortune, thousands of citizens, visitors, and notables assembled to unveil a fifty-foot modernistic obelisk placed beside a new theater complex and convention center. Music and color reverberated over the park area. Here had once stood the luxurious Kurgarten Hotel, local residence of the Count in his last decade and deluxe accommodation for airship travelers of the 1930s departing for transatlantic flights to South America. There was also promise in the air of a new zeppelin and technological museum to be completed by 1990.

The soaring obelisk carried two inscriptions. Under a bas-relief of the Count was inscribed: "One must only have determination and faith therein; then success will come." Another facet of the monument carried a longer inscription:

> 1900—ascent of the airship LZ 1 in
> the Bay of Manzell on its first flight
>
> 1924—LZ 126 crossed the Atlantic
>
> 1929—LZ 127 circumnavigated the world
> and penetrated the Arctic
>
> The gates to worldwide air travel were
> opened with scheduled air service
>
> 1932 to South America
>
> 1936 to North America

This essay is an abridged and refocused version of a more fully developed professional study entitled "Militarism and Nationalism in Count Zeppelin's Airship Venture: A Study in Massive Psychological Compensation." It is being published in Henry Cord Meyer, *Collected Works*, vol. 2: *"Drang nach Osten" and other Essays, 1960–1990*, due in 1992.

Understandable no doubt in 1985 was the omission of another aerial first zealously sought by Count Zeppelin and achieved by his collaborators: the opening of an era of aerial warfare with zeppelin raids upon civilian populations in London, Paris, Brussels, Antwerp, and Bucharest during World War I.

In his dedication address the mayor of Friedrichshafen recounted the legendary qualities of Count Zeppelin: his noble aristocratic spirit, his devotion to duty, his unshakeable conviction, his steadfastness and determination in the face of seemingly insuperable obstacles, his ability to win the cooperation of talented men from varied areas of competence, his quiet and firm religious spirit, his remarkable gentleness and modesty. "He was," the mayor averred, "positively enraptured with his idea of making an important contribution to the technological and cultural progress of mankind, with his unshakeable belief in the verity of his conception and its ultimate accomplishment." The mayor concluded by recommending the Count as a model for civic behavior and willingness to pursue technological improvement toward a better future.[1]

Only one small incident marred the continuing festivities of the summer. Shortly after its dedication someone defaced the glistening surface of the obelisk with a crudely lettered objection:

We are the youth of our era. We want the truth.[2]

Who knows what kind of truth the unknown graffitist sought? It is difficult enough to reach agreement about the qualities of an ordinary person. In the case of Count Zeppelin, we are dealing with the determined Württemberg cavalry-general-turned-aeronaut who, within a decade (1900–10), had changed from an object of local ridicule into Germany's greatest folk hero since Bismarck. Thousands of books, pamphlets, articles, and news accounts have appeared about him since that time. These have created a monument of fact and fiction that almost defies contemporary reconstruction in the light of reconsidered evidence. Accurate technical studies of the development of Zeppelin's work are readily available. Much more difficult are the problems of dealing with the Count and his personality in the context of the bureaucracy, business, and politics of his times. Viewed in a very personal context, there are really only two first-rate biographies of Graf Zeppelin: Hugo Eckener's very sympathetic study of 1938 (based partially on the resources of the family archives) and Rolf Italiaander's brilliant photographic compilation of 1980, together with its selected documents.[3] To these can be added several intimate accounts of his immediate collaborators, a basic German Luftwaffe study of German military aviation before World War I (which, of course, deals with airships as a military weapon), and a remarkable sociological study of Zeppelin and his times.[4] Beyond these books stretches a whole landscape of works variously laced with factual errors, patriotism, and mythology.

The single, glaring defect in all writings about Count Zeppelin prior to

1925 is their failure to mention the most significant and traumatic event of his life, namely, the abrupt and enforced termination (in the prime of his life) of the military career to which he was passionately devoted. This skeleton was kept securely locked in its closet by the military-political pressures on social and literary convention in Imperial Germany. Since 1925, no work, with the exception of Eckener's biography, has tried to deal in any analytical detail with the psychological and motivational results of the trauma the Count suffered. In this respect even Eckener does not go much beyond the immediate impact of the shock in 1890–91.[5]

Let us examine briefly three central aspects of Zeppelin's earlier life: the social milieu in which he matured, the qualities of his personality, and his attitude toward his chosen military career. The German aristocracy of the mid-nineteenth century into which he was born on July 8, 1838, was a very comfortable and civilized descendant from feudal times. Here still survived the aggressive spirit of the feudal warrior, with his fealty and obeisance to those above him nicely domesticated to social convention. The Count grew up within an elite social network, with its clearly defined but largely unwritten pecking order, derived from centuries of accumulated behavior patterns and protocol. The principal hallmarks of this semifeudal world were its ritualized social gallantry and romantic devotion to the passage of arms and the arts of war. Here the cavalry still held a preeminently prestigious position. Actively, the aristocratic social network channeled the ambitions of subgroups and individuals competing for influence. Passively, as an essentially protective order it shielded its nonentities, incompetents, and even minor charlatans. In this context alone—and without considering his undeniable personal qualities and accomplishments—Count Zeppelin automatically achieved standing at home and abroad. He maintained these inborn semifeudal attitudes throughout his life in a somewhat naive but bold patriotic sense. Until 1890, as a steadily advancing cavalry officer, he enjoyed the active benefits of the system. When his military career was then abruptly and traumatically terminated, the same social network gave him the passive protection of its psychological support and sympathy. More important, it also gave him continued and unimpeded access to its most influential personalities and to the seats of power. This would be the framework within which he would promptly and primarily move in determined efforts to rehabilitate his tarnished military reputation and honor.

What were the character and major personality traits of this well-connected aristocratic cavalry officer? Answers to this question are reliably found in the many quotations that biographer Eckener took from Zeppelin's voluminous journals. Begun in 1858, when Zeppelin was twenty, and continued until just before his death in 1917, these journals testify in several thousand pages to an individual of remarkable willpower, thoroughness, and candor about himself. His later and younger contemporaries found the Count admirably firm of character, stalwart in bearing, yet withal a generous and gentle man. Tenacious persistence, unswerving commitment to his objective, keen mental alertness, and genteel amiability: these were the qualities that Eckener stressed in his admiring biography. He also found them sometimes offset by petulant impatience, peevish stubbornness, occasional flashes of anger when crossed, and resistance to accepting advice from those more sophisticated or technically competent. Bridging these contradictory qualities were his fundamental honesty, his strong sense of justice, and a basic religious attitude uncomplicated by devotion to dogma or ritual. Finally, Zeppelin had much of a characteristic Swabian temperament: pertinacity and a deep attachment to his provincial homeland, both contained within an unswerving loyalty to the conservative order of his times, beginning with devotion to his Württemberg state and its ruling dynasty.[6] These details, and many others, were derived by biographer Eckener from the abundant archives of the Brandenstein-Zeppelin family resources closed to all other scholars then, and since then.

The young Count was brought up within a congenial family—a generous and loving mother, whom he lost at the age of fourteen, and a firm and well-educated father with whom he developed an uncommonly close relationship. His formal education came initially from a pious tutor properly versed in the requisite subjects. At age fifteen he entered the Stuttgart Polytechnic School and two years later began his training at the Württemberg Military Academy. Thenceforth his career was focused upon the service of arms. His subsequent advanced studies at the University of Tübingen were interrupted, never to be resumed, by the call to duty during the Franco-Austrian War of 1859. Shortly thereafter he set out upon his three *Wanderjahre* abroad. He dubbed these *militärische Studienreisen*, travels to study and understand other societies, their characteristic ways of thinking, their degrees of military preparedness, and their qualities of military behavior. They were meant to inform and sharpen his military perception and training.

These observations are summarized from Eckener's very detailed account of Zeppelin's maturing thoughts and experiences. His choice of a military career was one of the very few honorable vocations open to a young nobleman. Very likely, the young Count was fascinated by the soldierly traditions of his family. He could trace these usages back to his thirteenth-century Mecklenburg forebears, who over the succeeding centuries served as knights in the Swedish, Danish, and Prussian armies. His grand-uncle, Carl von Zepelin (*sic*), had joined the entourage of the Württemberg then-ducal heir apparent in 1787 and found his fame and fortune in the Habsburg armies of the French revolutionary and Napoleonic wars. This association raised the Mecklenburg knight to a count, added the characteristic second "p" to the family name, and transferred its residence and fortunes to Württemberg. His grandfather served the Duke of Württemberg, who became king in 1806, and thus the Swabian roots of the family were deeply struck. Through his marriage, however, Zeppelin's father opted for a career as manufacturer and landed aristocrat. With all the respect he had for his father, young Zeppelin was still evidently deeply impressed by a romantic notion of his family's past military glories. By his own choice of career he sought to reestablish its earlier semifeudal warrior identity.[7]

Such revived perceptions of the glories of the passage of arms appear vividly in the accounts of Zeppelin's military career. In recounting the future aeronaut's activities as a military observer with the Union armies in America, Eckener observed the characteristics of the Count's combat behavior there: cool demeanor under fire (which he eagerly sought), calm calculation of changing military circumstances, and yet a contradictory impulsiveness to be certain of participation in any action at hand.[8] Zeppelin himself recorded his excitement at first encountering "the romance of military combat" in America in 1863 at several small skirmishes together with a northern observer group on the Virginia front. In the opening weeks of the Franco-Prussian War in 1870, the Count galloped off with a small unit of soldiers on an impulsive "reconnaissance" charge behind French lines in Alsace. Though widely and popularly celebrated in later years when the Count had achieved fame with his airship, the maverick combat episode was judged poorly at the time and by later military authorities as well.[9] Six weeks later, he wrote to his wife from the battlefield at Sedan:

> It is magnificent to have experienced the greatest day of this century! Share with me my impressions! I rode up to the height where the king of Prussia stood. The picturesque fortress lay below in the last rays of the sinking sun and compressed therein was the shattered army of France. In wide surrounding circles stood the German armies, now at rest from the bloody struggle and joyously shouting, "The emperor has been captured!" Adjutants are hurrying about, bands are playing, and the thundering artillery salvos are writing world history—proclaiming Germany's grandeur. The next morning I witnessed God's punishing justice: there in front of a little hutment sat the crushed emperor and with him were powerful figures, Prussian guards officers more to defend than to detain Napoleon III. Wondrous are the ways of God![10]

Obviously a war like that of 1870–71 was an exciting affair. Many wars were thus, before the wholesale mechanized massacres of the twentieth century, when war as a social institution was viewed as a proper instrument of policy and the ultimate court of honor. Count Zeppelin was certainly a child of the military enthusiasm of his times, though more impulsively so inclined than others. Still, one misses in the data currently available a fuller explanation of the Count's motivations and psychological characteristics that determined his vibrant enthusiasm for passage of arms. As we shall see, his thoughts of military preeminence are frequently expressed after 1890, when his own military career had been abruptly terminated and as he tried to develop a radically new and superior military weapon for his German nation. Just before the war he wrote a friend, "The most important aspect of my life was my long period of military service in which I was permitted to participate in the [sociopsychological] education of the German people. That is, after all, the basic sense of our army and thus represents the highest and most significant values of our nation."[11] Ultimately, during World War I, his attitudes escalated into fanaticism. Obviously, he was not alone in crying "*Gott strafe England!*" Coming from this prewar folk hero, however, these attitudes had a far greater impact than those routinely mouthed by conservative propaganda. Possibly Eckener passed over some pertinent background data in the journals or papers of the Count, not wishing in 1938 to nourish from a hallowed source the rising tide of German militarism reborn under the Nazis.

In the development of his political attitudes, Zeppelin had a characteristic South German experience. Like most individuals of that time, he was caught up in the thoughts and excitement of German unification. Before 1866 he was in favor of a broader German union, the *grossdeutsch* alternative under Austria's leadership, which also meant the defeat of Prussia. In those days he perceived Bismarck as a "Prussian robber baron," a man with little sensibility for nobility and law, just brutal and ruthless. Later he adjusted to the realities of Prussian power, though barely tolerating the Prussians themselves. After 1871, however, the Count was like a great many younger Germans of the time. He waxed rhapsodic over the consummation of German unification under the aegis of the Prussian warrior-state. Now Bismarck was fully acceptable to him in ways the Count had not contemplated before.[12]

For the next twenty years Zeppelin lived, worked, and rose within the ranks of the new combined German armies, which were seen physically and ideologically as the embodiment of the new German Empire. The traditional officers' code of honor and spiritual mystique were enhanced in obeisance to the new German emperor as *Oberster Kriegsherr*—Supreme War Lord. Zeppelin thrived in this heady atmosphere. He was never content with sedentary assignments and purposefully sought active service. He relished the open-air exercises with his men, insisting upon repeated and thorough training with them in horsemanship and varied weaponry. All evidence points to his constant concern for the welfare of his cavalrymen, coupled with his insistence upon their superior performance in duty. These qualities of solicitous leadership earned him the respect and loyalty of his soldiers in bonds of association rather different from those of a characteristic Prussian unit, where the spirit of *Kadavergehorsam* (unquestioning, corpselike obedience) was more likely to prevail. Zeppelin's encouragement of innovations in training and weaponry were bound to grate upon his Prussian associates, all the more so when they were pursued with his energy and determination. These circumstances no doubt created an adverse reputation for him in Berlin and contributed to the unfavorable atmosphere in which his decisive career misfortune occurred.[13] There, quite simply, he ran afoul of an ambiguity in the German Constitution of 1871.

The new German Empire was a curious mixture of political modernity and remnants of feudalism. Bismarck had dominated the creation of the North German Confederation of 1867, partially negotiating its terms and generally

Count Zeppelin as member of the German Federal Council [Bundesrat], 1889; Count Zeppelin (left), Count Moltke (seated middle). (Luftschiffbau Zeppelin)

imposing it upon the losers of the 1866 war. Here the Prussian tail wagged the German dog. During the heat of conflict in 1870–71, further negotiations were conducted with the South German states. Each joined the new empire under different stipulations, depending upon relative size and political importance. Of crucial significance in these arrangements was the degree to which each of the new partners maintained its autonomous identity and differing privileges. Here was paramount the role of the formerly independent royal armies of Saxony, Bavaria—and Württemberg. By separate but coordinated military treaties these armies were rapidly and fully transformed and standardized to Prussian specifications in organization and equipment. They maintained, however, their separate identities, traditions, and various procedural niceties of appointment, promotion, command, and honors. Precise as they might have seemed in 1871, these arrangements (not only in military matters) still left enough elbowroom for aggressive Prussian bureaucratic maneuvering further to confine or co-opt the few remaining areas of independent identity for the southern states. This was the area of contention that would be Zeppelin's nemesis.[14]

All through his rising military career the Count had maintained very close and cordial relationships with the royal court in Stuttgart. In 1885 he was appointed military attaché to the Württemberg embassy in Berlin, and here he dealt with continuing problems to bring the Württemberg army into more complete conformity with overall Prussian patterns. Two years later he became ambassador himself, and member of the prestigious upper house of parliament, the Bundesrat. Indeed, Bismarck himself pressed Zeppelin to accept the appointment, which the Count did reluctantly and with the express promise of his king that he would be released within two years to resume his coveted military career. By now the new empire had lasted nearly twenty years, the ecstasies of unification and victory over France had subsided. Sensitivities sharpened in both Berlin and Stuttgart. A lingering bureaucratic dispute over the exact procedures in certain crucial military appointments found Prussians overstepping bounds of propriety and Swabians becoming incensed at "constitutional violations." Swabian patriots of all political shades resented having their sons serving under a Prussian at Stuttgart. Zeppelin's last official action was to confer with Stuttgart authorities and to submit a secret memorandum to the German emperor which began:

> The arrangement whereby the [Prussian] Commanding General is responsible for all changes in assignments of Württemberg officers has no justification either in the Imperial Constitution or in the Military Convention. Most particularly, this arrangement through the manner of its operation casts H. M. the King in the role of a mere rubber stamp, while the Commanding General determines the fate of Württemberg officers.[15]

While explicitly rejecting any thought of changing the constitution or the military convention, Zeppelin did convey Stuttgart's proposal to establish a military cabinet in Württemberg, parallel to that of Prussia. This measure was proposed to inhibit any further undesirable Prussification of the valued Swabian army and to maintain the federative character of the German Empire. No wonder the kaiser wrote his marginal comment: "Am very astonished at these particularist ideas here being revealed."[16]

No doubt the tenor of the message, and the way it was received, determined the fate of the messenger. During the summer of 1890, the Prussian ambassador in Stuttgart, Count Philipp Eulenburg (a notorious gossip and scandalmonger, and already a confidant of William II), reported on the atmosphere of popular anti-Prussian ridicule and insults there. Count Zeppelin also received unfavorable mention. By late summer of 1890, the kaiser relented and appointed a Swabian officer to command the Württemberg General Staff. Opinion in Stuttgart was jubilant. Count Zeppelin, however, had evidently become a marked man.[17]

The annual autumn maneuvers offered a favorable opportunity for Prussian military-political retaliation. Traditionally these war games served the important ritualistic side purpose of disposing of incompetent or unwanted officers. Just happily returned to his military career, Count Zeppelin was assigned command of a composite cavalry division at these *Kaisermanöver* of September 1890. Two months later, in mid-November, he was notified by

Prussian General von Kleist that his assigned exercise was a failure. He was shortly relieved of his command, whereupon he resigned from the Württemberg army and was promoted to Lt. General (ret.). His king, no doubt sympathetic and certainly comprehending the larger dimensions of the whole situation, promptly gave him an intimate honorary appointment directly at his side. Still, it was at best a pale amelioration for the lifelong career that the Count had lost.[18]

It was a staggering blow to a man of Zeppelin's basic competence and sense of honor, with his devotion to a romantically sentimentalized idealism about war and the passage of arms, and with his hitherto complete devotion to a lifelong career of military service for his revered German *Vaterland*. He was cut to the heart by the implications of derogation of his Swabian loyalty and the affront to his keen sense of personal honor by this transparent, shabby treatment. On November 23, 1890 he confided to his journal:

> My former commanding officer, General von Heuduck, could not believe that I was to be denied command of a division. . . . I fall by the verdict passed upon me by Cavalry Inspector von Kleist, though I do not as yet know what its exact terms will be. If he is referring particularly to my uncertain and faulty conduct on September 5th, he is perfectly justified, for I was myself not content with my performance that day. But on the first and second days I did not do badly and had success. . . . Heuduck said of the day he was present [and witnessed Kleist's own errors] "I have never seen anything like it. I infinitely prefer Zeppelin to Kleist. To whom are we to give our divisions, if we let men like Zeppelin go?" Kleist and I are too different in character and temperament. I suppose he mistook my pliancy for weakness and my quiet way with subordinates for lack of firmness.
>
> It is hard that I should be judged by this one experience with the Cavalry Division and on Kleist's verdict alone. It is God's will. May He give me strength to bear it and to do the best I can. Amen.[19]

For all his resignation to the vagaries of Divine Providence, Count Zeppelin was not unaware of what he must have perceived as skullduggery at work. His journal entry of February 23, 1891 is indicative:

> E. heard from Steinheil [then Württemberg minister of war] that he was promptly informed that I would not be given a division. That was *prior* to Kleist's unfavorable verdict. Heuduck had already told me: "You must have an enemy in high places in Berlin." I am now almost certain that Kleist's negative report was only a pretext. The real cause is resentment of my memorandum (though rooted in misunderstanding.) I must take comfort in the thought that I am the victim of convictions candidly expressed for the good of the Empire.[20]

Thus fate cleared the way for a determined airship inventor to emerge from the chrysalis of a rather naive dismissed cavalry general. It did not, however, dispel the atmosphere of disdain and ridicule that he would encounter for years to come, whenever he moved beyond his native Swabian precincts. There would be other significant change. Foremost would be a psychologically modified Count Zeppelin. Beneath his quiet and courtly demeanor

Count Zeppelin, wife, and daughter, 1889. (Luftschiffbau Zeppelin)

would be a patriot even more fervent for his German *Vaterland* and even firmer in his Swabian loyalty. No one would trespass upon his sincerity or find him pliant again.

Count Zeppelin was just fifty-two years old when the chosen career of his life was ruthlessly terminated with all the force of a stinging and professionally crippling insult. Biographer Eckener judges that his essential mental and physical vigor, the encouragement of his wife and daughter, and his "general philanthropic and cultural ideals" then directed the Count toward "the solution of the great contemporary problem of human flight."[21] A further motivation seems most likely and more basic. Not only was any further positive military activity denied him, but the ignoble circumstances of his abrupt retirement (which were no doubt the subject of malicious gossip in higher circles) also precluded his service in any civilian political or diplomatic position outside his native Württemberg. Unless he found some alternative and effective way of self-expression, he was doomed to enforced retirement and social-psychological deterioration on his Swabian estate—with occasional sops of provincial preferment. The Count had far too vital a personality and much too sensitive a character to accept such a blow from his detractors. Though we have no further journal entries from this traumatic period in Zeppelin's life, he was no doubt also moved by a burning determination to set aright the outrageous wrong that had been done him. It would require a supreme effort, outside of existing professional development and beyond the contemporary bonds of things and circumstances. In social and psychological *extremis*, Zeppelin stayed within the limits of his career and national perceptions, but projected his drive for professional and personal rehabilitation onto a new plane of activism—quite literally into an aerial machine that would move majestically above his beloved Germany, humble his enemies at home, and defeat imperial enemies abroad.

The Count wrote the first significant elaboration of his nascent airship thoughts in a memorandum to his king in May 1887, while he was still military attaché to the Stuttgart embassy in Berlin. He expressed his dismay at the operational cul-de-sac into which the Prussian Airship Battalion was moving—focusing on further developing earthbound balloons useful only in siege warfare, while the French enemy was experimenting with dirigible balloons. He argued further:

> To achieve genuine military effectiveness of untethered ballons, they need only be able to move against contrary winds and remain airborne for at least twenty-four hours. Then they could make broad reconnaissance flights, with lift enough to carry a larger number of persons, supplies, or explosive projectiles. All three essentials will require larger gas containers, therefore large airships. . . . Were it possible to solve these problems, then airships would become enormously useful in the conduct of war and could also serve for general transportation (shortest distance over mountains and seas) or for geographical exploration (North Pole, Inner Africa).[22]

Eckener's detailed account of Zeppelin's first efforts in 1891–92 indicates how the Count wrestled with various problems of construction and potential flight characteristics at a time when there were very few basic physical data available and even less experimental evidence for guidance in his work. All the more one admires his determination and energy in writing about his project, first to his king, and then directly to the top of the Prussian military hierarchy, to Count von Schlieffen, newly arrived as Chief of the Great General Staff:

> You will perhaps recall a conversation we had about dirigible airships during a ride in the Tiergarten. I did not at the time attempt to put my ideas into practice, as I was too busy to work them out. Besides, it would have worried me to be regarded, even temporarily, as a candidate for an insane asylum. Now that I have nothing better to do, and when public reaction can only hurt me personally, and not the profession in which I am engaged, I have been reverting to those ideas and have given them substance—so far only on paper.[23]

Thereupon followed some initial technical details. He ended by asking von Schlieffen to send an expert officer to Stuttgart to evaluate his designs and estimates.

Barely half a year after his devastating career termination, Count Zeppelin had stabilized several lines of action that would remain constant over the next generation. He indissolubly linked his name and reputation with the airship, even at the risk of anticipated malicious ridicule by fellow officers. He established contact with the most important decision-making or policy-influencing centers likely to affect his venture. By consulting with contemporary

Model of Count Zeppelin's airship-train, 1895. (Luftschiffbau Zeppelin)

lighter-than-air experts, he projected himself into the internecine competition among proponents and opponents of balloons, nonrigids, semirigids, and rigid airships.

During the subsequent years Zeppelin's enthusiasm and ideas rose, fell, and rose again, as he dealt with balloonists, engineers, and motor designers. The details of these technological and aeronautical aspects have been systematically and accurately described.[24] What has generally *not* been portrayed are the ideological contexts of the Count's self-expressed motivations for his endeavors. In the proliferating succession of his journal entries, letters, and memoranda (with all their wealth of technical concern) one perceives the emotional drives that constantly fostered the aeronaut's responses to alternating promise and disappointment. These included his pressing concern to compete effectively with emerging French military aviation and his commitment to increase the security and power of the *Vaterland*. Eckener commented on the unending series of explanations, replies, appeals, and entreaties which Zeppelin addressed in the 1890s to influential men in Germany, all containing the same cry: "'Help me to build the airship for Germany's defense and security!'" In the light of such evidence, is it reasonable to restrict interpretation of the Count's determination, as Eckener writes, to just "the optimism of all inventors?"[25]

By late 1894 Zeppelin had a fully developed project for an airship-train in hand and submitted it to the German army by way of memoranda to both Count Schlieffen and the emperor. Two committees of experts subsequently appointed found the proposals ingenious but so faulty as not to merit official support. A further memorandum of late 1895, with vistas of airship support for the German navy, the colonial empire, the development of meteorology and earth sciences, and the fostering of world communications found little favor and merited only the marginal comment—"pure Jules Verne." There was good reason to suspect that the major opposition came not from technical experts, but from the army itself, which had shown its dubious devotion to the Count five years before.

Rejected again, Zeppelin cast about for support outside his military-social network. In 1896 he gained the cautious endorsement of the prestigious Union of German Engineers with ideas for airships in both military and nonmilitary uses. Thus encouraged he further worked on refinement of his design—with the cooperation now of young Dr. Ludwig Dürr—toward a single-unit airship. He established the Association to Foster Airship Development, got loyal financial support from his Swabian well-wishers, but still had to subscribe more than half of the 800,000 marks required. By now he was both fearing, and rejecting, comparable nonrigid progress with kite-balloons and other improvements of the Prussian Airship Battalion (at work since 1884). He was convinced of his superior design, writing, "my system is the best, the only conceivable one for military purposes; and, if airships are ever possible at all, they will be mine."[26]

As the new century approached, the first Zeppelin airship took shape in a large floating hangar on the coastal water of Lake Constance. The Count supervised the construction in psychological and social loneliness. There is abundant detail of his technical progress (and error) in several excellent studies, but only scant evidence so far of his continuing thoughts and reactions—they must number many pages in his journals of that time. The first ascent of LZ 1 in July 1900 was successful, but the airship itself was not. If he was now noticed at all in the wider German world, it was as the "fool-count" at Lake Constance, or more sympathetically among his fellow-Swabians as the "aerial dreamer down at the lake"—*der Luftikus am Bodensee*. Certainly Zeppelin did not seek or welcome publicity. He turned a reporter away with the brusque comment, "I am not a circus rider performing for the public; I am completing a serious task in service of the *Vaterland*."[27]

The task, however, was neither quickly nor easily completed. With the failure of LZ 1, Zeppelin had to liquidate his enterprise at a heavy loss. With a decoration from the kaiser, faint praise from the Prussian Airship Battalion, and another cautious endorsement from the Union of German Engineers, Zeppelin persisted with his endeavors. Industrialist Carl Berg supported him with a new alloy, duralumin. Daimler built better engines. The king sponsored a Württemberg lottery that produced 125,000 marks. Still, Zeppelin had to raise the rest of 400,000 marks by mortgaging his wife's estates. The results were another failed airship in 1906 and financial exhaustion. Again the Count turned to the German army: could the empire consider purchasing his accumulated experience, records, and remaining construction facilities and materials—not for his personal benefit, but to serve the *Vaterland* and meet that alarming competition of French military aviation? At about this time Eckener records a personal comment of Zeppelin's, when the uncharacteristically dispirited aeronaut exclaimed, "I shall not go on building any more. The world will never know how good my airship is!"[28]

It had been an exasperating decade for the old Count. That quotation of Eckener's is one of the very few indications he gives from what must be hundreds of pages of Zeppelin's journal in these frustrating years. Exactly

Count Zeppelin with king and
queen of Württemberg, 1906.
(Luftschiffbau Zeppelin)

how Zeppelin recorded his feelings and how he steeled himself through the positive steps and the negative circumstances is not yet known. To what degree was he still driven by his need to satisfy honor and rehabilitate his career? How much did he continue to fear for the security and military might of his *Vaterland* among the competing European powers? One thing is certain. It can be read from the pages of Alan Sillitoe's *Loneliness of the Long-distance Runner*, "The work didn't break me; if anything, it made me stronger in many ways. . . . I worked out my systems, . . . planned my outward life of innocence and honest work, yet at the same time grew perfect in my craft for what I knew I had to do."[29]

During 1906 Zeppelin's fortunes began to change for the better. Using the yield of yet another lottery and straining his suppliers to the limit, the aeronaut began construction on LZ 3. Publicist Eckener came to his side with enthusiastic reports. The German public began to notice Zeppelin favorably, represented by the hundreds of vacationers at Friedrichshafen, who turned their gaze from Alpine views to the great construction hangar offshore. As the Count began to enjoy renewed contact with official circles, the same basic arguments reappeared in his memoranda: failure to heed his appeals presaged a disaster for the *Vaterland*; the empire must press ahead to acquire the best possible airship advantage over France. With his new success he could anticipate construction of airships carrying five hundred men, fully equipped, over long distances. He concluded that appeal to the minister of the interior with a stirring coda: "In days to come my airships are destined to erase the advantages or disadvantages of the geographical location of nations. For Germany, as the power most capable of supplying proficient crews, *they will assure her world military domination* [emphasis supplied], as indeed they will cause a complete revolution in commerce and transportation."[30]

At a subsequent conference in that ministry on December 19, 1906, and in the presence of General von Moltke and a representative of Admiral von Tirpitz, Zeppelin pleaded for further support to develop his airships. According to the protocol of that meeting, the Count argued that,

> The accomplishments of his airship in relation to an outbreak of war were already extraordinary. From Emden it could safely reach all English harbors and those of northern France. From Metz it would fly over all of France. Given its general cultural benefit, one must still primarily build airships for military purposes. One must take steps to conceal these advances, lest they be imitated and Germany lose her advantage. Once spearheading such technological superiority, Germany could then maintain the lead. Rapid and decisive action in defense of the nation was required.

Later in the session he was reported as expressing himself very personally:

> Of all German airshipmen he had known . . . only Captain von Sigsfeld had possessed full understanding of his [the Count's] airship. Awkward though it

Count Zeppelin (right), his daughter (middle), and Dr. Dürr (left) in LZ 3, 1907. (Luftschiff-bau Zeppelin)

might be for him personally, he must still declare that he was the only expert in Germany who was also an inventor. He was, moreover, not just an ordinary inventor, but a *German general* [emphasis supplied], and as such must stress that it was the height of official irresponsibility not to utilize his airship.[31]

In this long and crucial official document were foreshadowed three basic elements in Count Zeppelin's advocacy of airships during the last decade of his life: (1) the new but still hesitant support from German military circles; (2) a premonition of the tremendous popular acclaim for the aeronaut; and (3) a reassertion of the psychologically intensified personality of the Count himself, with a usually reserved but very pricklish dimension of self-esteem.

The scales turned rapidly in Zeppelin's favor. In early 1907 the first nationwide lottery on his behalf attracted broad participation. In spring all parties of the Reichstag voted to spend half a million marks for construction of a new floating hangar. Even the Social Democrats gave their support, averring that the larger scientific and cultural dimensions of the enterprise overshadowed its initial predominantly military purpose.[32] During the summer LZ 3 was rebuilt and improved. Visitors by the hundreds thronged the lakeside promenade in Friedrichshafen to view the construction from a distance. In late September four flights in four days had the airship in airborne movement from three to eight hours on each occasion. The German crown prince himself was aboard an early October flight. Zeppelin and his airship were becoming national celebrities. Early in November 1907, General von Moltke, stressing that Germany's only chance of competing effectively with France in airships lay with Zeppelin, granted him 400,000 marks and promised to purchase LZ 3 and LZ 4 (under construction) if the craft stayed aloft twenty-four hours over a distance of 435 miles toward a predetermined destination.[33]

The aeronaut was no longer isolated. Increasingly the national press had focused attention on his activities. There were the nationwide lottery of spring 1907 and the Reichstag concern for his enterprise. Multiplying human-interest accounts featured his lonely endeavors of the past two decades and the negativism of government circles. All these made for an accumulation of fact and myth about the heroic inventor. During the spring and early summer of 1908, as LZ 4 slowly took shape, crowds by the thousands watched from afar on the lakeside promenade or ventured closer in boats toward the great floating construction hangar. The first trials in June culminated in a twelve-hour flight over major cities of Switzerland. It was a worldwide press sensation. Eckener later wrote that this flight established Zeppelin's reputation, on which later events would build and enlarge. A firm image of the aeronaut was established: a quiet genius, a national patriot prevented from achieving his goal only by narrow-minded or inimical government authorities. Enthusiasm reached a fever pitch on July 8, his seventieth birthday. Congratulations poured in. Cities began to name streets in his honor. His Württemberg king capped these events with heartiest congratulations and conferred upon him the Golden Medal of Arts and Sciences. The fool at Lake Constance had become a national hero.[34]

Now events moved toward the incredible climax of the Zeppelin drama. After further brief trials, the Count set out in early August to achieve the prescribed distance and endurance goal. Down the Rhine valley he flew to the accompaniment of hourly newspaper extras and special trains to accommodate the fascinated crowds. *"Zeppelin kommt!"* was the cry now heard along the Rhine. Over the next six years it would attain nationwide currency and bring thousands to the streets, rooftops, and open spaces whenever an airship appearance seemed imminent or was rumored. At an emergency stop along the Rhine, crowds broke out in song with *"Deutschland, Deutschland über alles!"* Early on August 5 the airship landed at Echterdingen, close to the Daimler motor works, to repair a malfunctioning engine. Briefly secured there, the airship broke from its moorings in gusts from a midafternoon storm and was destroyed by fire. Eckener records that the Count was not only dismayed by the disaster itself, but even more so by the implications that his fourth airship had still not achieved the necessary airborne stability and engine power to complete the prescribed trials successfully.[35]

The "Miracle of Echterdingen"—the outpouring of public sympathy and financial assistance—is the very stuff of dramatic social history. Predominantly in the forefront is the image of the Count himself, stoically reserved,

Kaiser Wilhelm II visits Count Zeppelin, Friedrichshafen, Nov. 10, 1908. (Colsman Family Archives)

Count Zeppelin with Field Marshal von Haeseler, 1912. (Luftschiffbau Zeppelin)

Count Zeppelin on maneuvers with Kaiser Wilhelm II, 1913. (Bildarchiv Preussischer Kulturbesitz)

a heroic figure beset by malicious fate. One is touched by the stories of school childrens' pennies; but the bulk of the six-million-marks national gift came from business, the wealthy aristocracy, and major figures of the imperial government. The skeptic is less impressed by the volume of this support than by the spectacle of urgent scramble to get aboard the train of public enthusiasm before it had left the station.

The crowning success occurred on November 10, 1908, when the emperor of Germany, with the full panoply of retinue and publicity, paid a personal visit to the Count and his construction works in Friedrichshafen. Now the aeronaut had realized the first of his two basic objectives: his honor was restored. The full rehabilitation of his career was in progress. What thoughts he confided to his journal are still unknown, but photographic records convey the significance. Beginning with the autumn of 1909—almost twenty years since his humiliation in 1890—the aeronaut was recalled to regular attendance at the great annual *Kaisermanöver* of the combined German armies. One sees him jovially greeting his Württemberg sovereign, the Count's left chest weighted with decorations, the plumes of his helmet waving in the breeze. Other photographs show him on the field of honor in the uniform of a Stuttgart Uhlan general, binoculars in hand and earnestly poring over terrain maps. On another occasion he is seen engaged in convivial conversation with Field Marshal General Haeseler, the same professional colleague who two decades before could not believe that Zeppelin had been cashiered. Another photograph of the 1912 maneuvers speaks eloquently. There the aeronaut sits

LZ 6 at Bitterfeld, en route to
Berlin, Aug. 28, 1909. (Luftschiffbau Zeppelin)

in an improvised Elbe River ferry, somewhat overshadowed, but still at the
center of power with General von der Goltz Pascha, the kaiser himself, General von Moltke, Prince Maximilian Egon von Fürstenberg, and the king of
Bavaria. His rehabilitation was spectacular.[36]

For the next six years, until the outbreak of World War I, the Count rode
the crest of his wave of popularity. He moved publicly with quiet composure,
general affability, and expressive patriotism. Here was the model of a man
representing the conservative monarchical social order, within whose hierarchy he had now established a secure place close to the top. With his financial
woes eliminated by the national gift, the aeronaut could give all attention to
the full achievement of the second of his two basic objectives—the perfection
of a reliably constructed and performing aerial weapon of war. Still, despite
the important advantages he had gained, all was not smooth sailing for the
Count on that wave of public enthusiasm. Successive designs of his airships
and continuing bad experiences with operations still fell short of minimal
reliability. The German military still only doled out its financial-operational
support in unsatisfactory installments. The airplane began to emerge as a
troublesome competitor to airships of any kind.

In autumn of 1909 the army undertook a serious comparative test of all
three airship types in the first systematic airship maneuvers in military aviation
history. It was time to see how well nonrigid Parseval, semirigid Gross-
Basenach, and rigid Zeppelin could fulfill their military requirements. None
of the ships adequately passed their trials, but the anti-Zeppelin proponents

Arrival of LZ 6 at Berlin, Aug.
29, 1909. (Northrup University
and Lee Payne)

Dr. Ludwig Dürr. (Luftschiffbau
Zeppelin)

Major Hans Gross. (Strumann
Archives)

Dr. August von Parseval. (Strumann Archives)

could make a case that necessary further airship improvement could be accomplished with their types at far less expense than the rigid would require. The army had refused to purchase further rigids. Yet, fortified by his national financial gift, Zeppelin went on building with determination, his mind closed to certain basic problems of design and operation. If the crowds thrilled at the elegant ships aloft in flight, they also shuddered at the news of airship accidents. Four zeppelins crashed or burned in the year after April 1910, fortunately with no loss of life. There were no immediate further orders from the army.[37]

In desperation—to judge from the tone of the memorandum—the Count again reactivated his social network. In August 1911 he addressed a plea to the kaiser on "Contemporary and Soon-to-be-realized Performance of Z-ships and their Utilization in War." With selective attention he praised various performance characteristics of past, present, and future airships. Convinced of his argument, he continued:

> With the accomplishments and qualities of existing airships, or of those soon to be built, hereby established, [it is clear] that *they have great versatility and distinction as weapons of war, as they were conceived and developed by me from the very beginning* [emphasis supplied]. . . . Recognizing these facts, if a significant number of these well-performing airships were speedily procured, and if provision were made for crews and officers properly trained in their use, then Germany would in the very shortest time possess a most valuable auxiliary weapon of war in support of its forces by land and sea.

With pathos the Count continued:

> Is it not depressing for a man, whose anxiety for the *Vaterland* overrides all other concerns, to see that up to this very day recognition of that basic fact [usefulness of his airships] has been absent in leading circles and that they have failed in a related duty to take effective action? . . . My prophecies, declarations, warnings, and pleas have all been spoken into the wind. I have been ridiculed, pitied, and variously held suspect—*the same as in earlier times* [emphasis supplied]. The negative opinion of my airships held by the Prussian Airship Battalion has been accepted by the General Staff and instructors of the War Academy without any serious independent investigation. . . . Saddest of all is the fact that now, when an airship of superior performance already exists, no thought appears to be given to its potential usefulness, in ways I recently set forth in my address at the War Academy. . . . If I should die before I am given an opportunity to show what I can accomplish, it will be a great loss for Germany. Should war break out, as long as I am still in any way fit, I hope that I will be permitted myself to lead the best one of my available airships into battle, for its most effective use in our war-making power.[38]

This revealing document stands virtually alone. Little more, if anything, can be expected from the German Heeresarchiv: its resources were almost completely destroyed in World War II. The archives of Luftschiffbau Zeppelin in Friedrichshafen suffered considerably from wartime bombing; apparently nothing pertaining to these matters has survived. Any clues as to further

LZ 10, "Schwaben," early passenger airship, 1911–12. (Luftschiffbau Zeppelin)

correspondence between Count Zeppelin and empire authorities, indeed, as to his own reactions to the events of these years, will have to await opening of the aeronaut's own archives.

Faced with an empty factory and no orders, Managing Director Alfred Colsman of the Luftschiffbau Zeppelin had proposed the solution that would sustain the business until larger military and naval orders began to take hold in 1912. He suggested a passenger-service operating company (DELAG) to capitalize on public aviation enthusiasm. It would be part of the emerging Zeppelin industrial conglomerate and place orders for airship construction with the Luftschiffbau. The plan was accepted by the governing board in late 1909, but only over the Count's vehement objection. Half a century later Eckener still recalled Zeppelin's ardent disapproval: "I detest any notion of commercializing my invention!"[39] Even though the DELAG was enthusiastically supported by the mayors of a dozen major German cities and easily obtained capital investment of three million marks, Count Zeppelin kept his distance. As Colsman later wrote: "He saw his conception profaned if the airships were used to earn money through the DELAG. That enterprise thus remained for him, the feudal aristocrat and old soldier, a tradesman's venture. . . . In an aristocratic context such as his, a merchant was just not socially acceptable."[40]

The aeronaut's negative posture in the creation of the DELAG was a clear reflection of an industrial generational conflict characteristic of Wilhelmian Germany. The older, simpler individualistic enterprises were being superseded by modern companies and conglomerates directed by calculating, profit-oriented managers and technocrats like Colsman. In light of these circumstances and the emotionally laden year of airship accidents and resultant military disfavor, Zeppelin could pause to consider broader areas of public life being affected by aviation generally and airships particularly. He spoke publicly of the airship as benefiting the natural and social sciences. He urged the study and promulgation of international aeronautical law, notably of international treaties to regulate commerce by airship. With his old scientific friend and supporter, Hugo Hergesell, the Count made a trip to Spitzbergen in 1910 to examine possibilities of arctic exploration by airship, and contributed an article on meteorology to the volume of studies about the trip subsequently published.[41]

If the Count recognized the foregoing opportunities as important, he may also have derived greater stimulation from another phenomenon. All over Europe the air was redolent with gunpowder. Novels and stories of future wars entertained men young and old. Germans particularly enjoyed one variety of that reading, which exaggerated their zeppelin enthusiasm—accounts of aerial warfare. This *Luftmilitarismus* was hardly foreign to the Count. Aeronaut Georg von Tschudi, who was aboard LZ 6 with General von Eichhorn en route to the *Kaisermanöver* of 1909, recounts an incident symptomatic of the Count's inclination. Zeppelin knew that they would meet a Gross-Basenach semirigid on the way. For that occasion he had mounted a small artillery piece on one of the gondolas to fire a loud and smoky blank shot at his disdained rival. With some difficulty Tschudi talked him out of the demonstration.[42] Much different were the impressive and destructive aerial cruisers that filled the skies of airship warfare fantasy, especially in the ways they defied the basic laws of physics and meteorology. Dime novels and weekly installments of the war thrillers satisfied the youth. Their elders could enjoy more solid fare, like that supplied by Rudolf Martin with his seriously propounded strategic and tactical battle details in *Berlin-Baghdad: The German World Empire in the Airship Age, 1910–1931*, which went through several editions. Letters to editors and reports directly to Zeppelin raised the same themes. Wrote one patriot to the Count: "Just returned last week from a trip to England, I sent the Imperial War Ministry a detailed report on my impression of what incredible destruction of property and war material twenty zeppelins could wreak in one day on London with its billions of marks worth of structures, goods, banks, etc." The Count responded: "I fully share your patriotic anxiety, and *all the more am I determined to develop my airships as splendid instruments of war* [emphasis added], whereby of course I trust they will harm only the weapons of our enemies and not the unwarlike citizenry." A few years later he would no longer make such distinctions.[43]

The appearance of an effective competitor to Zeppelin (Schütte-Lanz) and a rapidly emerging airplane alternative for aerial warfare found the imperial military authorities divided several ways as to aerial strategies and types. Simultaneously France, the perceived enemy by land, had virtually abandoned the airship in preference for the airplane, while England, the perceived enemy by sea, was far behind in any type of aerial warfare. General von Stein of the General Staff urged abandonment of the airship in favor of the airplane.

General von Lyncker, Inspector-General of Military Transport, urged vigorous continuing competitive development of all airship types. With an oblique eye on Schütte-Lanz, the Count addressed the crown prince in the spring of 1912, thereby also reaching the kaiser, stressing again actual LZ accomplishments and rosy pictures of future achievements. Once again the Luftschiffbau needed a customer. Later that year Zeppelin informed the General Staff of bombing trajectory experiments carried out by the Company at his behest. After the autumn *Kaisermanöver*, the aeronaut sent the kaiser a long evaluation of the allegedly superior performance of several LZ ships involved, which hardly agreed with the realities observed by army judges. By the end of the year, however, a major corner was turned. Two further LZ ships were ordered, and, no doubt much to Zeppelin's chagrin, the first Schütte-Lanz ship had also appeared. With the active participation of Colsman and Eckener from the Luftschiffbau, the army had made its major decisions as to specifications and locations of a nationwide airship station plan. By 1913 the rigid airship had at long last arrived as a fully accepted, but no longer unique, weapon of aerial warfare.[44]

During 1911 the German navy ended several years of hesitant consideration and decided to develop its airship arm. Naval personnel had closely watched and sometimes participated in the LZ flights between 1907 and 1911. The Count had sent the chief of the admiralty two memoranda in May 1908, stressing the capabilities of his airship in reconnoitering and bombing ships at sea. The frailty of the airship in adverse weather, however, was the major stumbling block; it would have to become operationally more reliable to avoid the inevitably fatal results of unwanted descents at sea. That objective now seemed reasonably obtainable. Since 1910 a naval technical adviser had been present at the Luftschiffbau, indicating sole preference for rigid airships and beginning to penetrate the wall of secrecy that the Count had erected against his military nonrigid competitors. Still, this circumstance did not prevent the navy from equally favoring the Schütte-Lanz airships and thus positively encouraging competition within that industry. As a relative latecomer on the rigid airship scene, the German navy had none of the traumatic baggage of Zeppelin's two decades of relations with the German army, where the antagonisms still flared up until the war broke out in 1914. Still, in October 1913, the Count initiated a loud and intemperate public quarrel with Admiral Tirpitz at the burial of the crew of L 2. Zeppelin was never forgiven for this appalling display of petulance.[45] He was quietly maneuvered "upstairs," whence he would have neither the authority nor the opportunity further to complicate company relations with the armed services. Thenceforth negotiations of the Luftschiffbau were conducted on very professional levels mostly by director Colsman and flight specialist Eckener of the DELAG. In autumn 1913, the annual maneuvers of the High Seas Fleet saw the first full-scale employment of airships and airplanes in the most technologically advanced navy in the world.[46]

By 1914 Imperial Germany, with its military and civilian airship fleets, with its extended network of bases and terminals, was visibly the greatest air power of its time. A forced landing of army airship Z IV in eastern France in 1912 only strengthened the apprehension of German might. Historian Ludwig Dehio, later commenting on the imperialist and power-justifying vindications of leading German intellectuals in that era, saw prewar Germany caught up in an aggressive "dry war" mentality.[47] No doubt Count Zeppelin was in tune with this mode of thought and its shadow, the German fear of "encirclement" by Britain, France, and Russia. On his seventy-fifth birthday in 1913, congratulations flowed in to the Count from all over the Germanic world. Colonel Erich Ludendorff, who had forcefully participated in various army deliberations about acquiring and positioning the zeppelins between 1908 and 1911, and had himself made trial bombing runs with airships, wired, "With firm confidence in the accomplishments of the Zeppelin airships in the war that at long last is coming, I send your Excellency in deep admiration my most respectful best wishes." The Count replied with "heartfelt thanks for your warm birthday wishes."[48] In June 1914, Zeppelin's nephew, Baron von Gemmingen, wrote an article in which he conjured up the possibility that some island empire allied with a continental power would, in the event of war, send troops in support by sea. "Could there be a more beautiful task," he asked rhetorically, "than to interdict these troop transports by bombs thrown from our airships?"[49] The precise dimensions of Zeppelin's attitudes in these kinds of company remain to be clarified from his unpublished writings, but their trend would seem to be clear.

The great European war broke out in early August 1914. It promised to be the crowning event in Zeppelin's checkered military-technological career, but the fulfillment was never complete. Both the honors and the airships would fall short of perfection. After hostilities began, the Count requested the kaiser for assignment on one of his airships as a General Staff officer. Apparently he drew the bow too taut, for the kaiser offered in response only to grant him an appointment as a technical adviser to an already experienced staff officer. No doubt the Count's heart stirred with the same sentiments expressed by the German ambassador to Stockholm in late August 1914:

> The war must be brought in every possible way [into the heart of Britain] so that its people will be held in constant quivering fear. Therefore . . . I hope that we will soon control the northern continental coast from Ostend to Cherbourg. There, in a safe distance from the sea, we can build hangars, whose airships and airplanes will continually crisscross England with their bombing, while submarines and torpedo boats are relentlessly engaged in probing attacks against the British shore.[50]

Two months later Zeppelin addressed another request to his war lord—rephrasing his emotional plea of 1911—to command an airship in combat "because all Germany expects me to make the first flight over London."[51] The request was denied on grounds that he was far too valuable to risk his life in action. Instead, he was made a patriotic advertisement for the nation. On frequent appearances in various parts of Germany, he arrived in his splendid Uhlan uniform, with glittering medals and a requisite aide in tow. Except for occasional ceremony, there was no longer a place for him at the Luftschiffbau. Here the men of war were now in command, soon to speed up the production of airships to one per month and to require melding of some undeniably superior Schütte-Lanz technical innovations with the established LZ designs.[52]

As the initial military success of rapid movement bogged down in the statics of trench warfare and the German navy remained hesitant in the North Sea, the Count's frustration with events grew. Aircraft constructor Heinkel later recorded a characteristic circumstance. Zeppelin proposed dropping a single massive bomb into a British harbor, so that (as he claimed) the resulting explosive pressure through the water would sink all ships there present. In the ensuing heated discussion, which required correction of the Count's inadequate grasp of basic physics, all the aeronaut's least positive qualities were manifest: firm dogmatism, innocence of scientific details, pained obstinacy, and peevish grumbling when he was finally proven wrong.[53]

The Count was more successful as a political agitator and armchair strategist. Ideologically he became an assertive Pan-German and his military enthusiasm escalated into fanaticism. He berated civilian and military authorities for their failure to utilize fully all weapons at their command. Though he privately may have understood the operational difficulties and serious losses of both the army and the navy airships, by late 1915 the Count was crying for all-out war and massive commitment of airships to the destruction of the enemy. General von Einem recalled from 1916:

> It was near the front the last time I saw Count Zeppelin, as he visited me at my command headquarters. Standing before me in his Uhlan uniform, he exclaimed: "All England must burn!" and his eyes sparkled. As we shook hands in departure, I asked him not to forget us in our deadly struggle on the Western Front. "How could that be possible?" he replied, and that boundless generosity illuminated his expression.[54]

This charismatic personality of the Count, together with his equally boundless enthusiasm for politics and warmaking became a serious liability to military and civilian authorities alike. In early 1916, in pursuance of laws prohibiting public agitation about war aims, the imperial chancellor put Zeppelin under censorship for both his written and spoken word. Such prohibition did not deter his appearance before selected discreet audiences. In mid-1916 he spoke to a gathering of the Prussian State Assembly and their friends. With frequent interruptions by applause he called for radical measures ("the most devastating war is ultimately the most merciful"), proclaimed Germany's right to worldwide naval power, and demanded unrestricted submarine and airship warfare.[55] His private correspondence dealt with the same subjects. Later in 1916, one of his correspondents urged him again to press the authorities "fully to

Count Zeppelin at his bomber factory, 1917. (Luftschiffbau Zeppelin)

utilize the British seasonal fogs, so favorable to our cause, to annihilate London and destroy the British people." The Count responded, "Please be assured that I am doing what I can to realize your objectives. We can certainly anticipate that it will come to pass under our new military chief command [Ludendorff], as it becomes feasible in his future planning."[56]

If his airships were not proving very successful and he was politically under some restraint, the Count could still enjoy a new aerial dimension for his endeavors. Virtually barred from the Luftschiffbau in Friedrichschafen by the new generation of navy engineers, he turned to designing heavy, winged bombers. These were to be huge four-engined aircraft, capable of carrying the large bombs he thought suitable for inflicting that erroneously conceived damage on British harbors. These became the Giant Staaken airplanes that subsequently destroyed more British targets than did the vaunted zeppelins.[57] By then the Count had died (March 8, 1917) and had been buried with great pomp and circumstance. The obituaries were numerous, magnificent, and hyperbolic. His mortal cares and frustrations behind him, Count Zeppelin would no doubt have been content with the sentiment expressed in Germany's most distinguished publication of otherwise irreverent commentary. It showed a cartoon of the aeronaut in heaven, in the background a chorus of angels carrying an airship, in the foreground St. Peter conducting him on a tour of the premises. The caption read:

St. Peter: We have provided the best spot for our war hero and gifted inventor.
Count Zeppelin: Can one see Germany from there?[58]

It is unlikely that the Zeppelin rigid airship, even if devised, would have been constructed and developed in the way and to the degree that it had matured by 1914, had its inventor been permitted to continue his career as a German cavalry officer. That was the life work to which he was fully and professionally committed. That service in arms for the German *Vaterland* was his personal fulfillment—until it was suddenly irreversibly terminated by his abrupt rejection in the autumn of 1890. As he wrote to General von Schlieffen in 1891, he normally would not have been in a position to pursue his thoughts about airships because he would not have had the time and certainly not the occasion, lest his fellow officers consider him a candidate for an insane asylum. Barring that personal disaster of 1890, he would have continued the adequate military career to which he was devoted, arriving no doubt at an honorable statutory retirement at some time between 1903 and 1908. In unperturbed retirement he might then have returned to his airship hobby. He could easily have become more serious about it, as he contemplated his basic conception as an alternative to the nonrigid and semirigid types favored by the Prussian Airship Battalion and still being developed by the French army. Possibly the limitations of these craft (as exemplified by the Parseval, Gross-Basenach,

Funeral of Count Zeppelin, March 12, 1917. King Wilhelm II of Württemberg following directly behind coffin. (Luftschiffbau Zeppelin)

and Siemens ships) might have prompted his serious commentary, with suggestions that a rigid sky-train would offer greater opportunities for personnel transport and logistical supply. In view of the accident with David Schwarz's all-metal airship in 1897, however, and missing the consistent writings, experiments, and constructions of Count Zeppelin, it is doubtful if any one else, not endowed as the Count was with purpose, funds, and military-political connections, would have advanced rigid airship technology so far.

Without that stimulus, it is further quite conceivable that engineer Johann Schütte might not have studied airships at all. Had the rigid airship at best only begun to be developed and experimentally constructed around 1905, then it is likely that it would have been overtaken by the airplane before it could have made a significant military-technological impact on prewar society or during World War I.

It is also highly unlikely that the Zeppelin rigid airship would have been devised and constructed, even after the Count had experienced his humiliating personal disaster, had he not possessed a unique combination of character and qualities. Here was a man well-born and well-bred, possessed of remarkable honesty about himself and toward others. His deeply felt sense of loyalty expressed itself in dignified deference to his social superiors, amiable poise with equals, and unobtrusive paternalism toward social inferiors. A profound sense of honor marked his personal bearing and dealings with others. He generally possessed a confident self-assurance about his place in society and his mission in life. His personality expressed itself with affability, intellectual liveliness, energy, and pluck. His firmly self-disciplining willpower and stubborn pertinacity supported these qualities. They all came uniquely to bear in his time of contention with fate by giving him dignified endurance together with quiet determination to turn his life toward a new course of action.

Count Zeppelin's humiliation at the *Kaisermanöver* of 1890 caused him extreme psychological trauma. Here was a man passionately devoted to military service, who had asked to be relieved from the highest civilian post his king could confer upon him—Württemberg ambassador to the king of Prussia and member of the prestigious German *Bundesrat*—in order that he might return to his profession of arms. In those circumstances he was subjected to stinging and unjust mortification in the company of his professional peers. Most unbearable must have been the perceivably manipulated taint upon his sense of honor and the thinly veiled disparagement of his loyalty to his Swabian homeland. Only such a profound shock could produce the kind of motivation for action that would move him to risk his personal reputation and family fortune in what was so easily perceived as a ridiculous enterprise, especially for a German *officer*! This was not the situation of a retired gentleman turning contentedly to tinkering and inventing as a hitherto sometime hobby. Quite the contrary! Here was a man driven by a profound psychological need to compensate for great and unjust dishonor to his person and family name. Only such motivation explains the deep-seated urge and single-minded devotion to an enterprise to satisfy honor and rehabilitate his career by circumventing his enemies and detractors in devising a new and spectacular weapon of war for his *Vaterland*. In these circumstances his positive qualities were an indispensable support. If he contended nobly with fate, it is not surprising that in his often frustrating dealings with other individuals (and their bureaucratic extensions), he could lapse, especially in later years, into less attractive traits: mulish obstinacy, pedantic irritability, resistance to correction of his ideas, and occasional ruthlessness.

Still, all these circumstances and qualities together would not have sufficed to see the Count successfully through to his objective, had he not been fortuitously situated within the protective and facilitating aristocratic social network of his time. Rejected though he was as a professional active in the German army, his social military status remained unimpaired and he enjoyed the highest honorary military position in the Württemberg army. This favorable situation gave him easy access even to the chief of the German General Staff in a continuing fraternal context. These opportunities were equally evident in access to the civilian bureaucracy that uniformly gave a gracious hearing to any military officer. Indeed, most remarkably, the Count had unimpeded access to the kaiser himself, either by his presence at court social functions or through various memoranda that seldom failed to reach the desk of the All Highest. In these endeavors the Count was diligently supported by his Württemberg king, who no doubt vicariously felt Zeppelin's manipulated Prussian dishonor and was correspondingly anxious to see honor restored and respect for his state of Württemberg reaffirmed. The Count found the advantages of this social network psychologically very supportive. He shrewdly manipulated these opportunities, cautiously at first and then with increasing aggressiveness—much to the chagrin and often ill-concealed hostility of those who had to suffer and bend in face of his importunities. No doubt the Count also derived passing psychological satisfaction from the discomfort of those whom he annoyed as he pressed for attention and support. Crucial is the fact that without the opportunities and advantages offered by his social network before 1908, Zeppelin would never have got as far as he did in that time. These were the circumstances that helped bring him to the point where public acclaim could take him up and carry him on thereafter.

The social-aristocratic network of Zeppelin's era vibrated with a Germanic enhancement of the nationalism and militarism prevalent in all of Europe at the time. The intense loyalty that the Count initially felt for his native Württemberg was transfigured during the third decade of his life into a higher emotional devotion to the German nation. That transformation, however, did not occur in some sense of modernization, for beneath his fealty to the German kaiser he retained his subinfeudated loyalties to his Württemberg king and his own aristocratic peers. In that semifeudal social world he early found his way to its most characteristic mode of self-expression, a professional career in the warrior caste. He took to the passage of arms with commitment and passion, in a romantic aura of selfless dedication on the field of battle, in the cause of warfare that was both glorious and meant to be won. In short, he was a militarist. His great discomfort in 1909, when Colsman founded the DELAG in order to find a commercial outlet for the faltering airship business, clearly expressed the Count's subordination of civilian precepts to the military spirit. Colsman established in his account that Zeppelin always believed in his military destiny, indeed, as World War I began, in his advanced years, Zeppelin still sought fulfillment of his military duty in order thus finally to win back the full favor of his war lord.[59]

Zeppelin's intense psychological drive to repair his shattered professional reputation, to restore his honor, and to fulfill his soldierly mission occurred within a variegated German milieu of modern nationalism, semifeudal militarism, and up-to-date technological progress. With but a rudimentary mid-century technical education, the Count's native intelligence and capacity to learn took him well beyond the threshold of airship conceptualization. For the rest, he had his personal resources, the financial influence of his king, and the investments of his suppliers to move him toward his objective. Thus he could engage the necessary engineering talent to verify, expand, and correct his own shrewd technological initiatives. The airships he built were meant above all to be superior weapons of war. So his mid-nineteenth-century romantic idealization of arms was harnessed to the rapidly accelerating technological change in war weapons themselves at the opening of the twentieth century. When he memorialized his kaiser in 1911 and 1914 with requests for personal wartime service, he did so in phraseology that applied nineteenth-century cavalry thinking to twentieth-century airships. His technology was modern, but he still thought in terms of semifeudal romanticism. At least, that was the case until World War I broke out. Thereafter, as with so many of his time in Germany and elsewhere, the Count's attitudes and demands on the means and objectives of warfare escalated into extremes of destruction and retribution. The aeronaut, who had earlier represented humane dimensions of conflict and expressed the need to protect noncombatants and civilians, now urged intensive concentration of aerial bombardment over the defenseless cities of England and the Continent. Despite their ultimate inadequacies, these zeppelins and their inventor inaugurated the contemporary era of mass destruction of civilian populations by air. Author Clausberg has summarized it cogently:

> It was more than just tragic mental confusion that saw Count Zeppelin moved to advocate such an inhumane war of annihilation at the end of his life. The fact signaled the end of that fiction of individualized combat between nations that had so long been a common denominator of military and Christian virtues. In Colsman's words, here collapsed the work with which the Count had been closely entwined from earliest youth and through his entire life. It was an irony of history that he had himself created the weapon that affirmed this collapse in terms of impossible alternatives.[60]

In February 1915, just as the dimensions of aerial warfare over England began to appear, Zeppelin had a long interview with journalist Karl von Wiegand about the future of airships in war and peace. After the Count had sketched his then still moderate notions of aerial warfare, he turned to another aspect of his work, which would follow upon Germany's military aerial victory:

> I still have one great ambition. I would wish that a zeppelin would be the first vehicle to link Europe and America by air. I would like to live long enough to

pilot one of my cruisers over the ocean to America, where many years ago I made my first balloon ascent. . . . This war has interrupted my plans in that direction. Some day travel by air will be the quickest and safest way possible. In this respect zeppelins have a great future. Relatively few people know the feeling of comfort and security that a zeppelin gives. They will play a great role in the future of travel and conduct of the mails.[61]

These visions of the peacetime possibilities of the airship would charm the creators of Zeppelin's monument in Friedrichshafen today. These were the possibilities that indeed began to be realized, not by Zeppelin but by his lieutenants, notably Hugo Eckener, even in the last decade of the aeronaut's life.

Author Clausberg gave his study of Count Zeppelin and his time a striking subtitle—*The Story of an Improbable Success*. Despite its appearance at first glance as just another book of text and many pictures for airship buffs, it is a serious work that brings to bear very modern insights from psychology and sociology on the aeronaut and his times. For all that new analysis, and despite its ironic tone, Count Zeppelin retains some dimensions of a classic image. He is much of a Promethean figure. He wrests secrets of flight from unwilling nature, benefits mankind with invention, and suffers the torments of fate until released by destiny to assume an honored position among the gods of his time. Indeed, by 1910 the Count had become a charismatic father figure for the German nation. He was its greatest popular hero since Bismarck, confirming German enthusiasm for nationalism and militarism.

These dimensions of popular emotion and enthusiasm for war have been clearly identified by contemporary experts in the study of German airship development. Robinson devotes two chapters of his authoritative work on airship history to the zeppelin as a nationalistic symbol and as a war-winning weapon.[62] Author Knäusel shows by documents and analysis how much the development of the aeronaut's ideas and the building of the first airship were related to military circumstances, though he avers that the Count was not a militarist—an interpretation that this essay would contravene.[63] Yet, in each of these standard works the focus and fascination of the study is concentrated on the technological and engineering details. As a result, the milieu in which this progress occurred, and the motivations that prompted Count Zeppelin himself, are by emphasis (not by intent) obscured and easily lost, especially on the reader interested only in aviation history and technological development. What is obscured most of all is the awareness that in a world where technology is easily subject to political manipulation, in Count Zeppelin can be seen an original example of man manipulating technology for combined personal and national political advantage.

Has this essay brought a clearer view of the real Count Zeppelin? Is this reconstruction and interpretation of the driving forces in the personality and decisive circumstances in the life of the cavalry-officer-turned-aeronaut believable? Most important of all, is it accurate? None of this can be fully ascertained until there is a new biography of the airship inventor based upon the voluminous resources of the Zeppelin family archives. The origins of this essay lie in the author's appreciation of the books of Hugo Eckener and Rolf Italiaander, one a verbal portrait, the other a photographic account. Eckener's book of fifty years ago is a wonderfully documented study of the Count's personality and reactions to events, based on the candid revelations of his detailed journal. Still, these intimate details cease as author Eckener approaches the turn of the century. Thereafter the original sources are no longer used and the more obvious information appears. Why is this? Was the narrative becoming too long? Or were there details of the Count's personal attitudes and reactions after 1890 that blurred the heroic image of the general-inventor that Eckener wished to convey in 1938 as a preferred alternative to the militaristic *hazardeurs* of the Nazi regime? Italiaander's beautifully illustrated work is actually a detailed photographic essay of the Count and his times, especially if the pictures are carefully studied for their content. Such study is necessary, for Italiaander limits himself to brief explanatory captions or short introductions to the documents. Thus the most evocative sources are either incomplete or not fully explained.

There is clear need for a new biography of Count Zeppelin that will fully capture the contents of the rich family archives and render their significance without reserve or embellishment. Such a study need not embarrass the good citizens of Friedrichshafen. The selective presentation of facts in the address of the mayor can be left in the city archives as an understandable document of its time. A new study of Count Zeppelin will fill in the missing gaps on the memorial obelisk between LZ 1 and LZ 126. The wording need not be changed. Dials that record only the sunny hours have their aesthetic and psychologically comprehensible purposes too. And the graffiti that so crudely bespoke the demand of contemporary German youth to have the truth? Even if they have been long since erased, their legitimate request will have been fulfilled.

CHAPTER 2 In the Shadow of the Titan: Thoughts on the Life and Work of Naval Engineer Johann Schütte

Prof. Johann Schütte, 1935. (Landesmuseum f. Technik, Mannheim)

It was time to redeem the reputation of Johann Schütte. On a bright summer morning the American professor and his German friend, both students of airship history, walked through the modernized streets of the old city of Oldenburg, with its treasures of late medieval half-timbered houses and profusion of flowers. They arrived at the spacious seat of the local cultural society, Oldenburgische Landschaft, to meet its officers and to celebrate the restoration of the airship designer's personal archives. Champagne sparkled in tall fluted glasses and spirits rose among the gathered group. There was hearty reminiscence of favorite son "Jan" Schütte, who had contributed so significantly to the design of the modern German airship—always an airship (*Luftschiff*) in those quarters, never a zeppelin! Remembered too, with appreciation and wry smiles, were the peccadilloes of young Jan, who once in his late teens had climbed the walls of the castle of Oldenburg to an unscheduled rendezvous with the daughter of the resident grand duke. The meeting was forestalled and young Schütte subsequently sought his fame and fortune elsewhere.

Less hearty was the remembrance, now with a sober mien, of Schütte's later days. He had greeted the creation of the Luftwaffe in 1934 with enthusiasm and some of that had slipped over from technology to admiration of the national sponsorship. In 1938 followed the dedication of the Johann Schütte Hall of Honor and a Schütte-Lanz museum in that same castle where he had been caught half a century before. At the same time he was inscribed in the Golden Book of Oldenburg, by then of course fully synchronized with Nazi propaganda. The Burgomaster then proclaimed with importance, "Just as Friedrichshafen preserves the tradition of Zeppelin, so now will Oldenburg affirm the significance of Schütte-Lanz!" Seven years later Nazism was expunged from the German scene and so also disappeared the official appreciation of Jan Schütte. His name was eradicated from the Golden Book, the museum disbanded, and the large mural celebrating the native son covered with a wall hanging. Now, in 1979, the memory of Johann Schütte was being revived. And with it reappeared memories of the sharp antagonism between enthusiasts for the zeppelin and admirers of the later Schütte-Lanz designs.[1]

Elderly Oldenburg citizen Johann Friedrich Jahn was primarily responsible for this reawakened interest. Retired in the mid-1960s, Jahn took instruction from several trained archivists. Over the following decade he systematically identified, ordered, and catalogued an immense collection of Schütte's professional and business papers and artifacts. These had been left to the city of Oldenburg in 1938 and were spared the destruction wrought on many other national and business archives during World War II. The collection contained a major specialized library of aeronautical design and engineering, a great many pictures and photographs, and over six thousand construction drawings of Schütte's actualized and projected airships. Indeed, the celebration was as much a tribute to Herr Jahn as to Schütte himself; for the archivist had rescued from musty attics what is probably the most complete, self-contained collection of data about airship design and construction extant today. Thanks to Jahn's devotion, the full dimensions of Johann Schütte's contributions can at last be appreciated. The archive also throws light on the details and fate of Schütte's abortive airship efforts between 1919 and 1929, the same decade that saw Hugo Eckener and Alfred Colsman preside at the rebirth and triumph of the zeppelin—with its fundamental Schütte-inspired improvements.[2]

As the son of an Oldenburg ducal civil servant, Johann Schütte was born in Oldenburg in 1873, and he spent much of his youth on the East Frisian coast of the North Sea. His thorough education gave him a solid background for a characteristic Oldenburg preoccupation with sailing and shipbuilding. These interests predominated in his engineering studies at the Technical University at Berlin-Charlottenburg, with intervals of practical seamanship and professional apprenticeship at the imperial naval shipyards at Kiel. In 1897–98 he received his engineering degree, passed exams as a naval architect, and joined the construction division of Germany's largest shipping enterprise, the North German Lloyd, where he remained till 1904.

These were heady years of accelerating technological progress in steamship design and construction. Within Germany the Lloyd of Bremen was competing aggressively with its major competitor, the rapidly rising Hamburg-America Line in the city of its old Hanseatic rival. More important, through the initiative of these two companies, Germany, and the kaiser himself, were determined to snatch the mythical Blue Riband of the North Atlantic from England and her shipbuilders. Just as Schütte joined the Lloyd, there was a grave design crisis in the company. Its newest entry for the fastest North Atlantic crossing had failed to achieve the speed that its builders had promised. Young Schütte was put in charge of studying the comparative underwater resistance to ship hulls of various configurations. He took carefully constructed models of several competing hull designs to a testing facility in

Italy and there determined which one was hydrodynamically least resistant and therefore speediest. On the basis of his research the Lloyd refused delivery of the ship. Schütte was then made responsible for the Lloyd's design research and put in charge of a large, newly built testing facility. Soon he was at work on difficult studies about the reduction of keel resistance and the redesign of the stern components of more powerfully engined oceanliners. In recognition of these accomplishments and other significant engineering innovations, Schütte was called to a professorship at the Technological University in Danzig in 1904, at the remarkably young age of thirty. Here he specialized in theory of ship design and began training a succession of talented naval engineers.[3]

The zeppelin disaster at Echterdingen in August 1908 was as much a fateful turn in the career of Johann Schütte as for the aeronaut Count himself. Applying his experience with hydrodynamics, propulsion systems, and structures, within a week the engineer proposed a series of improved designs for airship hulls and propulsion. In a memorandum of August 14, 1908, Schütte explained that the problems of the zeppelin airship lay less with the specific cause of the disaster than in certain basic design flaws. The airship (like its naval counterpart) required its own terminals protected from unfavorable weather, but even more than that was required to establish reliability in an airship. Schütte suggested a strengthened double frame, analogous to the double bottom in a steamship hull. He argued further that, like a naval vessel, the airship must have a strong keel which would also facilitate unimpeded movement within the ship from bow to stern. The airship should have single-unit horizontal and vertical stabilizers only at the stern, as long since proven by rudders in naval design. Propellers should be attached directly to engines mounted in gondolas suspended outside the airship hull, thus reducing power loss and improving direct thrust away from the stern of the ship. (Schütte's major contributions of streamlined hull configuration and self-contained internal exhaust shafts for valving hydrogen lifting gas were developed a bit later.) When Count Zeppelin was informed of these proposals, he politely but firmly rejected them for application to any of his projects. Had that not been the case, Schütte might well have had no further interest in airship design. As it was, his psyche was picqued, his interest aroused, and his intelligence stimulated.

For all his young professional brilliance, Schütte did not overtly set himself up in direct competition with Count Zeppelin. Indeed, he himself originated the notion that he lived and functioned professionally "in the shadow of the titan." He was always an admirer of the old aeronaut. When the Count finally succeeded in flying LZ 6 to Berlin in late August 1909, Schütte sent him a telegram of hearty felicitation. The Count replied graciously that he welcomed the contributions of other Germans working for Germany. In fact, that was probably not the case; but Schütte's respect for the old aeronaut remained unimpaired. In an essay, "At the Bier of Count Zeppelin," Schütte wrote in

Transatlantic Airship Can Be Built To-day Says Great German Engineer

Dr. Johann Schuette, Whose Name Is Grouped with That of Zeppelin in the Designing and Building of Aircraft, Believes All Technical Difficulties Opposing the Aerial Passage of the Atlantic Have Been Overcome, but Study of Winds Is Still Needed.

DR. JOHANN SCHUETTE, inventor and constructor of the Schuette-Lanz airship, the latest development of the German dirigible, arrived in town a few days ago from Mannheim, Germany, and talked frankly to the Tribune man at the Waldorf. Dr. Schuette's ships of the air are not experimental. He has already built and successfully navigated one of the most perfect German dirigibles. This ship was finished in 1911, and has run perfectly through storms and rain from Mannheim to Berlin, over 340 miles. The vessel holds 600,000 cubic feet of gas and travels forty-five miles an hour. The largest diameter is 60 feet and its length 450 feet. The cargo weight is five tons. It cost 650,000 marks, or $162,500.

Zeppelin, Schuette and Parseval are the great designers and builders of successful German airships. Dr. Schuette is the greatest airship builder who has ever visited America. Zeppelin builds the rigid aluminum type, Schuette the rigid wooden type and Parseval the most successful non-rigid type.

Dr. Schuette ranks among the greatest of German engineers. For a period he was naval constructor in the North German Lloyd service. He now occupies the chair of naval construction in the Royal Technical High School of Dantzic. He brought a letter from the military attaché of the American Embassy at Berlin to Brigadier General James Allen, chief of the United States army signal corps.

It being understood that Dr. Schuette would soon build a new airship, to be the largest in Germany, and which, if it attains a certain efficiency, the German government will purchase, the Tribune man sought him at his hotel.

He is an impulsive type of the German engineer. His whole appearance suggests the man who has arrived. He bristles with Prussian alacrity. He received the Tribune man in the Palm Room at the Waldorf.

When the reporter stated his mission Dr. Schuette seemed to fail to understand. He said:

"What is the proposition?"

As well as he could the reporter restated the object of his call. The great inventor thereupon motioned to a seat at the table, inquired "What beer will you have?" and, taking a cigar from his leather case, he carefully clipped the end and stowed the expensively constructed weed between his teeth. The waiter lit it for him.

Dr. Schuette gave a guttural of deep enjoyment and again said:

"What is the proposition? You want to go into the airship business, yes? Well, if not, what iss? It is a good business, but no foolishness. Vanniman, Wellman.

"Are you going to bring an airship to America?" he was asked.

"For why?" he inquired. "Why should we bring it over here—an airship? For the money? Why should we bring an airship here—simply to send her up for the amusement of the people to look at and go away and talk about it?

"Tell me, why should we do it? We have it as many as we need, and we need what money we've got to develop more.

"Of course," the reporter hastened to reply, "Germany does not need to send an airship to the United States, but among aeronautical students here there is a strong hope that somehow, some way, we will be permitted to learn by observation of tried and proven airships to develop their usefulness in America."

"Bah! We subsidize airships in Germany," replied Dr. Schuette, much as a professor would chide a delinquent scholar. "The German nation helps Zeppelin."

"Well, our Congress as yet has failed to subsidize any scientific development in aeronautics," he was told.

"But your rich men, your private enterprise, would do it for a few millions, yes? I cannot understand it. Surely, if I go out and I talk with rich men and they see what in Germany we are doing, is it not so? What beer will you have—Muenchner, Pilsner?"

Dr. Schuette's friend, a Mr. Schaefer, of Dantzig, who had accompanied him from Germany, here withdrew from his pocket a large leather case filled with cigars, chose one, carefully clipped its end and deposited the weed, in appearance much like Dr. Schuette's, between his teeth. Throughout the interview the friend, who sat at the doctor's left, said no word, but appeared to obtain genuine solace from his dark beer and smoke rings.

To lead the conversation back to the fatherland, Dr. Schuette was asked how Mr. Lanz was brought into the name of the airship.

"By the very good reason," Dr. Schuette promptly replied, "that he and his family put 2,000,000 marks into the business."

Asked for his views concerning the future of aeronautics, Dr. Schuette said that with three to five years more of development the airship will easily cross the Atlantic.

"There are no technical difficulties in the way of building an airship to-day

Dr. Johann Schuette, inventor of the Schuette-Lanz Airship, who has just returned to Germany after a short visit to this country.

March 1917, praising "this grand, untiring, restlessly creative, heroically fighting man, whom the German nation loves and worships."[4] Considerably unkinder thoughts would characterize his relations with the business heirs of the Count after 1918.

Later a commentator suggested that Zeppelin's blunt refusal to accept Schütte's proposals aroused in the engineer "that well-known trait of German contrariness." Yet, the naval architect had no reason to be defensive. It was his firm conviction that a proper engineering analysis, based on scientific methods and insight, was needed to remove the rigid airship from its conceptual blind alley of rule of thumb design and flight experiment by trial and error. Photographs of his later years show him in his full professorial dignity: stern and erect; graying hair meticulously parted in the middle and smartly combed to either side; noble goatee and dark mustache upwardly twirled at the ends that would have aroused the admiration of William II himself. In earlier years he had an enviable reputation as a very approachable teacher, a concerned mentor, and a man of easy conviviality with his students on academic social occasions. His energy and intellectual vitality were proverbial. He was a scintillating individual. These qualities dominated his personality until the end of World War I. Then, with the collapse of the monarchy that he admired, the coming of a socialist-dominated republic that he distrusted, and an ever-losing struggle to reestablish his airship business, his somewhat less attractive qualities asserted themselves.[5]

In rapid succession Schütte improved on his original proposals and devised further new improvements in airship design. During the fall and winter of 1908–09 various memoranda went forth to State Secretary Lewald at the Interior Ministry; to Major Gross of the Prussian Airship Battalion; to the War Ministry, the General Staff, and the Naval Cabinet; indeed, to the kaiser himself. The encouraging and positive responses from these circles no doubt reflected their appreciation of the technological improvements proposed by Schütte. They also probably expressed some relief at dealing with an obviously capable designer who worked from scientific principles, in contrast to the difficult Count with his failing products and annoying pressures by way of his influential social network. The result was the establishment in April 1909 of the Luftschiffbau Schütte-Lanz at Mannheim-Rheinau, with the support of industrialists Dr. Karl Lanz and August Röchling and capitalization at 350,000 marks. Various imperial circles breathed more easily at the appearance of this businesslike alternative to the prickish national hero down at the shores of Lake Constance.[6]

Despite the naval architect's scientific methods and engineering experience, construction of the first SL (Schütte-Lanz) airship was fraught with unanticipated design changes, delays, and massive cost overruns. Like most pioneering airship designers, from Count Zeppelin to the British builders of R 101 in the later 1920s, Schütte changed his specifications and added improvements as the ship was under construction. Subcontractors failed to meet their deadlines or exact specifications. The most important structural innovation, and subsequently the Achilles' heel of the SL design, was the use of girders made from plywood of three or more layers held together with casein glue. Historian Robinson ascribes the engineer's choice of this structural material to its alleged lightness and elasticity. Analyst Haaland found that, since the airship initially was considered primarily as a vehicle for aerial reconnaissance and depended on wireless for transmission of its sightings, Schütte hoped to avoid potential interference from a huge metal airship structure. He may also have wished to gain a competitive edge over Count Zeppelin. At any rate, the laminated wood girders were uneven in quality, vulnerable to humidity, and prone to failure under stress. Nevertheless, Schütte held to this less-than-successful alternative until 1916 and even then delayed unduly in seeking the better girder construction with duralumin. Like Zeppelin, Schütte had his firm convictions and strong opinions.[7]

While simplicity and efficiency marked some of the design of airship SL 1, the single factors that immediately struck even the most technologically uninitiated observers were the beautiful streamlining of the hull and the ultimate, uncomplicated rudders and elevators at the stern—both innovations carried into aerodynamics from Schütte's hydrodynamic studies for the North German Lloyd. Though beauty was thus in the eyes of the beholder, the fliers had their difficulties with the airship, and Lanz was sorely pressed to meet the cost overruns that had come to two million marks. Possibly he was persuaded to continue the enterprise in hopes of achieving coveted social distinction by building "zeppelins," but certainly German official circles found the scientific approach to airship development promising enough to warrant further contracts and to maintain airship building as a competitive enterprise. As it was, SL 1 underwent various design and operational improvements and achieved a notable success for an initial airship construction in that pioneering age. In private trials and official service it made some sixty shorter and longer flights over a period of twenty months. In early July 1913, it flew from Berlin to Danzig, where the citizens cheered the accomplishments of their professor. Ten days later it was lost at its moorings when a violent storm arose, a meteorological repetition of the Echterdingen disaster of 1908. In more ways than one, the engineer and the industrialist moved "in the shadow of the titan"—the engineer seeking to exceed the success of Count Zeppelin, the industrialist to achieve some of the aeronaut's social preferment.

With a firm contract from the government in hand, Schütte-Lanz rapidly moved to build SL 2. Historian Robinson has stated its significance succinctly: "This SL 2, differing in many ways from [its] predecessor, showed Schütte's genius in every line and feature and was the first modern airship. Not only did [it] set the pattern for all the firm's later products, which were merely enlargements of the SL 2, but [it] also profoundly influenced later Zeppelin designs."[8]

What were these unique improvements? The viewer of any recent "zeppelin" photograph will immediately observe three external characteristics: (1) the elegant streamlining of the hull; (2) the single-unit rudders and stabilizers at the stern of the airship; and (3) the placement of engines with direct-drive propellers in gondolas suspended outside the hull. An expert in airship design would explain two further unique features: (1) a triangular interior keel running the length of the ship and (2) vertical enclosed shafts to carry off the lifting gas, some of which every airship must release at some point in flight or landing. These innovations finally made the airship much more opera-

SL 2 in construction, 1912: separate motor gondola. (Author's Collection)

tionally feasible and led the way to the giant rigids of the 1920s and 1930s in Germany, Britain, and America.[9]

Schütte's crucial improvements came just in time to make the airship really useful as a military weapon. SL 2 first flew in late February of 1914; six months later SLs and LZs were reconnoitering the German eastern front in emerging World War I and bombing fortresses and towns in Belgium. Now the German army and navy both discovered new uses for the airship. The construction works at Friedrichshafen and Mannheim-Rheinau became national assets. The engineering staff at Schütte-Lanz expanded, and for the first time "outside" engineers moved into the Luftschiffbau Zeppelin, which then had the larger and more sophisticated construction facilities. With the old aeronaut Count pushed aside and elevated into a prime patriotic propaganda figure, the constructors and engineers of the imperial navy moved decisively to improve the zeppelins with Schütte's innovations and continuing further Zeppelin advancements. Among the new team was Dr. Karl Arnstein, later chief designer of the American *Akron* and *Macon*, who led the way toward doubling the size of zeppelins by 1918 and sending them to 22,000 feet with three tons of bombs. Matters relating to patent rights and royalties, or any potential disputes about manufacturing rights and payments, were put on ice by the German government for the duration of the war—to await adjustment and full accounting when the great victory was won.

Both airship construction firms boomed with war orders. While Dr. Hugo

SL 2 in construction, 1912: laminated wood girders, keel, deflated
ballonets at stern. (Landesmuseum f. Technik, Mannheim)

Eckener took leave to command the navy airship training school in northern
Germany, Alfred Colsman remained in Friedrichshafen as managing director.
Quite probably Schütte and Colsman developed a creative business relationship, for fragments of their correspondence in the 1920s (preserved in Friedrichshafen and Oldenburg) find them addressing each other with the familiar
du—a social distinction in Germany restricted to closest personal friends.
Zeppelin thrived, but Schütte-Lanz was financially weak under its glossy
veneer of busy wartime production. By war's end there were four thousand

SL 2 in construction, 1912:
hydrogen exhaust shaft in place.
(Landesmuseum f. Technik,
Mannheim)

Aerodynamics of SL 2 in flight,
1914. (Landesmuseum f. Technik,
Mannheim)

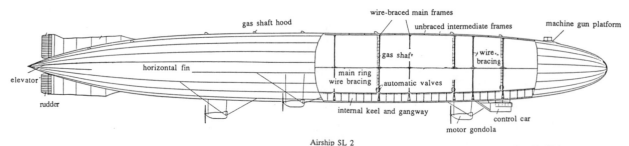

Airship SL 2

L - 144 m, H - 22.7 m, Gas vol - 24,500 m³, HP - 720, Speed - 24.5 m/s, Built 1913, First Flight - Feb. 28, 1914

Technical diagram SL 2, 1914. (*Der Luftschiffbau Schütte-Lanz, 1909–1925*, p. 6)

airship workers with Zeppelin and more than a thousand with Schütte-Lanz. Both firms built new construction hangars in Berlin, one at Staaken, the other at Zeesen. Both firms also developed airplane designs. Count Zeppelin was enthusiastic about the four-engined bomber built by Versuchsbau-Gotha-Ost, a camouflage name for a totally owned Zeppelin enterprise.[10] Schütte-Lanz developed six fighter prototypes and one four-engined bomber; ultimately almost a thousand of the fighters were built for the German army and navy.[11] Together both airship firms built more than a hundred dirigibles during the war. Two-thirds of these were destroyed either in combat or in operational accidents. Since construction figures were concealed from the public by military censorship, the further teething troubles of the airship, as well as the losses, were publicly quite unknown. Thus the national euphoria for the "zeppelin" remained high even into the waning months of the war. From there it could easily be stimulated again into the rousing zeppelin fever of the later 1920s and 1930s.

Even in these favorable circumstances, and with some significant additional technological improvements of his own, Schütte still remained constructionally "in the shadow of the titan," whose zeppelins, though fundamentally improved by the engineer's technical advances, saw further significant improvements by its own builders. Both the army and the navy took SL ships. Those flying for the army in eastern and southeastern Europe performed tolerably, though often in clumsy hands. The SL ships for the navy, however, were a disaster. The damp North Sea air hastened failure of the wooden girders and the crews' complaints were chronic after almost every flight. Captain Peter Strasser, the most prestigious of the wartime naval airship commanders, argued by early 1917 that no more SL ships of that design should be built. He found them almost useless for combat and subsequently refused to accept SL 22 for service. By this time Schütte was shifting to the use of duralumin, but he had lost two precious years—both technologically and financially—experimenting with tube girders instead of adopting the LZ construction methods. It is hard to know whether he entered this technological blind alley because of his stubborn competitiveness with "the titan," or by a designer's tunnel vision in pursuing a particular solution to a technical problem. These expensive delays and the declining orders for airships made serious financial difficulties for Schütte-Lanz in the final year of the war. The last two SL ships were laid down in late 1917 with the tube girder construction, but they were never completed. When the war ended and the victorious Allies pressed the defeated Germans to surrender their remaining airships, thirteen of them were available. Only one was a Schütte-Lanz—SL 22. The other twelve were zeppelins, including several of the most recent and advanced construction. For all his significant scientific expertise, and for all his innovative adaptation of naval architecture to airship redesign, at war's end Johann Schütte was dead in the water.[12]

With peace in prospect, airship building and flying discarded its military-naval uniform. The aeronaut Count had occasionally thought before the war of crossing oceans in his airships and was quite specific in his interview with journalist Karl von Wiegand in 1915, about postwar flying to America. Then a wartime flight pointed prophetically toward the future. In November 1917 zeppelin L 59 had attempted an aerial supply mission to imperial forces beleaguered in German East Africa. The effort was abortive, for the airship turned back to its base in Bulgaria when only halfway to its African destination. In other respects, however, the flight was epoch-making. The zeppelin had carried twenty-two men and over thirty tons of supplies and fuel on a flight equivalent to a nonstop trip from Friedrichshafen to Chicago, a distance of 4,200 miles in 95 hours. On landing it still had ten tons of unexpended fuel aboard. This was the performance beacon that beckoned all subsequent planners for transoceanic flight. The anticipation was fulfilled barely two years later, when in May 1919, the British airship R 34 made a one-stop, round-trip flight across the North Atlantic with similarly impressive performance statistics. No airplane could match such accomplishments. A new era was dawning for the airship.[13]

The builders and fliers of the Zeppelin Company arrived promptly at the starting gate. Eckener returned to Friedrichshafen shortly after the armistice. There Captain Ernst Lehmann was urging an early demonstration flight to New York with the nearly finished L 72 (LZ 114), quite heedless of the fact that Germany and the Allies were still technically at war and that the zeppelin had not yet shed its "baby killer" image in England and America. The saner heads of Eckener and Colsman prevailed. Instead, various materials in stock at the Company works were mobilized to build a new small airship for service within Germany. This was LZ 120, *Bodensee*, built with all the innovations of Johann Schütte and Zeppelin experiences of wartime construction. Beginning in August 1919, this remarkable ship made a hundred flights to Berlin, and one to Stockholm, under DELAG management until December 1919, when the Interallied Control Commission in Germany ordered a suspension of operations. Still, the postwar passenger airship had arrived.[14]

Meanwhile, though Schütte had his own aspirations and preliminary drawings for passenger airships, he had none of his rival's opportunities. His airship SL 22 could not be operated or sold and was subsequently dismantled.

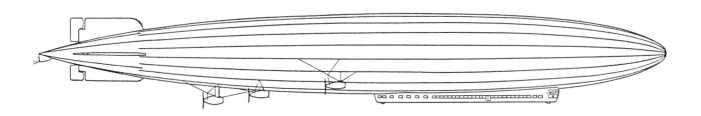

SL design for "Atlantic"-type airship, 1920. (*Der Luftschiffbau Schütte-Lanz, 1909–1925,* p. 45)

The construction hangar at Zeesen was cluttered with incomplete airplanes under construction. Uncertain subcontractors could not be relied upon to deliver engines or any other supplementary components. The prohibitions of the Allies that grounded the DELAG, applied to any future prospects for Schütte as well.

Just as the Zeppelin Company would do, Schütte sought to transfer his prospects abroad. In late 1919 he associated with Dutch partners in Rotterdam to found N. V. Schütte-Lanz Holland, with plans to acquire the Zeesen construction hangar and to build two newly designed, fifty-passenger airships of his projected "Atlantic" type. Fortune seemed to favor his hopes. In May 1920 he traveled in style to America. Here he sought orders for SL airships (or the sale of SL patents and construction experience), together with markets for his patented casein glue and various electrical products. He subsequently reported on an endless round of bewildering and tiring conferences in the best American business and social clubs. Still, he was buoyed by his perception that the Americans were incredibly naive politically, completely ignorant of airships, and ripe for his manipulation of them for Germany in general and Schütte-Lanz in particular. His contacts in New York included Panama Canal builder General George W. Goethals, Gerard W. Swope of General Electric, and representatives of the Submarine Boat, Wright Airplane, and W. R. Grace companies. None of these associations, however, led to any definitive results.

Already Schütte was in the capable hands of Washington engineer-attorney Frederick S. Hardesty. Largely thanks to him alone, Schütte spent a day at the aviation section of the U.S. Army. Armed with reams of documentation, piles of blueprints, and a dozen photo albums, Schütte spent hours conducting veritable seminars in airship building and flying, much to the gratification of army airshipmen and General William B. Mitchell himself. The whole process was repeated the next day—with a new set of materials—in the airship offices of the U.S. Navy, in the presence of Admiral D. W. Taylor, Commander Garland Fulton, Starr Truscott, Navy Secretary Josephus Daniels, and others. The American armed forces were thus expertly brought up-to-date on alleged SL achievements and prospects, while the impressionable Schütte now fully committed himself to Hardesty's representation on behalf of Schütte-Lanz.

The culmination of the trip was Schütte's visit to Akron. By fortunate coincidence, he had met Ralph H. Upson, Goodyear's chief engineer, on his voyage to America, and accepted an invitation to visit the Rubber City. He spent a day at Wingfoot Lake, finding the l-t-a installations there on a par with those of the Prussian Airship Battalion about the year 1900. In long discussion with Akronites, Schütte sensed warning implications of their contacts with Colsman's delegation from Friedrichshafen just a few days before. Accordingly, as he put it, "I declined with thanks [to give instruction in rigid airship matters], for I had come to America on business, not as a professor of aeronautics." After a hurried return to New York, Schütte was entertained by Goethals at a farewell dinner, where spirits glowed despite Prohibition and toasts were drunk to an early reunion aboard an SL "Atlantic" airship on a transatlantic flight.[15]

Curiously, this *tour d'horizon* coincided almost exactly with a similar business reconnaissance by a trio from the Zeppelin Company to some of the same destinations and interviewing some of the same potential customers. Possibly Schütte had heard of Colsman's intentions and thus rushed to America to cover his bets. For his part, Colsman's letters and final report to the home office commented guardedly on his awareness of Schütte's presence, for Schütte-Lanz and Zeppelin were already engaged in fierce publicity combat in Germany over Schütte's claims that the modern "zeppelin" was largely successful only because of his crucial improvements. Several complicated lawsuits underlay this vehement feud. In this context Colsman wrote his home office: "It is time that we started working towards some enlightenment over here in America and in Amsterdam. That could best be done by publicising the facts from our most recent press feud with Schütte." If Colsman made potentially the best contacts in America in mid-1920 (Goodyear, Ford, the U.S. Navy, and a financial group in New York), Schütte came home with a talented attorney already engaged on his behalf, looking after the fate of his endangered American patents and prospecting for American clients.[16]

These two prospecting journeys by Schütte and Colsman seem rather fanciful, but it must be understood that at this time everything was quite tenuous about the future of German airship building and flying. The Treaty of Versailles took effect on January 1, 1920. According to article 202 of the settlement, Germany was prohibited from building, possessing, or flying airships of any kind. No doubt the Allies recalled the civilian deaths and psychological terror of the wartime zeppelin raids. They also anticipated using confiscated German patents, construction techniques, and experienced airshipmen in pursuance of their own transatlantic flight expectations. America, however, had failed to ratify the Versailles Treaty, and though still technically at war with Germany, might conceivably make other arrangements with Germans about airships. At the same time that Schütte moved to Holland and flirted with Britain, the Zeppelin Company (Eckener) was talking with Spaniards about building airships there and opening passenger service to Brazil and Argentina. Concurrently the Disarmament Control Commissions of the European victors were busily destroying German war material and dismantling armaments factories. Shadows of these activities fell on the Zeppelin and Schütte-Lanz construction hangars. The German airshipmen felt disaster closing in upon them while the Americans perceived bright opportunities opening up ahead. Under these circumstances the German feelers toward potential American partners were not unrealistic for either sets of negotiators.

If Schütte was early on the American scene, the fate of his factories was already sealed: Mannheim was in the French zone of occupation and Zeesen was right under the noses of the Allied dismantlers in Berlin. With American prospects brightening, Schütte opened a design office in Heidelberg and closed out his Dutch company, encountering yet another sticky lawsuit in the process. Now began his fateful association with a remarkable enterprise called the American Investigation Corporation (AIC). His lawyer Hardesty had found a likely prospect, S. R. Bertron of Bertron, Griscom and Co. (40 Wall Street). On January 10, 1921, Bertron invited a former assistant secretary of the navy—Franklin D. Roosevelt by name—to lunch with him. Also present were Hardesty and Owen D. Young, Vice-President of the General Electric Company. Young later achieved fame as author of the Young Plan of 1929 that salvaged German reparations payments for the Allies. A week later the four men drew up a preliminary agreement to form a syndicate to "investigate all phases of aerial navigation, legislation required, and methods of fund raising."[17] Hardesty made available all his rights and data (earlier acquired from Schütte), in return for reimbursement of expenses incurred to date on behalf of Schütte and an interest in the syndicate. While the fund raisers began their canvassing in New York, the Midwest, and on the Pacific Coast, Roosevelt began to play a key role in Washington. The future president had more than a financial interest in the venture. He disliked and distrusted airplanes. He wrote a friend in mid-July of 1921: "I was horrified to get a cable from London the other day saying that my mother also had flown across from London to Paris. Wait until my dirigibles are running, and then you will be able to take a form of transportation that is absolutely safe."[18] "His" dirigibles, of course, were to be derived from the patents and the accumulated experience of Johann Schütte.[19]

Roosevelt lost no time. Early in February 1921 he wrote Hardesty, "I agree with you that we should do something immediately in regard to the Schütte patents, and at least make the try before the present [Wilson] administration goes out."[20] He was in Washington on February 9 and 17, meeting with the Alien Property Custodian and renewing his contacts in the Navy Department. He was asking about any navy claims to the Schütte patents and checked with Lt. Comdr. Richard E. Byrd in the Office of Naval Operations about rights for the emerging syndicate to use the Lakehurst facilities for his future airships. Shortly thereafter Schütte granted power of attorney to Hardesty and the patents were soon released by the Alien Property Custodian. Thus AIC bought the patents for a nominal sum, without the obligatory auction and competitive bidding, and with some interest accruing to their former

German holder. All these actions may have been in violation of stipulations of the Trading with the Enemy Act of 1917.[21]

By early 1922 the American Investigation Corporation had acquired an impressive group of investors. Among them were W. E. Boeing, Edward H. Clark (Homestake Mining), Arthur V. Davis (Aluminum Company of America), Allen Dulles (Gold Dust Corporation), Marshall Field III, E. M. Herr (Westinghouse Electric), W. L. Mellon (Gulf Oil), Theodore Pratt (Standard Oil), Owen D. Young, and Franklin D. Roosevelt, together with a covey of respectable financiers—everything needed to build, equip, and operate a budding airship line.[22] A contract was signed on March 11, 1922 between AIC and the Schütte-Lanz Company. There followed very quickly on May 9, 1922 another contract between AIC and (this time) Johann Schütte alone—possibly reflecting the demise of Schütte-Lanz in Germany and the establishment of a German successor business of Schütte and Company. The later contract paid Schütte $38,000 in cash and promised $220,000 further in monthly installments until July 1, 1923. In the event of payment lapses, the patents would be returned to Schütte. He was also granted a generous stock allowance to compensate him for his potential services as technical adviser to AIC.[23]

Now the greater American public was treated to a preview of the proposed airship services. The widely read magazine, *Current History*, published as a subsidiary of the *New York Times*, wrote very positively in June 1922 about the "Advent of the American Air Liner." Within the context of generalities about the history of airship passenger flights, pros and cons of airships vs. airplanes, and the importance of helium for safe operation, the article gave these specific details:

> The intention is to make the first route a practical demonstration between New York and Chicago, which by air is only 750 miles. The traveling public will need, and should have, proof of reliability and safety before undertaking overseas voyages in airships. All details of improved construction and operation will be assured on this short run before attempting the cross-continent and transatlantic routes. . . . The first airship will have a capacity of 4,000,000 cubic feet of helium and should cover the distance between New York and Chicago in ten hours' average time. About 100 passengers will be transported at night in berths similar to those on steamships. In addition to passengers, an airship of that size will be able to carry thirty tons of mail, express, or other cargo. The method of mooring to a tower and means of supplying gas, fuel, and water to a moored airship are interesting; so are the details of the engineering planning data; but those subjects cannot be discussed in brief space and are more appropriate for a technical article. . . . The airship has passed from the experimental to the reliable commercial stage. . . . Coast lines or mountain ranges no longer are barriers requiring a change in transport methods. St. Louis and Denver are as likely as any seacoast cities to have direct airship communication with Europe, South America and Asia.[24]

Quite probably the article was describing Schütte's much larger post-"Atlantic" design with passenger access by way of a high, solid mooring mast—

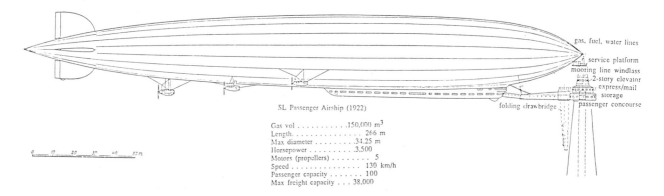

SL Passenger Airship (1922)

gas, fuel, water lines
service platform
mooring line windlass
2-story elevator
express/mail
storage
folding drawbridge
passenger concourse

Gas vol . . . . .150,000 m³
Length. . . . . 266 m
Max diameter . . . . .34.25 m
Horsepower 3,500
Motors (propellers) 5
Speed . . . . 130 km/h
Passenger capacity 100
Max freight capacity . . . 38,000

SL design for advanced transoce-anic passenger airship, 1922. (*Der Luftschiffbau Schütte-Lanz, 1909–1925*, p. 73)

anticipating the British constructions of the later 1920s for R 100 and R 101. There were two inviting illustrations of a promenade deck and of a passenger at an observation window. These pictures were characteristic products of the Schütte design staff in 1921–22. There was only one error, and it must have irked Schütte: Count Zeppelin was praised as the inventor, and thrice there was mention of the Zeppelin Company, but no reference either to Schütte or to his innovations. Here he was obliterated by the "shadow of the titan."

The engineer was not relying alone on the restoration of his airship enterprise in order to give his life meaning. He accepted as final neither the collapse of the Hohenzollern monarchy nor the terms of the Versailles Treaty. The revolution of 1918 and the Weimar Republic were anathema to him. No doubt he hoped and worked for the restoration of the kaiser. While Colsman and Eckener as moderate conservatives of the Zeppelin Company trimmed their sails to the Weimar wind, Schütte disdained democrats and detested "Marxists." As a counterpart to his gradually failing airship endeavors, and in pursuit of his monarchist hopes, he was active in a variety of conservative and nationalist causes. Most closely associated with his vocation was the Aviation Science Society (*Wissenschaftliche Gesellschaft für Luftfahrt*) over which he presided from 1919 to 1936. He gave enthusiastic support to the "sport" of gliding, which was the only viable private aviation activity open to Germans under the Versailles Treaty until 1926. In 1922 he was called to the chair of theoretical naval architecture at the Technical University of Berlin-Charlottenburg, Germany's most prestigious institute of higher engineering learning. Here also conservatism and technology went hand in hand.

Schütte's manifold activities and deserved academic honors hardly lessened his personal frustrations and attitudes deriving from his airship endeavors. He had become quite wealthy during the war years, acquiring a palatial villa near Zeesen, when he moved there in 1917. Apparently he conserved his fortune successfully, though his experiences with the German treasury were hardly indicative. The imperial tax authorities had him in court in 1917 for an alleged half-million mark evasion of wartime excess profits tax by the Schütte-Lanz Company. He initiated a vehement protest, but the company had to pay by December 1918. His efforts to rectify this injustice to his firm produced a partial refund of 300,000 marks in 1921 and a remaining payment of 190,000 marks in December 1923—in each case at the inflation-ravaged mark value of the later time. The first refund was in actual value just one-fifth of what was originally paid, the second was worth one ten-billionth of a pfennig in the currency of original payment! These transactions were no doubt infuriating, but otherwise Schütte survived quite well financially. The chateau in Zeesen was sold when he moved to a lovely villa in another Berlin suburb, an expensive engraving of which graced his personal stationery until his death. Psychological stress, however, took its toll on him. In his struggles to preserve the Schütte-Lanz properties, and to obtain payment for the unsold SL 22 and the unfinished SL 23 and 24, his combative attitude no doubt affected these negative circumstances even more negatively. His struggle to win recognition for his innovations in airship design after 1919 strengthened his opinions that airships could never have been successful without his design contributions and exaggerated his views about the shortcomings of Count Zeppelin's efforts. As his great lawsuit against the German treasury and the Zeppelin Company (between 1919 and 1924) spilled over into periodic press feuds, his never-absent egotism developed a sense of martyrdom and perception of alleged conspiracies against him. Despite his further effective career as a professor of naval architecture, he never overcame this psychological trauma.[25]

Meanwhile, things still looked promising in America. Schütte made three trips for consultation across the Atlantic between 1920 and 1924. He maintained a technical staff in Germany working up various aspects of the designs for AIC, notably the post-"Atlantic" type. At the same time further studies were made on various aspects of transoceanic airship operation in general. From this era also came the detailed project of an airship especially designed for arctic exploration. Schütte later complained that inadequate payments were made by AIC for these services and even these were substantially in arrears. The promoters at AIC were optimistic. A "strategy memorandum" of later 1922 identified achievements in working with Schütte, possible cooperation with engineers of the Ford Motor Company, and proposals to seek leases of U. S. Navy facilities at Lakehurst. The memo ended on an ambiguous note about "What we Need"—that turned out to be simply (1) funds and (2) orders. The AIC annual report for 1922 (dated January 8, 1923) indicated that the Allied Reparations Commission refused to allow large airship construction in Germany—indeed, by then the Schütte-Lanz construction hangar at Zeesen was already being dismantled. There was concern about the possibilities and reliability of obtaining helium from the American Bureau of Mines, all the more important since the loss of ZR 2 in England in 1921 and of the army semirigid *Roma* in early 1922. The final goal was still envisaged to establish airship service in America and possibly to found a dirigible construction business in the United States.[26]

Early in 1923 Pickens Neagle, solicitor in the Office of the Naval Judge Advocate General, was exploring further aspects of U.S. Navy assistance for

69

AIC. He reported to Roosevelt on possibilities of using naval officers and leasing facilities at Cape May. More than that, there were thoughts in the air that AIC should acquire the German airship being built for the U.S. Navy.[27] At the same time Schütte was again visiting America to check on progress at AIC. Upon his departure he was accorded a long interview with the *New York Times*. Here he indicated that AIC was establishing an operating company, General Air Service, and that two helium ships were in prospect. He had visited Lakehurst to view ZR 1 under construction there and found American builders quite up to German standards. Editorially the *Times* emphasized Schütte's observations and concluded that "capital is available, and American promoters have never lacked courage."[28] The public relations desk at AIC was busily at work. On March 24, 1923 the widely read *Literary Digest* featured an article, "Coming: Overnight Airships, New York to Chicago." The piece praised the "authority, business judgment, and financial strength" of AIC and quoted at length from a special statement just published in the *Times*. In general the article was written with a solid grasp of airship history in Germany and Britain, and it should have delighted Johann Schütte with its careful distinctions between the Zeppelin Company and Schütte-Lanz and its acknowledgment that AIC had selected his design for its superior qualities.[29]

For all the glowing prospects, however, things were not going well behind the scenes at AIC. On his recent visit to America, Schütte had learned, contrary to the *Times*, that capital was virtually nonexistent and that interest of the financiers was flowing to other investments. In fact, the syndicate was disintegrating. There were vexatious difficulties because of the incompetence and procrastination of the financiers. Consultant Hardesty had teamed up with another Washington consulting engineer, Edward Schildhauer, who was also a member of the original syndicate group. They in turn procured the assistance of Owen D. Young to untangle the difficulties caused by a group of men too limited in vision and too much dispersed in other interests. Upon his advice, Hardesty and Schildhauer turned to Major General Clarence R. Edwards U.S.A. (ret.), who recommended reorganization, new men, and new financing from the Boston area so that affairs would be shaped "with a view to establishing airship transportation between New York, Chicago, and possibly St. Louis by placing orders for ships not later than July 1, 1923." Understandably serious difficulties arose with the other members of AIC. These were of particular concern to Schütte, for the extension of his contract with AIC and the payment of $220,000 to him were due on July 1, 1923. Among other things, Schildhauer wrote to Schütte on June 1, 1923: "We are firmly convinced that the present management will fail to pay you the amount due you on or before July 1 and that even if you should be inveigled into an agreement for an extension, they will still fail in the end. It is for this reason that I am approaching you now so that when the critical time arrives, we are in shape to save the wreck."[30]

It was an unholy mess. Schütte, Hardesty, and Schildhauer had, in fact, been conniving since early 1923, not only to rescue the German engineer's airship prospects, but to save the others' financial skins as well. The internal details of subsequent matters are unknown. What is clear, is that Schütte finally sent his own chief engineer and patent specialist, Walter Bleistein, to America in November 1923 to unscramble the situation. Schütte must have been frantic. Not only were his own former bright prospects apparently derailed, but "the shadow of the titan" loomed again. Just a month before, the Luftschiffbau Zeppelin had signed a contract with the Goodyear Tire and Rubber Company to found a new joint construction and operation enterprise to be called the Goodyear-Zeppelin Company. It was clear that the German Zeppelin Company's patents and expertise would now be going to America and, with them, everything that Schütte was still hoping to gain from his lawsuit against the German treasury and the Friedrichshafen builders. After four years the lawsuit was still dragging through the German courts unresolved.

Goodyear and the German Zeppelin Company had come together through the enthusiasm and entrepreneurship of cagey Chicago railway equipment supplier, Harry Vissering. This Chicagoan was in Germany in the autumn of 1919, seeking opportunities for his firm. Because of German railway strikes and delays, he chanced to travel in the DELAG airship *Bodensee* from the Swiss border to Berlin. Vissering became an instant convert and enthusiastic promoter of ideas and equipment for airship travel. How and where he functioned during 1920–21 is not clearly understood, for there are only fragments of records in America and Germany. It is quite clear, however, that by early 1922 he had become a spokesman for the German Zeppelin Company in America, that he had awakened the serious interest of Goodyear President Paul W. Litchfield, and that he was busily at work to bring the mutual interest of both firms together in a new American enterprise. He developed very cordial relationships with Eckener and an intimate knowledge of the German Zeppelin Company's political and economic dilemmas—including the contentions and lawsuits of Johann Schütte.[31]

Obviously Vissering was also abreast of Schütte's dealings with the nascent AIC in America. In mid-February 1922, as the Akron-Friedrichshafen negotiations were becoming very serious, Vissering sent Eckener a long letter analyzing the potential usefulness of a New York legal firm to oppose AIC. Since he thought that firm might be biased on Schütte's behalf, he urged Eckener to hire a Washington patent attorney to keep an eye on Hardesty and to protect the Zeppelin interests. Schütte, he warned, had a real head start, and there was no doubt that these patent matters required resolution.[32] Details are sparse on how things developed exactly over the next two years; but by mid-October 1923, Hardesty had heard of the imminent birth of Goodyear-Zeppelin and was seeking consultation with Vissering. At that time Vissering sent Edward G. Wilmer, chairman of the board at Goodyear Tire and Rubber, full information about the men and interests at AIC. Vissering argued now from strength: "The fact remains that Mr. Owen D. Young and his Group have interested a goodly number of very substantial American businessmen and as I told you during my short talk with you at F'hafen, it might be well to do everything possible to keep this interest alive with the view of capitalizing it for the benefit of our own account."[33] It is not clear to what extent Vissering or Wilmer by that time knew of the dissension within AIC, but one of those AIC parties was not long in contacting Goodyear. On November 15, 1923, Wilmer reported to Vissering on a long meeting at Akron with Franklin D. Roosevelt and two other AIC investors. After commenting on the patent quarrels, he continued:

> Roosevelt's mind seemed to be working in the direction of forming another company which might acquire both Zeppelin and Sch[ü]tte patents and form a joint engineering organization to proceed with construction. The whole thing savored very much of the desire on their part to get back their money, avoid a conflict and retain a position in an ultimate joint enterprise. . . . We said that off hand, if it is clearly established that we have real conflicts between us, we shall be only too happy to try to get together with them, that we shall be glad to have the interest of their subscribers with us . . . I believe that our announcements, the general reception accorded them, and the fact that we are actually going ahead with the engineering, has pretty much upset their plans. They have been discussing a possible get-together with the Upson group in Detroit and say also that they have been preparing to organize a construction company with a view to turning over their patent rights. I take it, it is their intention to try to finance it so as to pay off their present subscribers for what they have already invested. At any rate, when we left them yesterday afternoon they seemed inclined to do nothing further, pending our investigation of the patent situation. I think, all told, the conference was quite satisfactory."[34]

Vissering responded to the effect that he had been watching Schütte and AIC over the past four years and was glad that Goodyear now had a contact with the American group. He went on:

> No doubt by this time they fully realize that Sch[ü]tte is not the man that they would want to go on with. He is a difficult man to handle, seemingly has no set plans and is simply seeking capital to enable him to go ahead with the idea of constructing a "tubular frame" ship, because he has so many times publicly and on every possible occasion condemned the Zeppelin girder form of ship construction. As no one would consider building any more of his wooden frame ships, he naturally is compelled to go to some other form of construction, hence his advocacy of the so called "tubular frame" construction. If the AIC were to back this man, Sch[ü]tte, financially to the extent of building such "tubular frame" experimental ship, it would cost them millions of dollars and if Sch[ü]tte's former record is to be considered it would take from three to five years and with the possible result that the ship would be of little use when completed. . . . Possibly the time is approaching when they will have to make the final payment to Sch[ü]tte or hand him back his patents. . . . therefore their anxiety to do something quick.[35]

At this point Walter Bleistein, Schütte's chief engineer and legal envoy, stepped off the ship in New York City. He stayed in America for nearly four months, and what he finally had to report was the death knell for Schütte's American airship prospects. At the very outset he learned that AIC had bungled everything legally, that eventually only some participation with Goodyear-Zeppelin seemed feasible to rescue something for Schütte, and that the road to this outcome was by way of establishing Schütte's patent rights in America—so that Goodyear-Zeppelin could not build without coming to some agreement with him. Bleistein spent about one-third of his time in America (December 6, 1923 to March 15, 1924) with patent lawyers in New York and Washington, D.C. He concluded that Schütte's rights indeed were prior, but he shied away from pursuing the U.S. Navy for allegedly violating those rights in building its airships ZR 1 and ZR 3. The patent matters were relatively clear.

The same could hardly be said of relations with Schütte's American partners. Here Bleistein faced three distinct parties: (1) a major portion of the original AIC syndicate, (2) the Boston group gingered by Hardesty and Schildhauer, and (3) Hardesty and Schildhauer themselves constituting potentially injured parties against Schütte. The German naval engineer was in the peculiar position of standing apart from these parties, alternately being sought for some new dimension of participation with any one of them, or being threatened with legal action from each of them. Financial considerations were usually center stage. Would Schütte receive what was owed him by AIC, or would these obligations be deferred until the desired participation with Goodyear-Zeppelin had been arranged? Would Hardesty and Schildhauer ever cease making continually revised demands about what was owed them? Could the stockholders of AIC, or those dreamed of for the Boston group, be motivated to supply funds for Schütte or the needy American consulting engineers? It went on endlessly.

Visions of legal-financial sugarplums danced in their heads. The discussions were often focused on the great objective: would AIC achieve the breakthrough in negotiating with Goodyear-Zeppelin? Or could the Boston group maneuver a threesome, together with AIC and Akron? On the outside stood Schütte, presumably to receive the patents returned from AIC and then to negotiate their transfer to Goodyear-Zeppelin.

These may sound like staid legal proceedings, but they were often interrupted by elements of human drama. Resignations, frequent absences of crucial persons, and threats of cancellations or court proceedings brought excitement to Bleistein's interminable meetings and conferences. Hardesty and Schildhauer were called pipe dreamers and crooks. The Boston group was denounced as financially incompetent. Franklin D. Roosevelt was accused of giving away the store at Akron. Louis Howe, speaking for FDR, was caught lying and made to recant. Even Schütte was accused of being a swindler. It might have been comical, had it not been so tragic for Schütte.

Some aspects of airship actuality played into the scene. In mid-December

Bleistein conferred with Admiral Moffett, Starr Truscott, and Charles Burgess about possible applications of Schütte's tubular aluminum construction to future navy rigids. Just at Christmas the loss of the former German L 72 (LZ 114), now the French *Dixmude*, cast its shadow over the discussions. In mid-January Bleistein was at Lakehurst to visit the *Shenandoah*. He saw it fly over the field and went aboard for a tour the next day. That evening he saw its mooring fitting still attached to the mast from which it had been wrenched in heavy winds. These events apparently did little to bring all the talk down to earth.

In early March Bleistein concluded his negotiations. Schütte broke off definitively from AIC and Schütte canceled his relationships with Schildhauer. Some potential arrangements were left with the Boston group, where Hardesty continued to function on behalf of the German engineer and for himself. Schütte's all-important patents were still in limbo with AIC. Like the old soldier of barracks balladry, Schütte was just fading away—as far as America was concerned.[36]

There was an epilogue. In mid-July of 1924, Harry Vissering again reported to Wilmer at the Goodyear Company. Hardesty had been to see him and told him that the Boston group had incorporated as Airways Corporation of America and was seeking to take over what remained of AIC. The syndicate still had Schütte's patents in hand and the German engineer would have to sue to get them. Schütte (Hardesty) was negotiating with the Boston group. They had agreed that they would be turning the patents over to him, when and if they acquired them. The Airways Corporation would not seek to build airships, rather they hoped to buy one from Goodyear-Zeppelin. That, in fact, was a matter of corporate life or death for them. Vissering referred Hardesty to Goodyear. Beyond that the archives are silent.[37]

Johann Schütte, however, still had the last word in Germany. On March 28, 1928 he filed a formal protest with the German group of the International Chamber of Commerce in Berlin. The text read, in part, that Schütte-Lanz had met with AIC "and has been deceived in this [enterprise] in a most unprecedented manner." It went on:

> The AIC have not re-transferred the patents to Schütte-Lanz, so that we were not able, during the last four years, to control or dispose of our whole USA patents. . . . What has become of the AIC, we have no means of knowing. It is said that the Airways Corporation of America is a successor to AIC. . . .
> Merely in the general interest Schütte-Lanz have so far avoided discussion in full publicity of this incredible case, giving no names and details. It appears to us, however, now to be of the highest time [sic] that Schütte-Lanz should at last come into their rights and that they should receive reparation for what has been sinned against them in the unjustifiable manner. To this end we respectfully request the assistance of the Chamber of Commerce.[38]

What could the Berlin Chamber of Commerce do?

Schütte's preoccupation with his patents in America was simply the reverse of the coin that marked his protracted litigation over the same matters in Germany. Whereas in America the struggle centered primarily around liberation of the rights for production abroad from a former enemy nation, in Germany his struggles had a more basic double focus. First, Schütte sought technological satisfaction and financial reimbursement from Luftschiffbau Zeppelin for alleged pirating of his unique innovations in airship design, plus suitable civil damages. Second, in two separate suits against the German treasury Schütte sought (1) damages for the failure of the imperial government to order additional SL airships (together with reimbursement of construction on SL 23 and 24) and (2) indemnification from the government for pressing the forced technological marriage of Schütte and Zeppelin designs.[39] The several suits dragged on and on.

In the meantime, the Zeppelin Company had survived with the construction of LZ 126 for the U.S. Navy (as Schütte claimed, because of *his* crucially important technological improvements), while both the assets and the future prospects of the naval engineer wasted away. Of course, there were the obligatory countersuits by all affected parties.[40] Both the Zeppelin and Schütte archives contain reams of documentation about the lawsuits, about themselves, and about each other—materials more of interest to a student of business litigation than to an enjoyment of airship history. Succinctly put, the Zeppelin Company argued that in each of the instances of alleged patent infringement, the claims were without substance because (1) the Company was already using its own similar designs before Schütte arranged his patents, (2) the Company's designs differed enough from Schütte's so as not to constitute infringement, and (3) that some of Schütte's patents were either not relevant to the suit or were legally defective in some way. When the dust had settled in the final out-of-court agreement (August 27, 1924), Schütte-Lanz and Zeppelin dropped their suits against each other and agreed to an unreimbursed exchange of patents. The German treasury settled by paying Schütte and his colitigants (from the happier Schütte-Lanz days) forty thousand gold marks—not even enough to settle Schütte's legal fees. This was, ironically, the very same day that LZ 126 (the future American *Los Angeles*) first took to the skies over Friedrichshafen—a clearly identifiable descendant of SL 2.[41]

The lawsuits were settled, but the "scientific" and public relations feud continued. In July 1925 the Luftschiffbau Zeppelin celebrated the twenty-fifth anniversary of Count Zeppelin's first ascent with LZ 1 in 1900. It also marked the rebirth of German hopes for international airship travel. The Goodyear-Zeppelin Company had been founded and a dozen of the Zeppelin Company's best designers and engineers had moved to Akron. The transatlantic flight of LZ 126 in mid-October of 1924 had awakened worldwide attention. Now Eckener could reveal his plans to build an even larger experimental airship for use in polar exploration or transatlantic travel. The festivities in Friedrichshafen were celebrated in a sumptuously published commemorative book of articles and photographs about the legendary Count, the designs of his ships, and their achievements. Schütte responded promptly with his own volume, not quite as handsome, but all the more technically "scientific." Still, Schütte's indignation penetrated the many pages of engineering drawings and calculations in higher mathematics. There was also a section of telling photographs: the zeppelin before Schütte, the Schütte-Lanz airships before 1915, and the hybrids after 1914. Common sense should have prevailed.[42]

Yet on this occasion, and steadily thereafter, Schütte was falling behind in the contest for public recognition of the importance of his contributions. His book appeared more than a year after the Friedrichshafen celebrations, symbolizing what would henceforth be Schütte's fate—arriving breathless at the station after the train had left, and furious to boot. There was indignant correspondence with book review editors who failed to give his volume its requisite attention, or overlooked it altogether.[43] It was an unpropitious time for Schütte. The airship attention in Germany now focused on Hugo Eckener, who was crisscrossing the Teutonic world, raising funds for the *Zeppelin-Eckener-Spende* to build his new airship. If Schütte was once "in the shadow of the titan," he was now also face-to-face with a talented and experienced zeppelin commander with an international reputation in his own right.

The vehement passions of those years died only with their possessors. Half a century after these struggles, Schütte's major airplane engineer still held a fierce animosity that quite likely reflected Schütte's own exasperation:

> I probably knew Schütte even better than he did himself, was so-to-speak his shadow. [We were made of the same intellectual and emotional stuff.] I only experienced Eckener two or three times, never spoke with him. I also observed that there was never a conversation between the two men, only formal social recognition—that was all. . . . Whatever later appeared in the press about Eckener, his accomplishments and his capabilities was either a result of his own press releases or commissioned articles in various papers. From all this emerged the image of Hero Eckener. [Contrary to his truly negative qualities and genuine lack of accomplishments] he always appeared on board the airships as the genial host of the Zeppelin Company—no doubt a great organizer and advertising expert, mostly on his own behalf.[44]

The compliments were hardly flowing.

The Luftschiffbau Zeppelin, and Eckener himself, easily and wisely avoided engaging very much in further polemics. What was past was past, and they had great projects in hand. In 1927 Schütte apparently engineered a "scientific" paper and discussion at the Aviation Science Society of which he was president. The author of the presentation took a rather partisan view of Schütte *vs.* Zeppelin. An advance copy reached Friedrichshafen. Colsman was seriously concerned that this rekindling of the feud would adversely affect negotiations currently under way by the Luftschiffbau to obtain funding for its airship plans from the German transport ministry. Schütte promptly jumped in with an energetic defense of the proposed program, pleading public enlightenment and freedom of thought and press. Saner heads prevailed and the program came off without much confrontation.[45] In those years Colsman worked both sides of the street: on the one hand, restraining Eckener and his engineer-designer Dürr, on the other, calming Schütte and his adherents. He evidently had some success, for on one occasion he wrote to Schütte— using the familiar *du*—in reference to "our so harmoniously concluded Locarno-meeting of the airship builders."[46]

The competition between Eckener and Schütte continued vigorously to the end of the 1920s. In 1928, when the Bureau of Aeronautics of the American Navy sponsored a second design competition for two new rigid naval airships, Schütte was not absent. He was represented in two ways: in an American Brown-Boveri Electric Corporation proposal that seemed to pirate the secrets of Schütte-Lanz, and in a project of his own. Goodyear-Zeppelin won the contract, no doubt for its more persuasive design that incorporated Eckener's construction experience with LZ 126 and planning for LZ 127, now represented by Zeppelin Company personnel in Akron. Listed as second best, the naval engineer was left behind again.[47]

A final skirmish occurred a year later. It was at the beginning of the global flight of the airship *Graf Zeppelin*. In accordance with the wishes of the American news tycoon, William Randolph Hearst, who provided major funding for the flight in exchange for exclusive journalistic coverage by that old airship commentator, Karl von Wiegand, the dirigible flew first to Lakehurst in order then to make the world flight begin and end in America. Who else should appear there on August 6, 1929? It was Frederick S. Hardesty, together with legal talent from New York, armed with a court order to prevent departure of the zeppelin and secure it as collateral in yet another effort to obtain satisfaction for Schütte's remaining American and world patent rights—matters not covered by the German settlements five years before. The Lakehurst commandant refused to deal with Hardesty on grounds that a civilian court had no jurisdiction at a naval station. It was Hardesty's last legal move on Schütte's behalf.[48]

Thereupon followed all the acclaim for the *Graf Zeppelin* on its circumnavigation of the globe. The next year saw the opening of flights to South America, and the year after, a well-publicized expedition to the Arctic Circle. In 1931 regular transatlantic service began to Brazil, followed in the summer of 1936 with scheduled air service to North America. Even if his fury had subsided into sullen resentment, these must have been painful circumstances for Johann Schütte. Still, he continued to live well and pursued an effective academic career. His extracurricular activities continued in the directions of the 1920s, from which we see representative photographs: with General von Mackensen (of the historic Death Head Hussars of the Prussian army); at the dedication of the super-balloon *Westpreussen* (German territory lost to Poland in 1918); with Prince Henry of Prussia at the Aviation Science Society;

with General Ludendorff at a sailplane meet. His Oldenburg archives have various clippings and commentaries about airships at home and abroad. Marginal notations, corrections, and exclamation marks abound. When Colsman's book appeared in 1933, there was a long draft analysis with many corrections of Colsman's alleged errors. Was it meant to be published, or was it just self-satisfaction for the embittered commentator? Honorary titles, honorary degrees, and various decorations came his way. In 1930, he was appointed honorary chairman of the *Schiffbau Technische Gesellschaft*, Germany's premier organization for the study of shipbuilding in theory and practice. The city of Danzig celebrated his sixtieth birthday by naming a Johann-Schütte-Strasse. How much could this praise and honor compensate for his resentments over airship matters?

Johann Schütte was no doubt part of that large group of very conservative Germans who were cajoled by Nazi propaganda into believing that the arrival of Hitler would mean restoration of the themes and glories of the old empire—that phenomenon called the "National Resurgence," with its temporary reinstatement of the imperial colors and the glorification of the armed forces and military traditions. Soon followed the reemergence of the aerial weapon, the Luftwaffe. Schütte no doubt basked in these events, though he might have wondered at the Nazi "cleansing" of the Aviation Science Society in 1936, by recasting it into the Otto Lilienthal Society, wherein he retained only an honorary membership. The kudos at his retirement in 1938 were proper and fulsome. He certainly appreciated the honors from his native Oldenburg, which produced belated recognition of his airship achievements by way of the new archives, the museum, and his inscription in the Golden Book of the Grand Duchy. Schütte died quite suddenly in Dresden on March 29, 1940, almost exactly on the second anniversary of his Oldenburg honors.[49]

Upon the centennial of Schütte's birth in 1973, the Oldenburg Historical Society held a commemorative reception that featured an address on the history of airships and their possible future.[50] The native son was, of course, at the center of attention. His life was succinctly summarized: "God gave this man everything in full measure: success and adversity; poverty and wealth; struggle, defeat, and victory; the joy of life and the adverse blows of fate; exuberant health and a sudden demise."[51]

There can be no doubt that Johann Schütte made the most important contributions to airship design of anyone except Count Zeppelin himself, as these were expressed in his initial recommendations of 1908 and fulfilled in the construction of SL 2. Curiously, his perceptive and inventive mind was distracted into the blind alleys of persistent experimentation with the accident-prone laminated wood girders and then with the tubular variations on aluminum structures. It was as though he were seeking strenuously to escape from "the shadow of the titan." As of 1919, he had a genuine grievance against the German government that had compelled him to make his crucially important design improvements available to the Luftschiffbau Zeppelin without properly safeguarding his patent rights and without arranging for reimbursement for their use by others. From these circumstances the Zeppelin company derived the major technological benefits and business profits. It was his fateful misfortune that the treasury of the Weimar Republic understandably fought to dissociate itself from both the wartime reputation and the financial obligations of the preceding German Empire. A sense of generosity would have suggested some spontaneous recognition of Schütte by the Luftschiffbau Zeppelin, with corresponding compensation for the use of his patents. But businessmen are seldom generous, and these were not generous times. In the immediate postwar economic uncertainties both the Zeppelin Company and Schütte-Lanz were fighting for survival—against the punitive Allies, sometimes against the Weimar government, and always against each other. Each party, now personified by the emotional confrontation of Eckener and Schütte, used every legal resource to win its case. Schütte lost against an improbable supervening combination of German and international odds and circumstances.

Today Johann Schütte is forgotten, except among a handful of airship history enthusiasts. In Germany now anything that flies lighter-than-air (except a balloon) is popularly called a "zeppelin." The tiny band of Oldenburgers who keep Jan Schütte's memory alive, and who have resurrected his archives, now find themselves in danger of losing these material vestiges of their native son to the much larger, more important, and more influential resources of the Technological Museum in Mannheim.[52] That may be a painful loss to the emotionally committed Oldenburgers, but it will certainly make for the more effective reminder and presentation of the data that the accomplishments and reputation of Johann Schütte and his technical collaborators deserve.

CHAPTER 3

Building Rigid Airships: Three Communities and Their Changing Fortunes

The rigid airship has a poor reputation in popular memory today. It is recalled with titillated horror in those perennial replays of the news film showing the *Hindenburg* disaster in 1937. A few enthusiasts still marvel at the views of those featherweight sky ships with their luxurious accommodations. Generally, however, the rigid airship is dismissed as the dinosaur of the emerging aviation age. With that dismissal there also evaporates any appreciation of the great expectations that arose in three unique communities that built these gleaming soaring ships and that hoped to become terminals for their ocean-spanning aerial routes. Friedrichshafen in Germany, Cardington and Howden in England, and Akron, Ohio in the United States: Each had its unique relationship to the construction and flying of airships. Between 1900 and 1940, in these three locations, the maturing technology of airship construction, the business impact, and the industrial hopes associated with airship building made their greatest mark. Fate left to each of them a different afterglow of the airship era.

Two very contradictory perceptions highlighted the brief age of airships. The first was the conviction between 1910 and about 1930 that, given the state of general aviation technology in those two decades, only airships could provide transoceanic transport for passengers, mail, and express. Second, these expectations were constantly bedeviled by recurring and highly visible disasters with the very same sky ships heralded as the most promising technological achievements of their times and nations. Two further aspects need mention for an understanding of the times. First, airships were enormously expensive to build and usually required government assistance comparable to that of building a major transatlantic liner or battleship. For example, in 1932 a private enterprise like Douglas Aviation could develop the DC-2 pro-

This is the revised and expanded version of a paper, "The Rigid Airship in Western Society," given at the First Annual Irvine Seminar on Social History and Theory, University of California, Irvine, April 1, 1978.

totype for a hundred and fifty thousand dollars; that same year the naval airship *Akron* was building for over five million dollars. Second, while airplane development escalated rapidly through a wide variety of improvements, types, and quantities between 1919 and 1938, airship development moved with glacial tempo and produced only eleven quite newly designed craft in the same period: six in Germany, three in Britain, and two in the United States. The airplanes got commensurate attention as they hopped and skipped about in insectlike agility while the airships commanded wondrous admiration as they linked continents—and dread as they crashed infrequently but spectacularly.

As long as airships flew, their passage had a powerful psychological impact upon the multitudes that turned out to see them. The airships also had a corresponding echo into the communities that built and serviced them. Inevitably these impressive perceptions of technology were manipulated politically. Already before World War I, the zeppelin became a symbol of German aerial prowess, invoking widespread national egotism and aggressiveness. Britain and the United States took seriously to airship building in response to their wartime enemy. After the war, Britain sought to rule the skies, as it had once ruled the waves. Britain's effort of 1925–30, to make a great technological leap forward, produced a unique combination of airship advance and political disaster. The U.S. Navy built airships for battlefleet scouting. Their builders hoped to adapt the naval designs to commercial service, but found themselves gradually outflanked by the competitive technology of the maturing flying boat and the expertise of its pilots. Despite technological changes favoring the airplane, the airships continued to captivate the multitudes, except at those intervals of spectacular airship disasters.

The building of an airship brought together technological accomplishments from a wide variety of fields and combined them in a new construction process and product. This involved five already developing areas of skill and manufacture. First was the expertise of general design and computation. That was accompanied by the application of civil engineering to girder construction, together with the invention and manufacture of light-metal alloys. Third was the rapidly developing internal combustion engine. To that was added the experience of balloon making and the manufacture of hydrogen gas. Finally came the development of special materials for gas cells and strong fabrics for outer hull covering. Each of these manufacturing elements had an industrial place in its own right. What was new were the ways these diverse elements were brought together to produce a novel vehicle of aerial ascent and movement. These elements produced a slow sequence of gradually improving airships. Here the three communities in which they were built made their unique contributions, and here each of them was vitally affected by the airships it built.

Airship building was not restricted to the three communities here examined. These sites, however, most vividly illustrate the interactions of their societies and enterprises. Between 1900 and 1918, airships in Germany were actually built in several cities. One thinks of Friedrichshafen, idyllically located on the shores of Lake Constance and the scene of Count Zeppelin's many trials and eventual triumph. By 1911, however, Zeppelin had a strong competitor in Schütte-Lanz, which then began building in the large and industrially diversified city of Mannheim. During the breakneck production pace of World War I, Zeppelin also built twenty-eight ships at Potsdam and Staaken in the greater Berlin industrial area. At the same time Schütte-Lanz was building some of its twenty ships in Leipzig and Zeesen (Berlin). Overshadowed by the many other enterprises in those large industrial cities, airship building had little specific social or economic impact. In Friedrichshafen, however, which launched 85 of the 114 zeppelins constructed up to the end of 1918, the interaction of community and enterprise was spectacular.

The British built fourteen rigid airships between 1909 and 1921 at four different locations. Most of these ships were constructed largely on German designs derived from downed zeppelins or, in two instances, from technological data obtained from a dissident Swiss worker at Schütte-Lanz. One genuinely new airship, R 80 designed by young Barnes Wallis, suffered neglect in comparison with the attention focused on derivations from the zeppelin. Airship R 34 was one of these copies, which made aviation history in its round-trip Atlantic crossing of May 1919. Another was R 38, already sold to the Americans as ZR 2, which explosively disintegrated over Hull in England in August 1921. Now the British felt that their problems must stem from deficiencies inherent in the derivative zeppelin design. These convictions were strengthened, in their views of the time, by a variety of operational accidents with their remaining airships after 1921. In 1924, Britain devised its Imperial Airship Scheme to design and construct two entirely new experimental airships to overcome the alleged zeppelin faults. Both new airships would be built in industrial isolation: one at Cardington, the other at Howden. Though separated by 125 miles, these two sites would represent the opposite sides of a single social experience.

America's first rigid airship was fabricated in Philadelphia as a zeppelin copy and then assembled in a massive construction hangar at Lakehurst Naval Air Station sixty miles away. Thus ZR 1 was built between 1921 and 1923. It was joined a year later at that station by the German-built LZ 126 (ZR 3). The destruction of ZR 1 in 1925, and subsequent congressional political maneuvering, gave pause to American airship construction until 1928, when contracts were let for Goodyear-Zeppelin to build two new giant rigids at Akron, Ohio. Here, in a city stereotyped the "Rubber Capital of the World," would occur a promising effort to employ an early high tech enterprise in order to diversify an industrial base beyond its general smokestack character.

Between 1900 and 1939 the silvery paths of the airships in the skies were watched from below by fascinated millions all over the world. Conversely, their vividly reported disasters periodically depressed official and public expectations that these splendid ships could really fulfill certain naval and broad civilian transportation needs. It was constantly one step forward and two steps back—until there were no further steps to be made. Friedrichshafen, Cardington, and Akron: each moved in unique ways with this fluctuating rhythm.[1]

How did each of these communities originally come to build airships?

At the turn of the century Friedrichshafen was a small town of 5,000 with a modest cultural heritage from the German baroque age. It had some pretension to importance as a favorite summer residence of the kings of Württemberg. Far more significant was its location on Lake Constance across from a spectacular range of the Swiss Alps. By 1900 it had become a well-known German vacation resort with a modern *Kurhaus* (social center and spa). Count Zeppelin had spent most of the 1890s in Stuttgart for his basic airship research, business establishment, and correspondence. In 1898 the king of Württemberg gave the aeronaut free use of the construction site at Manzell on the lakeshore. The Count favored this location for its generally mild meteorological conditions and because the lake would permit construction of a floating wooden hangar that could swing with the most favorable wind direction. The sparsely populated surrounding agricultural areas offered convenient open space for unplanned airship descents. In 1909, when the Count had his generous gift from the German nation in hand, he moved from the lakeshore to a large undeveloped area on the northwestern edge of the town. Here was the nucleus of an industry that grew to prodigious size during World War I. Thereafter the Treaty of Versailles scheduled all German airship building for dismantling. By dint of the zeal and efforts of Dr. Hugo Eckener—and some very good luck—Friedrichshafen survived successive economic, political, and diplomatic crises, finally to become the leader of postwar airship activities in the 1930s.

The two widely separated, tiny communities that saw the culminating excitement of Britain's bid for airship predominance between 1924 and 1930 were each in very rural settings. They got their names from small nearby towns and drew on their larger surrounding areas for the human energies of their airship activity. Cardington stood in a prosperous rural area near Bedford, fifty miles north of London. Howden endured on a distant eastern Yorkshire moor, its town known best for a thirteenth-century church and a well-attended annual horse fair. From its beginning Cardington was by far the more officially favored of the two. From 1916 onward, airships had been stationed and built there. Howden had great importance as an airship station during the war years of contest with Germany for control of the North Sea but thereafter it was a hostage to successive official plans for demobilization. Between 1919 and 1921, British plans for postwar airship activity fluctuated between ambitious expansion and frustrating indecision. By 1921 Cardington had been designated the major focus of airship building and flying and had been elevated to the Royal Airship Works; then Howden fell into disuse. With the Imperial Airship Scheme of 1924, Britain set out to build and fly airships on a bold new theoretical basis. Here the Labour government of that time set out to test the efficiency of state-sponsored construction in competition with private enterprise. Cardington had the government job. The other went to the Airship Guarantee Company, an offshoot from the Vickers armaments conglomerate, which selected and refurbished a part of the derelict Howden station. Despite their distances from proximate industrial manufacture, each of these communities experienced similar intensities of airship construction—Cardington in a favored glare of publicity, Howden in distant obscurity.

At the turn of the century, Akron, Ohio, was a well-developed city of 40,000. It served primarily as a business and cultural center for the surrounding prosperous agricultural area. A small manufacturing enterprise in specially treated rubber products began to profit from the dawning automobile age. There were other products as well. A former Akron resident, Walter E. Wellman, undertook polar and transatlantic airship ventures between 1906 and 1909, both of which failed. Still the airship bug was biting in Akron. Wellman's engineer, Melvin Vaniman, came to Akron and aroused the interest of Goodyear leaders Frank A. Seiberling and Paul W. Litchfield. With their support, in 1912 Vaniman built a large airship for a transatlantic flight, with rubber and fabric elements from Goodyear, and dutifully christened it the *Akron*. The flight was a disaster, but Goodyear retained its faith in airships.

Just before World War I, history was made with various ballooning records. During that conflict both Goodyear and Goodrich manufactured many balloons and blimps for the U.S. Army and Navy. When the guns fell silent, Goodyear maintained its interest in airships of every kind. Alfred Colsman and Johann Schütte, both from Germany, visited Akron in 1920 to find a possible new home for their respective and competing airship enterprises, now threatened in their defeated homeland. More immediately influential between 1920 and 1923, was the enthusiastic activity of Harry Vissering, a Chicago railway equipment supplier, who had become a zeppelin enthusiast after flying with the DELAG *Bodensee* in the fall of 1919. He was the sagacious and tireless negotiator between Akron and Friedrichshafen, who brought their interests together in late 1923 in founding the Goodyear-Zeppelin Company. With an infusion of German Zeppelin Company personnel in 1924, Goodyear-Zeppelin was alert for business. Success finally came in 1928, when the U.S. Navy gave Goodyear-Zeppelin contracts to build two huge rigid airships as scouts for the American battlefleets. Now the culminating drama in American airship building could begin.[2]

There the three communities stood. Friedrichshafen was born great; Akron sought to achieve greatness; and Cardington had greatness thrust upon it.

How did the airship building enterprise affect the existing community and what was its long-range impact?

At the turn of the century Friedrichshafen was still a *Residenzstadt* of Württemberg royalty and a popular summer resort. It had some intrinsic business significance as well. In 1869 it had become an important regional railway and transshipment center, as rail and passenger ferry service was opened to Switzerland across the lake. Hereupon followed a regional rail maintenance and repair works and a local marine construction and repair facility. To these were added a quality leather products factory. By the turn of the century there were also small businesses to serve the tourist trade and the surrounding agricultural area.

When Count Zeppelin started building LZ 1 at Manzell in 1899, freight trains began moving in with aluminum from northwest Germany, Daimler engines from Stuttgart, hydrogen from a factory in Berlin, and various stuffs and cloths for gas cells and the outer covering from small Wüttemberg subcontractors. The floating hangar in the lake attracted tourist attention and hundreds pressed to the lakeside to watch the first ascents in early July 1900. Public wonder gave way to ridicule when the flights were unsuccessful and

King and queen of Württemberg at lakeside, Friedrichshafen, anticipating third ascent of LZ 1, Oct. 21, 1900. (Luftschiffbau Zeppelin)

LZ 5 in flight over floating
hangar at Friedrichshafen, 1909.
(Luftschiffbau Zeppelin)

the enterprise was disbanded. In 1904 the Count began again with more
substantial support and a more imposing hangar on the lakeshore at Manzell.
Despite his intermittent problems, from LZ 2 in 1904 thru LZ 4 in 1908, the
attitudes of the same fickle public changed from derision to wild enthusiasm,
as thousands now thronged along the shore or dotted the lake with their
sightseeing craft. Friedrichshafen had become the *Zeppelinstadt*.

Immediately upon the destruction of LZ 4 at Echterdingen on August 5,
1908, there began that remarkable outpouring of German sympathy and
funds for Count Zeppelin. For a month the *Seeblatt*, the busy small-town
newspaper of Friedrichshafen, published a daily tally of the contributions
flowing in locally, supplemented by graphic accounts of accumulations elsewhere in the German-speaking world. Sensation gave way to new planning
for airship building. By the summer of 1909 everything was set. The king
and the city helped acquire the immense new airfield, and construction began
on the first new hangar. Alfred Colsman arrived as a modern, experienced,
twentieth-century businessman to manage the newly established Luftschiffbau Zeppelin. The continuing dissatisfaction with performance of the Daimler engines prompted the recruitment of engineer Karl Maybach to found a
new factory for airship motors. A hydrogen production facility followed in
1910. Another talented engineer, young Claude Dornier, joined in 1913 and
was soon entrusted with special research activities on metal alloys that would
eventuate in a full-blown seaplane subsidiary of the Zeppelin Company.

After a small initial order for new airships by the German army there was
a hiatus. Who would buy the zeppelins that could now so readily be produced?
Very much against the Count's inclinations, Colsman urged establishing an
airship operating entity, the DELAG, for which the Company would build

the necessary passenger ships. It was a stroke of enterprising genius. As zeppelin fever continued to sweep Germany, there was prestige and potential profit for every large city that would establish an airfield, build a hangar, and welcome visits (or direct stationing) of DELAG zeppelins for passenger flights. Since the price of a ticket, two hundred marks, equaled several months of an average German income, business was prestigious but strictly limited. By 1914 DELAG had carried 40,000 passengers but lost three million marks. Still, the relative reliability of DELAG ships and flights made it clear that the airship had a future beyond warfare.

Amidst the sabre rattling and pleasure flying, Friedrichshafen flourished. Tourism boomed as citizens flocked to follow the kaiser and the imperial court, the various kings and their royal entourages, and the prosperous upper middle class to the home of the gallant Count and his wondrous airships. Real estate appreciated handsomely as new villas supplanted farmsteads on the lakefront or were built on newly opened tracts to the west. City planning appeared with new wide streets and an impressive promenade with gardens and a yacht harbor. Crowning this last achievement was the luxurious Kurgarten Hotel, residence of the Count himself until his death and subsequently well known to transatlantic airship travelers of the 1920s and 1930s. By 1913 Friedrichshafen had fully arrived, for in that year an airship battalion appeared, complete with a full garrison and army airship school. In the words of one observer, it was a real "California atmosphere" of beneficial climate, bustling tourism, and technological innovation.[3]

With the outbreak of war, Friedrichshafen, like southern California a generation later, became a center of production for military aviation. Epoch-making results were anticipated for the zeppelins. The citizens cheered the news of the airship raids on Liège in Belgium and the aerial pursuit of French troops retreating from the Alsatian borders. The first raid on Paris occurred on March 20, 1915, soon followed by the initial bombardment of London. A tiny fly in this delicious ointment, however, had been the visit of several British airplanes in November 1914, whose small bombs slightly damaged several houses in the city.[4] As the war progressed, the rainbow of tourism gave way to the battle gray of war production. Two additional construction hangars were built at the Zeppelin Company and the instructional hangar of the airship school was converted to military production. The labor force grew explosively from 400 to over 4,000 in the zeppelin works. Another 3,000 were employed at the related Flugzeugbau Friedrichshafen. In 1915 the Zeppelin Company established another subsidiary, the Zahnradfabrik, which specialized in transmissions, drive trains, and a host of related engineering developments. By then Friedrichshafen was building primarily for the German navy, whose naval architects and engineers expeditiously removed the aging Count. They proceeded to apply the technological innovations of Johann Schütte (and other indigenous improvements) that the old aeronaut had hitherto resisted. Though the airships themselves became dubious weapons as the war progressed, the Zeppelin Company was a prodigious money earner. In 1915 the Count was repaid a million marks for all his earlier investments and privations. No doubt with Colsman's perceptive management, the Zeppelin Company invested a significant proportion of these gains in businesses to supply the needs of its workers, in real estate, and in other enterprises. Thus the Company could successfully overcome the enormous economic dislocations of the immediate postwar era.[5]

With the defeat of Germany and the revolutionary upheavals of late 1918 came abrupt change. In the collapse of the military war economy, nine-tenths of the wartime labor force dispersed within a year and the community could seek to regain its prewar equilibrium. But that was difficult. The pomp, the glitter, and the wealth of imperial Germany was gone. With it had vanished the mainstay of Friedrichshafen tourism. The Zeppelin Company rapidly shrank to less than 100 employees, many of them on part time. Dr. Hugo Eckener returned from his wartime service of training airship fliers, imbued with determination to give the airship a new future in commercial aviation. In contrast, as managing director of the Zeppelin conglomerate, both in Friedrichshafen and Berlin, Alfred Colsman was not as fully convinced of a future for airships. Instead, he hoped to restructure the variety of Company manufacturing capabilities toward postwar consumer goods. Here began a growing rift between Colsman and Eckener that resulted in Colsman's resignation from the Company in 1929 when the world was cheering Eckener and the global flight of the *Graf Zeppelin*. Loyal believers in the airship destiny recalled disparagingly how Colsman was reduced to "making aluminum pots and pans," while Eckener struggled to make the commercial airship possible. Such memories do the somewhat stiff-necked managing director a disservice. With the well-invested wartime earnings as a sea anchor, Colsman navigated the stormy postwar economic and political waters with considerable skill. While Eckener focused on the zeppelin, Colsman budded several dozen smaller enterprises from the five basic Zeppelin subsidiaries. He also sought a great variety of subcontracts for the basic companies in burgeoning German consumer industries. Some of these projects failed, some never developed; but in the shadow of reborn zeppelin building and enthusiasm of the era 1925–38, Colsman's work would become the foundation of Friedrichshafen's postwar industrial-technological significance.[6]

From the summer of 1922 onward, Friedrichshafen's faded image as the *Zeppelinstadt* began to brighten. The great construction hangar had survived Allied postwar dismantling and was building an airship for the Americans. Tourism began to revive, more for the lake and the scenery, but still drawn by the zeppelin mythology. After LZ 126 was delivered to America, the Zeppelin Company and the city in 1925 celebrated the twenty-fifth anniversary of the Count's first flight. Here was announced a project to construct an experimental ship for potential polar exploration and to blaze the way for world air travel. LZ 127, the *Graf Zeppelin*, was the result. Now the city was in its element again, with a frenzied welcome for the globe-trotting airship in 1929. In the shadows of the Depression, however, optimism withered. By dint of prodigious activity and superb public relations at home and abroad, Eckener kept the Zeppelin Company alive, handsomely supplemented by the income from eager stamp collectors flying their letters by airship, together with admission fees and sale of zeppelin souvenirs at the hangar where the next airship was slowly taking shape. The city and the Company together drew and shared the tourists.

The Nazis came to power in early 1933 and promptly saw their own political advantage in the zeppelin enterprise. Though Führer Hitler would never set foot inside an airship (which he considered an "unnatural" phenomenon), and though Air Minister Hermann Göring would place all his wagers on his rebuilding Luftwaffe, Propaganda Minister Joseph Goebbels fully understood the political potential of the zeppelin for the Nazi cause. First the *Graf Zeppelin*, and later the *Hindenburg* and *Graf Zeppelin II*, were fully exploited to put the ships with their giant swastikas into the skies as symbols of German technology and Nazi superiority triumphant. While wealthy visitors still came to enjoy the comfort of the Kurgarten Hotel, or were part of a newly motorized version of tourism, these were both inundated by a new type of mass tourism promoted by the "Strength-through-Joy" movement of the Nazi Party. Friedrichshafen boomed again. Alongside the airships, the Zeppelin Company was making other products worthy of attention: diesel motors for a new generation of high-speed trains for the German railroads; all-metal flying boats of the Dornier Company (just recently separated from the Zeppelin conglomerate); and the prestigious Maybach-Zeppelin automobile, a luxury competitor to Mercedes-Benz. It could be seen as a "California atmosphere" all over again.

On July 8, 1938, Friedrichshafen and the Zeppelin Company celebrated the centennial of Count Zeppelin's birth. It was a splendid occasion, with the opening of a remarkable Zeppelin Museum, proper commemorative Nazi postage stamps, and distinguished airshipmen from at home and abroad. Still the pall that overlay the ceremonies could not be denied. The *Hindenburg* had crashed in flames a year before. Now the *Graf Zeppelin II* stood, impressive to be sure in its hangar, but caught between conversion to flight with helium and helium denied by the United States because Germany had recently invaded neighboring Austria. Nonetheless, Friedrichshafen was hard at work, in the image of the zeppelin apparently, but actually quite irrespective of the airship. Alfred Colsman's new ventures of the previous decade had fully matured. They were at work primarily on armaments orders for the Nazi government, including ultimately aerial weapons that Count Zeppelin could hardly have dreamed of—components and subassemblies for the V−2 rockets. When the war came, these facts were duly noted by Germany's opponents. Several smaller air raids struck Friedrichshafen before 1944, but in that year the city and its factories were almost totally demolished in two massive Allied air strikes. The good citizens have had a rather ambivalent attitude toward these matters since then. They bemoan the "senseless destruction" of their cultural monuments, but Friedrichshafen as a center of Nazi war production—that subject is still rather taboo. Thereafter it was back to square one for the *Zeppelinstadt*.

In complete contrast to Friedrichshafen, the communities of Cardington and distant Howden had little reciprocal relationship with their surrounding populations. Or, to put it differently, these two airship building entities, while largely dependent on a wider outside world for construction supplies and labor, were self-contained in their workaday activities. Building of the first hangar began at Cardington in the summer of 1916, but the first airship was not completed there until August 1918. By this time the Short Brothers Company of Rochester had established a branch enterprise at the new air station. The nearby city of Bedford housed some of the initial airship design facilities. When construction of the station was complete, everything moved to this location. Near an impressive, multistory stone administration building stood a characteristic series of workshops for girder assembly and a complete manufacturing facility for gas cells. Various ancillary services and backup facilities supplemented the fully developed hydrogen gas works. For the rest, spur railway lines brought all the necessary construction parts directly to the workshops and hangars. The little village of Cardington remained almost untouched by the airship enterprise. It was the Royal Airship Works that was the focus of activity and self-awareness.

In the early 1920s several airships were built and serviced at Cardington. Most notable was R 38, the latest British improvement on the basic zeppelin design, which was disastrously lost on a trial flight in 1921, carrying with it the cream of Cardington's flight personnel. In the continuing search for new alternatives, the Shorts' establishment was nationalized and Cardington became a completely government-run operation. In 1924 with the implementation of the Imperial Airship Scheme, Cardington reassessed all theoretical and practical matters related to airship building. Fresh teams of designers and builders were recruited from various walks of civilian life as well as from service leadership. By 1926 Cardington was thriving. The existing construction hangar was enlarged and a second one was moved from Pulham. The world's first giant cantilever mooring mast was under construction as R 101 began to take shape. Stainless steel came for the girders by rail from the works of Boulton and Paul, in Norwich 100 miles distant. The works throbbed with thoughts and experiments in innovation, as streams of theorists, technicians, and newsmen came north from London to consult and report on the airship wonder taking shape at Cardington. It appeared to be the center of the empire's airship future, soon to accommodate both ships being built under the Imperial Airship Scheme.[7]

R 101 leaving mast at Cardington, spring 1930. (R.A.E. Cardington Crown copyright, G. Chamberlain Archives)

R 100 at St. Hubert (Montreal, Canada), August 1930. (Canadian National Railways and Barry Countryman)

In mid-December 1929, R 100, the airship built by private enterprise at Howden, arrived for its permanent stationing at Cardington. How different had been its origin and development! The design and construction teams of the Airship Guarantee Company had grown out of Vickers's experience and Barnes Wallis's work with R 80. In 1925 their vanguard set up shop at the derelict airship station of Howden, which had been closed down in 1921 after the R 38 disaster. As one expert has described it.

> A single shed of corrugated iron, 750 feet long and 150 feet wide, stood on a steel framework rising above the marshland now strewn with the debris of wartime blimp sheds. Feathers and the remains of many hens littered one end of the shed and beneath the 7.5 acre floor the concrete trench that had housed the hydrogen and water mains there was a vixen's lair.[8]

Some order and minimal accommodations were introduced; but again Howden village would be only slightly affected by the airship activity. Various components of the new ship came by rail from far-off parts of England. The gas cells of goldbeaters' skins came from distant Berlin because the Cardington manufacture could not provide enough material for both ships. One singular difference was in the on-site construction of the girders. Engineer Wallis had devised a machine to make helically wound tubes from duralumin strips, which were then riveted with a helical seam. And so R 100 took shape over four years' time: frugally planned, with no opportunities for expensive innovation; a self-sufficient stepchild isolated and insulated by distance from the empire airship center.

The climax of the Imperial Airship Scheme came during 1930. The R 100 had left its Howden birthplace, never to return. Its builders dispersed, except for a standby watch. From its new base at Cardington, R 100 made its fortunate round trip to Canada in July—lionized in the Dominion, but barely appreciated at home.[9] Now Cardington buzzed with a sense of frustrated competition and much overwork, as R 101 was necessarily and hurriedly enlarged for a much-anticipated and heavily politicized trip to India. Britain's bid for airship supremacy was forever lost with the R 101's spectacular destruction on October 5, while barely under way to India. Only now did the village of Cardington play its single, poignant role in the airship drama. To its small church came the funeral procession, en route from London, where two million people had witnessed its passage. In the presence of a host of dignitaries from the nation, the empire, and the world at large, the airshipmen were laid to rest in a dignified common grave in the village cemetery. At the Royal Airship Works vitality ebbed to nothing. R 100 was briefly maintained and then reduced to scrap. Within half a year Cardington was converted to share its space with a Royal Air Force facility. Howden was simply abandoned.

In contrast to Friedrichshafen and Cardington, Akron was no stranger to industry when airships began building there. As of 1900 Akron had already developed a variegated pattern of smaller enterprises in milling, farm machinery, clay products, and other manufacturers. By 1924 this diversity was giving way to a predominance of rubber products under such familiar brand names as Goodyear, Goodrich, and Firestone. With the burgeoning demand for military requirements in World War I, the city grew apace and Goodyear established its preeminence as a manufacturer of all kinds of lighter-than-air equipment. Akron grew further with the postwar American automobile boom to a city of 200,000. Given its distinction by then as the Rubber Capital of America, Akron had also acquired industrial smog, a frequently pervasive malodor. Onto this somewhat murky scene came the promise of airship building. There were other industrial anticipations, notably in chemicals; but this promise spoke in noble terms of silver ships in aerial spheres and high tech cleanliness. Cinderella Akron could aspire to become a princess.

When Goodyear acquired the cooperation of the German Zeppelin Company in late 1923 and founded Goodyear-Zeppelin, expectations were generally high for America's airship future. The Germans were most likely out of the business. The British were still indecisive about their airship future. America's ZR 1, *Shenandoah*, was just taking to the skies to improve the power of the world's greatest navy. In later 1924 the German-built LZ 126 (ZR 3), *Los Angeles*, joined the fleet as well. Goodyear's public relations offices roused the expectations of the Akronites, punctuated with news about flights of America's two rigids and cheering the arrival of Dr. Karl Arnstein and twelve other airship-building experts from Friedrichshafen. All that was missing were the indispensable navy construction contracts.[10]

This rosy future was suddenly darkened by the loss of the *Shenandoah* during a fierce midwestern storm in September 1925. Thereupon followed a lengthy official investigation of the disaster, along the margins of which could be heard the negative arguments of a new breed of naval airmen—the emerging carrier captains and their fliers. Admiral William A. Moffett, chief of the Bureau of Aeronautics, however, was determined that all types of naval aviation should be experimentally developed and fully tested. The *Los Angeles* continued to make good airship news, though more with barnstorming trips and media attention than with fleet operations. Both navy designers and the Goodyear men were working at their drawing boards. After three years of delays, and through two design competitions, Goodyear finally won. In October 1928, contracts were signed for the construction of two new rigid airships—to be the largest, most advanced, and finest in the world.

The timing could not have been more propitious. Just a week later the *Graf Zeppelin* was en route from Germany to the United States, opening a decade of excitement for transatlantic passenger travel by airship. Zeppelin fever broke out in Akron. Goodyear manipulated the enthusiasm to good advantage. Earlier, in late 1927, the voters had rejected a one million-dollar bond issue to construct a new municipal airport, which the city council then resolved in early 1928 to build on its own authority at some time in the future. With its navy contract imminent, Goodyear now sought to ensure certainty in Akron by appearing to negotiate with San Diego, Los Angeles, or Cleveland for the most advantageous terms for establishing an airship building industry. "Akron's Greatest Chance!" cried the *Beacon Journal*; "Every citizen will encourage the organizations and committees that have this great project in charge!" Shortly after the contract signing, the *Los Angeles* was overhead and the city council indicated its willingness to build the airport forthwith. By mid-October Goodyear stock had risen within two weeks from 70 to 98. At that point Dr. Hugo Eckener and a contingent of his *Graf Zeppelin* officers made their triumphant entry into Akron, not by airship as hoped, but by special train. The *Beacon Journal* published a special edition, replete with zeppelin-theme advertisements. There was still suspense about the Goodyear negotiations, but the newspaper was certain that Akron was ready to take its place in the forefront of new transportation by zeppelin. With obvious relief the late October *Beacon Journal* described Goodyear's decision to build in the Rubber Capital as, "a barren field with tumbling shacks will be changed into the center of world zeppelin industry." Editorially the newspaper proclaimed "Akron's Genius Recognized," and "Akron Starts a March on the Future."[11]

During the month of November 1928, Akron's promise began to be realized. The pages of the *Beacon Journal* gave the news. Akron enterprise on the job had raised eighty thousand dollars to provide a site for the "zeppelin industry" (Nov. 1). Real estate men hailed the coming of the new airship enterprise and advertised homesites near the new airport-to-be (Nov. 3). Various editorials praised the funding efforts for the new airport. The groundbreaking for the new construction facility, done with a silvered shovel in the presence of official Washington became front-page news (Nov. 4). Goodyear President Litchfield always insisted upon calling this the Airship Dock, in order to mark its distinction from an airplane hangar, which he considered markedly inferior. At month's end, Akron's business leaders could picture the city's great future, with zeppelin-building a crown on its favorable but still heavily rubberized industry. Goodyear's public relations staff worked overtime for the next decade, and even in the face of disastrous news, stressed—and exaggerated—the significance of airship construction and flying for Akron and America.

The years 1929–30 brought what would later be recognized as a glamorous but premature climax to Akron's airship expectations. The *Graf Zeppelin* circled the globe in August of 1929, and Akronites followed its progress as though it were their own. Dr. Eckener, the "Zepp Master," as the *Beacon Journal* dubbed him, came to confer with Litchfield about transoceanic airship lines. Early in November the Airship Dock was completed and Admiral Moffett came to drive the golden rivet into the first ring assembly of ZRS 4—later to be named the *Akron*. Construction materials flowed to the site: duralumin from Pittsburgh, Maybach engines from Friedrichshafen, and other materials from 800 suppliers and subcontractors. As 1930 opened, the stock market decline and the first ebbing economic statistics only marginally reduced the zeppelin fever. The society pages of the *Beacon Journal* chronicled a succession of distinguished visitors and of social events in the mansions of the rubber barons: admirals and other high government officials, diplomats and congressmen, airshipmen and engineers. In mid-1930 the *Graf Zeppelin* made a widely publicized triangular flight between Germany, Brazil, and America. This event only confirmed the emerging studies of Dr. Jerome C. Hunsaker, founder of the Navy Bureau of Aeronautics now at work in Akron on basic operational plans and cadre formations for Goodyear's projected worldwide passenger services. Akron thrilled to the flight of British R 100 to Canada, but failed in its expectations of a neighborly visit from the English aerial traveler. Meanwhile ZRS 4 majestically took shape, while a new generation of blimps also took to the skies. It was an atmosphere in Akron such as Houston would later experience in the first years of the space age.

The crash of the British R 101 on October 5, 1930, marked the beginning of a four-year fluctuation in Akron's airship expectations—sometimes down, then up again, but ultimately always downward. It would never be quite the same again. The knowledge that inert helium would lift Akron's sky ships in the near future could not quite overcome a lingering pall. To be sure, throngs of tourists continued to visit the municipal airport and the Airship Dock. This holiday enthusiasm partially masked the inroads of Depression distress. But the times were out of joint. Akronites apparently enjoyed a succession of news exposés about skullduggery at the airship works, one after another, over three years' time. Momentarily things brightened when Mrs. Herbert Hoover arrived to christen the *Akron* on August 8, 1931. For a week festivities echoed in the presence of hundreds and thousands: distinguished visitors, singing school children, cheering spectators, flying pigeons, and autos seeking parking spaces. As it had before, the airship promise gave a disproportionate emphasis to the realities of life in Akron, always punctuated by Goodyear publicity hyperbole.

In an upbeat of zeppelin fever, the *Akron* was commissioned in late 1931 and flew off to service with the navy. The ZRS 5, was begun in the great Airship Dock. As the production of auto components sagged with stagnation in the motor industry, employment at Goodyear-Zeppelin remained a small Akron bright spot. The tourists continued to come and marvel at the giant taking shape. News of the *Akron's* continuing flights with the navy kept the faith, now with somewhat grim determination, as the city's economic spirits sagged during 1932. The German connection remained important. At Goodyear the steady record of the *Graf Zeppelin* in service between Germany and Brazil fortified efforts to procure legislation in Congress for an air merchant marine, giving airship building and operational service the same status and governmental subsidies as enjoyed by the American merchant marine—and guaranteeing further orders for passenger variations on the naval airships that Goodyear-Zeppelin would build. On March 11, 1933, in chilling winter weather and equally low economic temperature, Mrs. Moffett christened the *Macon* and wished it Godspeed. This would be her husband's last visit to Akron, for he perished with most of the crew a month later in the destruction of the *Akron* in stormy skies off the New Jersey coast.

If it was a loss for the navy and a blow to the minority of airshipmen in that service, the wreck of ZRS 4 was a disaster for Goodyear-Zeppelin and a terrible blow to the great hopes of the city of Akron. Soon thereafter the *Macon* was commissioned and left for service on the Pacific coast. Now the Airship Dock stood empty and the tourists dwindled. Unlike Friedrichshafen, airship building in Akron had not produced a group of related industries making component parts, firms that might now innovate new types of consumer goods. Even given that possibility, the woes of the Depression might well have foreclosed such opportunities. Goodyear returned to promotion of its other lighter-than-air activities with free ballooning and its always well-advertised blimps. When Akronites could divert their major attention away from worries about the economic crisis, they could still take pride in Goodyear products continuing to win in international ballooning contests and beginning to surge into the stratosphere. In October 1933 the German connection reasserted itself. The *Graf Zeppelin* visited en route to the World's Fair in Chicago. For the first and only time the transit and immigration facilities of Akron's new "international" airport building were put to use. Dr. Eckener spoke brave and encouraging words, but the blighted airship hopes got at best a mixed message of encouragement from the brilliant swastikas newly emblazoned on the fins of the zeppelin. Accounts of the *Macon's* flights in the *Beacon Journal* during 1934 receded somewhat in the presence of more diverse and positive news about other industrial and economic developments. The loss of the *Macon* off Big Sur in February 1935 took most of the starch out of the remaining Akron hopes for its airship future. Thenceforth the sky ships were only silver ghosts over the almost empty Airship Dock.[12]

In the face of these grim realities the Goodyear Company maintained an aggressive forward stance in its public relations locally, in Washington, and abroad. It had invested three million dollars in the original venture and had built the two navy sky giants at a loss. Its future hopes were now pinned on the culminating German zeppelin activity. Goodyear maintained a representative in Friedrichshafen who flew frequently on the transatlantic flights to North and South America. With the *Los Angeles* decommissioned, the tiny minority of navy airshipmen still in service also kept their skills alive by flying with the Germans. The widely publicized crossings of the *Hindenburg* in 1936 roused great expectations at Goodyear and renewed interest in Akron. For 1937 the Goodyear-sponsored American Zeppelin Transport Company (AZT) entered into joint operation of the North American flights, together with the Nazi-controlled German operating company, expecting to charter LZ 130 for 1938. The *Hindenburg* burned at Lakehurst while on AZT's first participation in May 1937. For almost the last time the familiar German names passed in the columns of the *Beacon Journal*, mourned especially by the shrunken contingent of former Akron airship builders. In September 1937 the U.S. Congress approved legislation permitting the export of helium abroad for the operation of foreign airships. A flicker of Akron hope was now pinned on plans for renewed service with German zeppelins, from which continued operations might then flow some orders for construction of commercial airships by Goodyear-Zeppelin. Now the only American airship builder had to contend not only with the scarred record of the airships, but also with a formidable phalanx of flying boat builders and operators, notably Sikorsky, Boeing, and Pan-American.[13] In addition, there was no help from the White House, which had traditionally welcomed all aviation heroes, including the German airshipmen. President Roosevelt, who had once come hat-in-hand to Goodyear in 1923 for help to save his own failing airship venture based on Schütte-Lanz designs, was reported as referring disdainfully to "that rubber company in Akron" when there was talk of reviving legislation for naval airships or for the air merchant marine.

With the Nazi invasion of Austria and the subsequent prohibition of helium exports to Germany, all prospects for airship building and travel vanished. Between 1939 and 1941, as the German associate of Goodyear-Zeppelin was booming with the production of Nazi armaments, the Friedrichshafen partner was dropped and the airship company became Goodyear Aircraft. All through the 1930s, Goodyear had continued to develop and fly its fleet of half a dozen blimps, creating therewith a widely recognized advertising symbol that would mark the entire enterprise for half a century. Other variations were developed for the armed services through the decade. When war broke out again, the military adapted the blimps and balloons to a wide range of uses; but the rigid airship glamour was gone. The dream of Cinderella Akron becoming a rigid airship princess vanished amidst the smokestack industries of Akron that enjoyed the general upswing of the wartime economy.

In all three of these airship building communities it was not only the prospect of light industry development and pride in a new kind of workmanship that stimulated the participation and expectations of the citizenry. There was also the high excitement of anticipation that each of these centers already was, or would become, a hub of world travel and noble commerce. The shining ships aloft in the skies quite literally raised the sense of citizen participation to a higher and more vivid purpose in a world of aviation progress. Friedrichshafen knew that excitement in the later 1920s and 1930s. Cardington aspired to be the hub of the empire, where the loosening ties of Britain's distant dominions would be drawn together again for higher Anglo-Saxon purposes. And at Akron's municipal airport today, in the shadow of the Airship Dock one can still see the murals in the little international terminal building displaying and symbolizing some Akronites' anticipation of the role their city would play as a center of intercontinental travel by airship.

Granted that business managers were caught up in the promises of airship building and flying; granted that they carried their enthusiasm successfully into the communities where they operated; what were the involvements and commitments of the men and women who actually built the sky ships and brought them to perfection for their flights?

When Count Zeppelin first began to assemble his airships on the shore of Lake Constance in 1899, there was no experienced industrial working class in the immediate area that he could call upon. In this dearth of native skilled labor, he brought in a handful of men with basic engineering and manufacturing skills from Stuttgart or nearby cities. These in turn trained a hodgepodge of small-town craftsmen and agricultural artisans in the necessary skills of assembling the partially prefabricated components for the first six airships built at Manzell by 1909. Thus was accumulated the core of workers that established Germany's best known airship industry. Many of them lived in the nearby countryside and came in daily on foot or by train and bicycle. Some of them combined farming with airship building. The gracious Count was readily in contact with the socially limited townsmen or rural workers and conversed with them in their common rustic Swabian dialect. In this context of interest and mutual respect the airship builders developed their heartfelt loyalty to the man and his incredible venture.

As work began in the new construction hangar adjacent to Friedrichshafen from 1909 onward, it attracted additional workers with somewhat more varied experience and talents to service the airship building, engine construction, and hydrogen production. The Zeppelin Company also favored a sufficient annual contingent of apprentices, who in turn often became lifelong employees and devoted participants in the Zeppelin mystique. Their loyalty was well placed, for the Count came to their assistance in a crucial circumstance. By 1913 there were nearly 700 men and a few women at work. With this growth in the number of workers, there developed a dearth of housing and a significant growth in demand for the basic necessities of life. It was not enough that local landlords and merchants enjoyed the enhanced tourist trade stimulated by the Zeppelin phenomenon; they also profited handsomely from rent-gouging and excessive prices for their goods and services. In doing so, they drew their financial bow too taut—and it was the patriarchial Count who snapped.[14]

Early in his adult life Count Zeppelin had shown social attitudes that were tolerant, sensible, and pragmatic. Eckener later commented that he had often heard the aeronaut say that it was "the privilege of an aristocracy to have a particularly strongly developed sense towards the community," a responsible essence of noblesse oblige. It angered Zeppelin to see how many of his fellow-aristocrats ignored these obligations. He was keenly aware of the rising social tensions between the emerging proletariat and the rest of German society in the 1860s. He was convinced that the privileged aristocracy had its responsibility to lead the nation—including the often insensitive and newly rich middle class—to a reasonable alleviation of the distress of the workers and toward some realization of their aspirations for a better life. Failing such concern by the aristocracy, the alternatives would be sharpening and dangerous social antagonisms and eventually civil disruption. Shortly before the war, Count Zeppelin began to put his views to the test in Friedrichshafen.[15]

Possibly the count was reminded of his obligations by some intermittent work stoppages in 1911 that culminated in a mass meeting to protest the rent-gouging and profiteering in Friedrichshafen. Certainly manager Colsman played a major role. He suggested to the aeronaut that he commemorate his seventy-fifth birthday by announcing to the 600 workers assembled to celebrate the occasion, that the Count would sponsor a workers' housing

"Dorfkrug," LZ employees' pub at Friedrichshafen, 1916–40. (Luftschiffbau Zeppelin)

"Zeppelindorf," housing for LZ employees at Friedrichshafen, 1917–40. (Luftschiffbau Zeppelin)

development. Shortly thereafter the *Zeppelin Wohlfahrt* (Zeppelin Welfare) was established as an integral part of the Zeppelin enterprises. Between 1913 and 1916 this socially sensitive organization created a whole community within the economic life of Friedrichshafen. First and foremost were the employees' own garden homes that put an end to real estate speculation and eventually comprised over 150 individual and row houses. By the later 1930s an additional 400 apartments and studios had been acquired for the use of the *Wohlfahrt* within the city limits. Separate residential quarters were built or made available for bachelors and unmarried women. There was a day-care center, together with consultation facilities for prenatal care. The singles' quarters provided public baths. A commissary supplied the daily needs of the employees. A packing house, dairies, truck gardens, bakery, and coal yard serviced the commissary. A large meeting hall was built that doubled for noontime meal service, eventually feeding 1,200 people daily. In 1916, great celebration attended the opening of the *Dorfkrug*—the workers' commodious and well-stocked pub supplied by its own winery. The Company athletic fields were just across the way from the pub and were always a steady source of customers. To complete the facilities, there were a savings bank and a library of several thousand volumes, with a comfortable reading room. A distinguished architect designed the various buildings, and for years the *Zeppelindorf* and all its interwoven services were a model for other workers' settlements in the rest of Germany. It should be emphasized that, although the notion of *Wohlfahrt* (welfare) was central to the whole concept, Colsman always insisted that the constituent parts of this autonomous enterprise of the Zeppelin Foundation should be financially self-supporting, either individually or in interrelationship. His governing assumptions were directly opposite to those underlying the modern welfare state.

If the *Zeppelin Wohlfahrt* at first appeared in some uncomfortable economic contrast to the business interests of Friedrichshafen, it was soon integrated into the larger community by the burgeoning dimensions of wartime economic expansion. In the difficult postwar years it was strong enough to bolster the whole business fabric of its city. The constituent business derivations from that remarkable socioeconomic enterprise are still clearly discernible in the affluent city of the 1990s.[16]

Wartime demands for zeppelins, airplanes, and component parts for other vehicles caused employment at the Zeppelin Company and the related Dornier works to increase tenfold. The more than 7,000 workers, many of these brought in from outside the Swabian homeland, were mostly untouched by the charisma of the Count. A tiny prewar socialist party group grew to several thousand with the outbreak of the German Revolution in early November of 1918. The streets sprouted red flags, while a Workers' and Soldiers' Council met in the *Rathaus* to take advantage of an orderly mass demonstration outside. It was a flash in the pan. By early 1919 three-fourths of the untypical workers had dispersed to other parts of Germany. Friedrichshafen reasserted its rustic Swabian character.[17]

There was a brief optimistic upsurge in airship building. Hugo Eckener returned from his wartime service as head of the airship school at Nordholz and promptly set to work building two small airships for peacetime travel from materials and parts left over from wartime construction. Between August and December of 1919, even the prewar DELAG was revived, catering to more than a thousand passengers between Friedrichshafen and Berlin. The year 1920 marked the Treaty of Versailles and the abrupt halt of most airship activity. The existing ships were maintained pending Allied decisions as to their future. While Colsman traveled to America in mid-1920 in a futile search for airship orders, his keen business mind conjured with other possibilities. As Eckener focused single-mindedly on an airship revival for Germany, Colsman kept a hard core of his men at work during frugal 1920–21: making aluminum wares for consumer use, repairing motor vehicles and railroad rolling stock, making transmissions and drive trains for other vehicle manufacturers. His efforts at diversification produced a dozen new enterprises; his staff had to learn marketing of consumer goods from scratch. His men were on full time, half time, part time; for the rest, the *Zeppelin Wohlfahrt* saw them and their families through. By 1924 a new production foundation was laid and the Zeppelin Company was doing significant sub-contracting for other solid manufacturers.[18]

Colsman's achievement, however, was completely overshadowed by a new wave of German zeppelin fever. The airship LZ 126 was completed and flown across the Atlantic to the United States. Eckener became a world-famous personality. He returned to Germany, and sought national support in a campaign for funds to build a modern airship for polar exploration and trans-oceanic travel. Despite the inadequate sums raised in a prodigious propaganda campaign, Eckener went ahead with building LZ 127, supported by the Zeppelin Company directors, including a lukewarm Colsman. Again the tourists thronged to the revived *Zeppelinstadt* and saw an airship slowly taking shape. The essential means for the construction, however, came not from them, but from the profits of Colsman's other enterprises. Still, all the workers were captivated by the expectation of the zeppelin revival. Their greatest hopes were realized when the *Graf Zeppelin* returned triumphant from its global flight in 1929, jubilantly welcomed by the entire Friedrichshafen community. Shortly thereafter Alfred Colsman resigned from the firm, a victim, incredibly, of zeppelin fever.

Friedrichshafen and its workers survived the Depression tolerably. Eckener kept the *Graf Zeppelin* flying with a host of financial stratagems, playing notably on its unique fascination for a world awakening to the promise of aviation. Construction began on a new super-airship with assistance from the state of Württemberg, reminiscent of the image of a struggling Count with

Building LZ 129: girder assembly, 1932–34. (Luftschiffbau Zeppelin)

Building LZ 129: ring assembly, 1931–32. (Luftschiffbau Zeppelin)

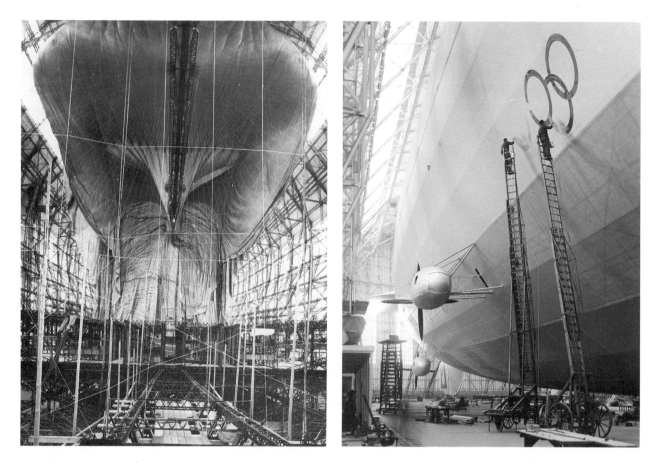

Building LZ 129: hanging
ballonets, 1935. (Luftschiffbau
Zeppelin)

Building LZ 129: painting Olympic rings on hull, 1936. (Luftschiffbau Zeppelin)

his supportive king. Total unemployment was minimal, combined with some
part-time work and the saving grace of Colsman's other, often hard-pressed
divisions. In extremis, there were the easy proximity of inexpensive agrarian
surroundings and the floor above disaster provided by the *Zeppelin Wohlfahrt*.

When Hitler came to power in 1933, a perceptible quickening of mood
and pace occurred. It was punctuated by flags, military bands, parades, and
other propaganda. Zeppelin building and flying became a state-sponsored
project, but not solely for its commercial value. The great, attention-getting
sky ship was put in service for May Day commemorations in Berlin and Nazi
Party rallies at Nürnberg. With its emblazoned swastikas, *der Zeppelin* now
became Germany's symbol of technological achievement and advertised political superiority. If the workers at the Zeppelin Company were inherently
a cohesive and conservative group, they still enjoyed all the nationalistic excitement of the Nazi revival. The younger men and women were likely to be
swept off their feet by the propaganda for the new ideology. Uniforms
sprouted. New salutes and greetings became the order of the day in the
workshops.[19]

The Nazi movement also introduced new organizational pressures. Together with all the rest of German industry, the Zeppelin companies were "synchronized." The Nazi-sponsored German Labor Front (DAF) was introduced perforce as sole bargaining agent—where there had been no labor unions at all before. In their guild-craftsman conservatism, the workers superbly maintained the *Graf Zeppelin* on its South American service and built the two new super-airships. A number of the workers were basically unresponsive to the agitation of the younger zealots. These attitudes infuriated the Nazi radicals in higher regional and national circles. For five years they steadily increased their pressures on key sectors in labor and management. The conservatives in both areas buttressed their positions by favoring pro forma Nazis less vehement than the local radical agitators. By 1939, however, the radicals won by pressure through the National Socialist Works Organization (NSBO)—a branch of the DAF allegedly seeking codetermination in all the Zeppelin companies by way of required labor-management committees. Director Hugo Eckener, world-famous in his own right, was a troublesome anti-Nazi hindrance who barely tolerated the regime in order to keep his airships flying. When he was targeted by the local NSBO, he made a few marginal compromises and went about his work—with the silent approval of a number of his workers. After the destruction of the *Hindenburg*, however, and when the new *Graf Zeppelin II* without helium could find service only in Nazi-sponsored flights, no further compromises were possible. Eckener retreated under pressure from the NSBO and the Nazification of the Zeppelin Company was completed.

By the time the war broke out, the image of *Zeppelinstadt* was only the façade of a different Friedrichshafen. Airship building had ceased in 1938, except for sporadic activity on LZ 131; both the Company and its workers went to other tasks in the booming business of armaments. In 1940 the last two zeppelins were scrapped and the Frankfurt passenger terminal was leveled to make way for a Luftwaffe fighter squadron. All that the zeppelin workers had left was a nostalgic memory of the silver sky ships and possibly a vague prescience of some impending destruction of their community by enemy bombers.

The airship builders in Britain had somewhat different experiences with their enterprise than did the Germans in their *Zeppelinstadt*. Cardington had remained on a standby basis all through the airship indecisiveness. It had the discipline, pride, and spirit of a preferred service. By the time the Imperial Airship Scheme had been resolved, it was the focal point and station of the elite nucleus of England's airshipmen. In mid-1924 the new designers and calculators arrived, the vanguard of an ultimate thousand in the hangar and workshops. Materials and parts rolled in from two dozen suppliers all over Britain. By 1927, 300 women were working in a spacious loft, fabricating the huge gas cells, for which one million cattle were to supply their guts. All these workers were, to some degree, caught up in the excitement and professionalism felt by the cadre of men in the service, either air force or governmental. Howden had no such advantage. With preliminary work already done at Vickers near London, engineer Barnes Wallis moved with his small expert staff to Yorkshire in mid-1926. Building began late that year, with basic worker training occurring on site, using Wallis's simplified fabrication machinery and procedures. The workers and staff at Howden seldom exceeded 500. Since building R 100 was a single manufacturing episode on a derelict station, morale was always a problem. Calculator Norway (Nevil Shute) later gave a hair-raising account of brutish and uncouth lasses recruited "straight from the plough" and requiring constant supervision of their behavior. The air in the hangar had whiffs of uric acid, as the men frequently relieved themselves from perches high up in the emerging structural framework. Thanks to Wallis's expertise and basic management, the work was completed within the terms of Vickers's tight contract. But the accomplishment was more in spite of the local elements than because of them.[20]

An important supplemental reason for the superior spirit at Cardington was the presence of Shortstown. This nicely designed, suburban garden colony had been built by the Short Brothers during their wartime tenure at the naval air station. Together with small stores and the indispensable pub, these several hundred houses and apartments supplied fine living accommodations for resident airshipmen, servicemen on station, and a number of workers building the R 101. Some senior builders lived in Bedford or in other nearby towns, as did many of the workers. Every workday morning they came streaming in by train, bus, car, and cycle. The men in the Royal Air Force and civilians in the British Civil Service enjoyed mutual respect and comradeship. Basic health and social facilities open to the services were apparently somewhat shared by the workers. The wages and the working conditions were evidently satisfactory, for there were no strikes. If it was a professional enterprise at Cardington, there was no comparable cohesiveness at Howden. Aside from two dozen indifferent accommodations on the construction site itself, all housing had to be found elsewhere, often distant. Here, too, the men and women streamed in daily, but hardly to joyous work. On its tight contract with the government, Vickers was also very tightfisted with its wages. There were strikes every year. Relations between the white-collar staff and general workers were not cordial, sometimes severely strained by the gap between those who worked with their heads and those who labored with their hands. Airshipmen visiting from Cardington were essentially outsiders to either the men of brains or those of brawn. Completion of both ships was delayed by about two years. In the case of Cardington, it was because of time needed to introduce innovations or conduct experiments. Howden had design problems tempered with bad blood and disruption. At Cardington there was distinct satisfaction with an important task that had prospects of much more to come. At Howden it was a one-job stand with a miserly employer and no prospect of a future.

R 101 cutaway for new bay insertion, summer 1930. (R.A.E. Cardington Crown copyright, G. Chamberlain Archives)

The Cardington-Howden contrast had even wider dimensions. Relatively close to London, and certainly close to the hearts of successive air ministers, Cardington was favored with frequent visitations of top-rank airmen and senior officials. The avid press department of the air ministry facilitated tours for engineers, politicians of every stripe, and varieties of laymen—notably other members of the press. Howden was largely ignored, by many for reasons of distance, by others in order to emphasize the implied superiority of the government ship in construction. A few British airshipmen occasionally visited to see R 100 taking shape, but the flying crews remained in training and waiting at Cardington. Conversely, Wallis and Norway visited their counterpart only once, very near the end of what had become an unseeming rivalry. Their peevish negativism toward their competitor was perpetuated in Norway's (Nevil Shute's) otherwise fascinating autobiography and by Barnes Wallis's remarkable longevity. At its completion, Wallis's airship best met its performance specifications. Whatever might ultimately have been achieved by the reconstructed government ship was obliterated by the disaster en route to India.

Many of the workers who built R 101, and the men who serviced her, lined the country roads that bore the funeral cortege of her dead to the Cardington church. For half a year the Labour government wrestled with plans and alternatives to hold workers and crews together for some possible future employment. With the deepening Depression and the loss of all confidence in the airship, the enterprise was terminated. Although the workers sought other employment, many went on the notorious dole. Now the flying boat emerged as the likely contender to hold together the bonds of the empire by air. The two great hangars were left standing at the RAF station at Cardington. Lingering memory continued of the airship hopes once nourished there. At Howden, by contrast, the moment R 100 departed for Cardington in late 1929, the workers were dispersed to the winds, with little understanding of the significance of their labors. Wallis and Norway went in new directions, each to achieve distinction of his own in different aspects of airplane design and building. For them, as for the rest, the airship was best gone and forgotten.

The first experts to arrive in Akron for rigid airship building in late 1924 were instant local celebrities. Akronites lionized Dr. Karl Arnstein and his so-called "twelve apostles"—all German design and construction specialists, sent from Friedrichshafen under terms of the Goodyear-Zeppelin agreement. The great reception was followed by a very long lull. Several dozen men from the old Aero Department were added to the German nucleus, but they all had much time on their hands. Designs and estimates for the U.S. Navy were made and remade in detail; so were those for passenger-carrying variations. Still, it was four years before the great Airship Dock—the futuristic airship construction hangar—began to rise at the edge of Akron's new municipal airport.

Goodyear employed nearly 1,000 men at the peak of its lighter-than-air building and services. In addition to rigid airship construction, there were six up-to-date blimps in the air and a number of record-breaking balloon flights. Unlike Friedrichshafen or Cardington, however, the airship builders and fliers were completely overshadowed by ten times their number in the rest of Goodyear's enterprises—not to mention the other tire manufacturers and still other industries in Akron. Yet, the airship people had unique visibility

R 100 under construction, 1926–28. (Vickers, Ltd. and Barry Countryman)

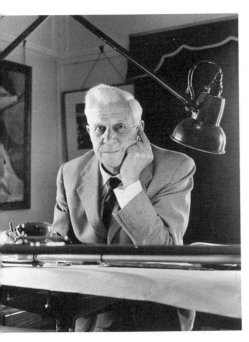

Sir Barnes Wallis, 1970. (Vickers, Ltd. and Barry Countryman)

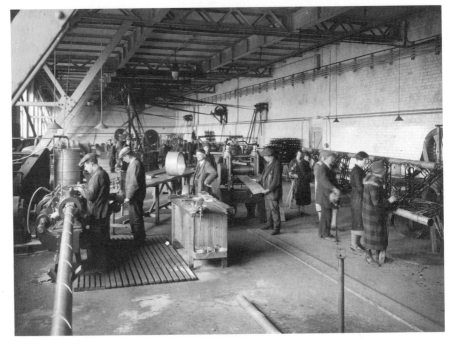

R 100: constructing the unique Wallis helical girder components. (Canadian Pacific Railway and Barry Countryman)

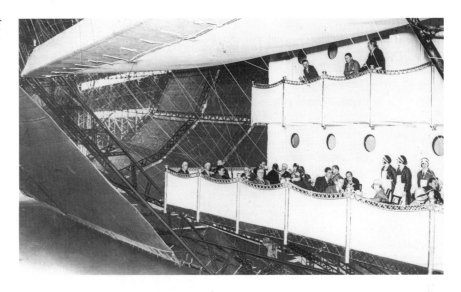

R 100: teatime for 50 members of Parliament and businessmen, July 5, 1928. (Smithsonian Institution, 77-1797)

Dr. Karl Arnstein (left) and Lt. Comdr. T.G.W. "Tex" Settle (right) at construction of airship *Akron*, ZRS 4, Goodyear-Zeppelin hangar, Akron, Ohio, 1930. (Goodyear Archives)

and cohesiveness. No doubt, some of this identity was a product of Goodyear's hyperactive exertions in public relations. But there was more than that. It was the cachet of building America's only industry of its kind that gave the employees a particular self-awareness. Young engineers, designers, and draughtsmen from universities sought opportunities at Goodyear-Zeppelin. At the Airship Dock itself, work was cleaner and more stimulating than many other jobs in the Rubber Capital. Several dozen officers and ratings staffed the offices of the naval inspector with their cooperative presence and frequent official visitors from the political and naval establishment, they made a positive and welcome impact. Inspectors, designers, engineers, and workers all had an interest in achieving a marked success; and they did so because their efforts were clearly and mutually focused on a single ultimate objective. Occasional visits by famous German zeppelin fliers were harbingers of Goodyear's successes to come. The Goodyear newspaper highlighted the airship progress, including reference to plans in the office developing cadres for two international airship transport companies. And among all these elements, the expertise, the experience and the optimism of the original German contingent worked as a facilitating psychological lubricant.[21]

The workers lived quite well by their expected American standards, very few of them without their own cars. In the shadow of the larger Goodyear enterprise, they fully shared in its unusual, if paternalistic, program of employee benefits. President Paul W. Litchfield had a sense of something comparable to Count Zeppelin's conviction of noblesse oblige, though the American expressed his views in characteristic free enterprise management terms. Unlike Colsman, Litchfield probably did not insist that the constituent parts of the program be necessarily financially self-supporting. He conceived of an "Industrial Republic," which sought to enlist and foster employee talent and

German-American Airship Coop-
eration; at Cleveland Air Races,
Oct. 29, 1929. Front row (left to
right): Fred Harpham [Good-
year], Jerome C. Hunsaker
[Goodyear Zeppelin], Paul W.
Litchfield [Goodyear Tire and
Rubber Co.], Dr. Hugo Eckener
[Luftschiffbau Zeppelin], Dr.
Karl Arnstein [Goodyear Zeppe-
lin], unknown. (Goodyear
Archives)

ambition, but he also tried to co-opt them for management objectives. The
results were materially beneficial, if not always psychologically successful from
the employees' point of view. Beginning in 1912, various benefits were established: in-house cafeterias; hospital facilities and medical insurance; athletic fields; opportunities for home ownership; Goodyear Hall with its sports,
educational, and entertainment facilities; a neighborhood bank; and a limited
program for profit sharing. Litchfield's broad conception, with its undeniable
advantages for his employees, did not survive the labor upheavals of the mid-
1930s; but these provisions found little criticism from members of the German
contingent, who considered them on a par with the aristocratic social engineering in Friedrichshafen.[22]

This invigorating construction climate was hardly affected by the destruction of the British R 101. Akron, after all, was building its airships for flight
with safe, nonflammable helium. Amidst the drop in tire production that
came with the Depression, Goodyear's airship employment alone remained
stable. Construction began on the naval ships and commercial variations
therefrom seemed not far behind. When the *Akron* was lost in April 1933,
the *Macon* was almost ready for its departure to West Coast naval service.
Now the plans for passenger airships went into limbo. Could Goodyear-
Zeppelin's highly trained work force be held together till times were again
more auspicious for rigid airship building? Railway supply tycoon Harry

Airship *Akron*, ZRS 4, in construction, 1931–32. (Goodyear Archives)

Vissering again supplied an innovative idea for Goodyear: why not build an experimental, lightweight passenger train, the kind that several railroads were just seeking? The floor of the Airship Dock became a car factory, as the metal and other component airship workers moved to build a three-car, articulated train for the New Haven Railroad. Unfortunately only the prototype was built, for no further orders followed.[23]

Goodyear-Zeppelin marked time. Some workers left to seek new jobs. Others were transferred to various Goodyear plants, where much of the force was already on three-fourths time. Only about 100 remained with Goodyear's actively sponsored blimps and balloons. With the loss of the *Macon* in February 1935, the holding operation ceased. The nucleus of designers and engineers, numbering little more than 100 around its German core, was absorbed into other divisions of the Goodyear Company. For a while longer the corporate identity of Goodyear-Zeppelin remained, as did the great Airship

Airship *Macon*, ZRS 5, in construction, 1933. (Goodyear Archives)

Rail Zeppelin, Goodyear Zeppelin, 1935. (Goodyear Archives and Zenon Hansen)

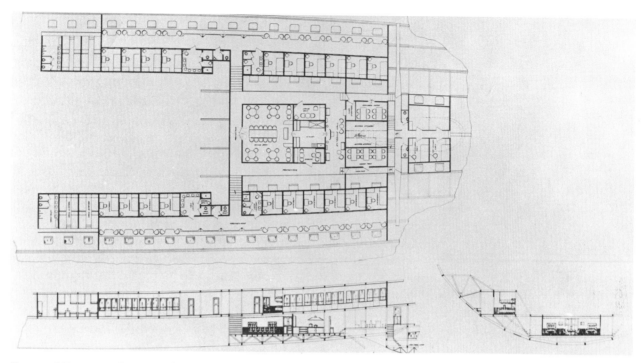

Proposed Passenger Accommodations, Goodyear Airship, 1938. (Goodyear Archives)

Proposed Passenger Accommodations, Goodyear Aircraft, artist's visualization, 1938. (Lufthansa Archives)

Dock. Engineering representatives from Goodyear continued on station with Luftschiffbau Zeppelin in Germany and flew regularly on the South and North American flights.[24] The bulk of the airship workers, however, were released into the turbulence of the labor troubles of the mid-1930s or onto the welfare rolls.

After the *Hindenburg* disaster of 1937, and the reimposition of helium-export controls in 1938, almost no hope for rigid airships remained. The Germans would build and fly commercially, but without helium they could not. Goodyear-Zeppelin could build, but would have no orders. Still, the U.S. Navy continued its interest in nonrigid airships and the varied uses of balloons. There was also the imminence of World War II, with its premonitions of need for great quantities of planes and aircraft parts. Very quietly, between 1939 and 1941, Goodyear-Zeppelin became Goodyear Aircraft. A new generation of aviation builders, with new skills and goals, appeared on the Akron scene. The Airship Dock, now pressed into new service, alone remained to symbolize the accomplishments of America's only corps of rigid airship builders.

Almost half a century has now passed since the last rigid airship flight occurred—this one the last of a series of Nazi propaganda and electronic spy flights in late August of 1939. Subsequently each of the construction communities participated industrially or in direct armed service during World War II. Friedrichshafen alone suffered heavily from enemy bombing. How have these communities fared in the postwar era of fantastic aviation and space developments? What remains in artifact or retrospect to commemorate the earlier industrial commitment to airship building, to celebrate its fragile accomplishments, and to recall the dreams of these builders?

At the end of the war Friedrichshafen was an industrial ruin and remained under French occupation until 1950. There was little to tie the postwar community to the romance of the zeppelin. In fact, quite grotesquely Dr. Eckener was formally accused by the French of being a Nazi industrial leader, was heavily fined, and was denied some basic citizenship rights—until saner heads prevailed upon appeal. The remnants of the once-impressive Zeppelin Museum went to storage in Paris. What little remained of the war-bloated industrial facilities was partially dismantled, the rest left to vegetate. Remarkably, electrostatic expert Erich Hilligardt of the old Zeppelin Company had managed before 1944 to collect thousands of blueprints of all zeppelin designs and other documents, and to place them in dispersed safekeeping in countryside lodges and barns of sympathetic farmers in the area—but these materials had only nostalgic value.[25] A revival of tourism alone seemed to offer any chance of prosperity for the future.

Then, almost miraculously, the old Count reached out from the past to aid the shattered *Zeppelinstadt*. A generation before, when the funds had flowed in from the German nation to rescue the work of the aeronaut, he had established the Zeppelin Foundation as an umbrella corporate entity to disburse and supervise the funding of the various industrial enterprises that formed the Zeppelin conglomerate. The control of its resources was placed in a directorate comprised of representatives from his family, from the several major component industries, and the mayor of Friedrichshafen. The generous charter of the Foundation included a singularly prophetic provision. Article Fifteen stated that, if at some future time the building and flying of airships was no longer possible, then the net profits of all the constituent enterprises (which flowed back into the Foundation) should annually be distributed to the city for charitable and communal purposes. In 1947 the French authorities readily concurred in the validation of this provision. Dr. Eckener resisted indignantly. When he failed to prevail, he rejected the honors the city had earlier bestowed upon him and turned his back upon the community. It was vintage Eckener; he would not disavow his airship heritage.

The full implementation of the Foundation provision coincided with the beginnings of the German "economic miracle" of the 1950s and 1960s. The various zeppelin companies have since prospered wondrously. Where airships once were built, now stand many new structures of the Zeppelin Metallwerke, clearly identified by its zeppelin logo. The myriad workshops of the Zahn-radfabrik today stretch nearly a mile into the farther suburbs of old Fried-richshafen. Maybach Motors is merged with the much larger Motor-Tur-binen-Union. All of these industries are geared into the German and worldwide equipment and consumer goods boom. Dornier is back to making planes for the new Luftwaffe, but far greater is its significance in electronics, bioengineering, and environmental equipment. As a result, the city has by now received nearly one hundred million dollars in proceeds from this post-war prosperity, invested annually in human services and community en-hancement. Shortly before his death, Dr. Eckener was reconciled with the *Zeppelinstadt*, but this fact should not obscure the role of the two prime movers in the rebirth of the community. Thanks be to the Count—but also to his farsighted business manager. For it was Alfred Colsman, in divisive conflicts with Eckener during the 1920s, who insisted upon the industrial diversification of the Zeppelin companies and thus made modern Friedrichs-hafen possible.

For the first decade after the war, the community almost forgot its zeppelin past. Then memories stirred. In 1956 a group of veteran airship designers worked out a detailed proposal to put an improved *Hindenburg* into the skies. The costs proved to be prohibitive: nearly a hundred million marks, including training a new generation of airshipmen.[26] The badly damaged Zeppelin Company archives became part of the public relations work of the Zeppelin Metallwerke; in the last generation both staff and documentation have been overworked. Annually on July first, the seniors of the various Zeppelin companies meet to commemorate the first airship flight of 1900. The past and the future are both present—a tiny handful of former airshipmen and builders, together with Count Albrecht Brandenstein-Zeppelin, great-grandson of the old aeronaut, who also guards the fully preserved family archives. Downtown, the *Schwäbische Zeitung* never fails to find ample space in its columns for zeppelin-related news. Nearby, the new conference center and a fifty-foot monolith at long last properly recognize the civic importance of the old count. An interim Zeppelin Museum, mostly stocked with materials returned from Paris a generation ago, will soon give way to a much larger exhibition, commemorating both the zeppelin era and the industrial vigor of Friedrichshafen since then. Time and the world move on, but Friedrichshafen has not lost its identity as the *Zeppelinstadt*.[27]

One approaches Cardington today along a quiet country road in an English garden landscape. At the right is the large airfield, still dominated by the bulk of its twin construction hangars. At the left is the little village of Cardington itself: scattered houses, a pub, and the lovely small neo-Gothic church. Within that quiet chapel, where the final services for the forty-seven victims of the R 101 were held, is preserved the scorched ensign that flew at the stern of the airship in its final moments. Just across the road, in a formally sunken garden, stands a simple memorial cenotaph inscribed with the names of the dead—alphabetically, without reference to status, whether just a service rating or a noble secretary of state for air. The great mooring tower at Cardington field is gone, its adjoining wooden structures collapsing in decay. An occasional "old hand" can be found to welcome and instruct a visitor on the spot. Still, that visitor has to bring most of his own mental baggage with him to fill the quiet empty spaces of the area.

Aside from the Bedford news files and many memorabilia in a closed museum room, the records of this airship community are held in fulsome economic and technical detail within the stacks of the official Public Record Office, near Kew Gardens in London. A few other papers repose in family archives. Howden, to the end, has drawn the shorter straw. There was no place for the sizeable personal files of enterpriser Dennistoun Burney, the flamboyant developer of the Imperial Airship Scheme and major force in the building of R 100. The files went to a public dump in 1962. The substantial records of Vickers airship activities, which had the contract for R 100, were reduced to pulp in the flooding of its Weybridge archives in 1974. Some Barnes Wallis papers about R 100 remain, a minor portion of his larger technological accomplishment placed with the London Science Museum. Historians can draw life from this documentation; for the general public the bold British airship dream is lost.

There is some small stirring of airship vitality in one of those Cardington hangars. The British government had built many balloons there between 1936 and 1943 to be aerial barrages around Britain's major cities and to be used with the armed forces. A generation later Goodyear used Cardington to launch its European advertising blimp that ranged the European NATO world from a base near Rome. Most recently, Airship Industries Ltd. is constructing a new series of blimps with synthetic materials and electronic controls, the Skyships 500 and 600. Among a few believers there is confidence that these "cathedrals of Cardington will echo to the song of airship engines for many a year to come."[28]

Like the rest of America, Akron overcame the Depression in the wartime economic boom. Goodyear Aircraft prospered with the rest. Paul Litchfield kept his airship hopes alive longer than anyone else. In late 1945 he launched his final effort to realize the commercial potential of the airships he had earlier built for the U.S. Navy. The nucleus of veteran German-American designers produced a new set of plans: a one hundred-passenger deluxe airship, a three hundred-passenger "economy" version, and a cargo ship. Publicity and lobbying flourished, with veteran airshipman, Vice Admiral Charles E. Rosendahl, at work in Washington.[29] Neither the public nor the government, however, was impressed. Aged Dr. Eckener visited the Rubber Capital in 1947, forgotten and unnoticed by a new generation of Akronites. Goodyear continued to service its blimps for their advertising advantages at crucial locations in America. It also built improved and larger airships for the U.S. Navy until 1962. New corporate leadership moved its vision from the past to the future. In 1962 Goodyear Aircraft became Goodyear Aerospace. There it has remained, prosperously covering a wide spectrum of aeronautical and aerospacial needs.

A small group of Akronites keeps the airship memories—both limp and rigid—alive and relates them to the continuing Goodyear blimp activity. This Lighter-Than-Air Society has a strong nucleus of local enthusiasts. Some of them are older or newer Goodyear employees; others are veteran nonrigid airship fliers. The bimonthly *Bulletin* of the Society reaches a membership of nearly 1,000 in five continents. With this unique publication, a group of former and present Akronites is the focus of a worldwide interest in airships rigid and limp, in the past, present, and future. The local membership has played a major role in preserving the records of all airship building in Akron.

The well-maintained Goodyear Archives have important records of the airship past, but there was never room for much, especially about the rigid airship era. Most companies do find it unproductive to maintain space and funding for records of their unsuccessful business ventures. Over the years the shelves and files of Goodyear-Zeppelin were emptied. Almost everything would have been lost, had it not been for the interest and devotion of airship enthusiasts still working at Goodyear. They watched the waste-baskets and disposal bins. Over time the Society has thus accumulated an eclectic but

Cardington Hangars, 1983. (Dr. Dorothea Haaland)

Akron Airship Dock, 1930. (Luftschiffbau Zeppelin)

Santa Cruz Hangar, south of Rio, 1936. (Luftschiffbau Zeppelin and Harold G. Dick)

remarkable store of information—fragments of zeppelin flight logs of World War I, brought over to Akron from Friedrichshafen in 1924; portions of German flight-testing data for LZ 126; a full set of studies from Dr. Hunsaker's offices relating to the establishment of commercial airship operations; bits and pieces of in-house documentation showing how rigid airship hopes were translated into technical blueprints or into business practice. The official records of all aspects of construction of the *Akron* and *Macon* repose with navy documentation in the National Archives. These various papers, rescued by members of the Society and preserved in the Archives of the University of Akron, give unusual episodic insights into the lives, hopes, and actualities of the Akron rigid airship builders.[30]

The great expectations of Goodyear-Zeppelin and the optimistic visions of the Akron Chamber of Commerce exaggerated the realities of airship building and its relative importance for a bright decade. Despite all the propaganda, this activity was never more than a small part of Akron's total industrial and business vitality. It was simply that it shone so brightly in the darkest days of the Depression. Since then Akron has moved to new industrial dimensions. The Rubber Capital image has faded; automobile tires are no longer even made there. At Goodyear designing continues for a new generation of blimps that are environmentally favorable, serving public safety, and watching far out on America's sea frontiers. Yet even here, time has now taken its full toll. During 1986 merger-mania invaded Akron. In self-defense against an outside corporate raider, Goodyear maintained its larger integrity by sacrificing an important and prosperous enterprise component. Goodyear Aerospace, the direct descendant of Goodyear-Zeppelin, has been sold to other hands, but Goodyear will still fly the blimps and retain its familiar airship logo.

Where are the monuments to the airship builders or the significant hallmarks of their industrial communities? In Akron the great Airship Dock should remind its citizens of Goodyear's bold initiative to grasp the hand of the future. If they will listen, a few fortunate children there can hear their grandfathers' tales of the pride and hope in building the two silver sky ships for the U.S. Navy. Although the great hangars at Cardington still dominate the countryside, hardly anyone remains there to remember the confidence and imperial aspirations that went into constructing the R 101. At Howden only the recurring fog can whisper something about the thrifty commitments and scant rewards that went into making R 100. Friedrichshafen finally enjoys its full measure of the transfigured Zeppelin resources and active memories of a century of airship endeavors. It does lack the hangars that distinguish Cardington and Akron. But if the prosperous citizen of the *Zeppelinstadt* jets to Rio de Janeiro, and can find an obliging *Carioca* to drive him thirty-five miles southwest of the Carnival City to Santa Cruz Airbase, he will there find still standing an exact duplicate, erected in 1936, of the last and most modern hangar originally built for the Zeppelin Company in Löwenthal, near Friedrichshafen, in 1932.

These monuments remain. Will our children's children lose their memories, so that like the medieval citizens of Rome who lived among the great ruins of antiquity, they will also look upon these structures with unseeing eyes, averring that a vanished race of giants had once built them?

CHAPTER 4   Eckener's Struggle to Save the Airship for Germany, 1919–1929

When one looks back upon the transatlantic flights of LZ 126 and Lz 127, the *Los Angeles* and the *Graf Zeppelin*, one inevitably thinks of the flying skill and daring of those German airshipmen, who (together with the British in R 34) opened the brief era of transoceanic travel by airship. The almost unknown and even more dramatic story, however, concerns of the efforts of Dr. Hugo Eckener to keep German airship building and flying alive, so that the later achievements of the *Graf Zeppelin* could be accomplished. This task required a man of dogged determination, great conviction, and unusual vigor in order to win that struggle. In the course of a decade he contended with four opponents. First was the group of victorious Allies of World War I and their interallied commissions to supervise the dismantling of Germany's capacities to make war—including elimination of the wartime terror bomber, the zeppelin. Second was a technological opponent, Dr. Johann Schütte, with his efforts to regain what he felt had been wrongly taken from him by the Luftschiffbau Zeppelin during World War I, and by the early postwar success of that company to revive airship building and flying. Third was the Berlin government that tried to hobble Eckener's steps to begin construction of the *Graf Zeppelin* between 1925 and 1927. Finally, there was an epic contest of wills between Eckener and Alfred Colsman, managing director of the industrial conglomerate that emerged out of Count Zeppelin's construction efforts. While Eckener, as head of one component of the conglomerate, Luftschiffbau Zeppelin, devoted his entire efforts to airships, Colsman was willing to de-emphasize zeppelin building in order to make the entire conglomerate industrially more viable. Eckener had to win each one of these struggles, if the German rigid airship was to triumph as it did between 1928 and 1937.

This essay is an extended version of an address delivered at the annual meeting of the Lighter-Than-Air Society in Akron, Ohio, on October 17, 1981. Reprinted by permission from *Bouyant Flight*, vol. 29, no. 2 (Jan.–Feb. 1982), pp. 2–9.

Dr. Hugo Eckener. Engraving by Hans P. Eckener, 1929. (Uwe Eckener Archives)

His career as an airshipman was already firmly established before 1914, when he was director of the DELAG, the passenger-flight subsidiary of the Zeppelin enterprise. It is interesting to note, however, that he did not find his calling until he was forty years of age. What had he been doing before then? He came of a good bourgeois family in Flensburg, Germany's northernmost city. With an early interest in social phenomena and aesthetics, he attended several universities between 1888 and 1892. In his culminating studies at Leipzig, he worked with the pioneering behavioral psychologist, Wilhelm Wundt; and ever after, Hugo Eckener had a perceptive insight into the psychological dimensions of the circumstances through which he moved. Evidently not driven toward an academic career, he could afford to live as an independent scholar and occasional commentator for various newspapers on art, music, and literature. In 1899 he sought the isolation of distant Friedrichshafen to write a serious study about the interaction between finance and workers' employment. Here he was occasionally distracted by the early airship ventures of Count Zeppelin and wrote various accounts about them for the *Frankfurter Zeitung* between 1900 and 1906. Between 1907 and 1909 he was back in the north, completing his book on social economics and regularly contributing aesthetic commentaries to the *Hamburger Fremdenblatt*. Here Alfred Colsman found him in 1909 and persuaded him to come south again, initially as public relations agent for the DELAG.[1]

The various eclectic elements of Eckener's earlier interests now came together to form the foundation for a unique career as airship propagandist, airship flier, businessman, and internationally acclaimed German diplomat-without-portfolio. Once Eckener had been won to the cause of the Count's rigid airship, he remained a single-minded, energetic, and consistent champion of the zeppelin to the very end. As a behavioral psychologist he understood the effect of this great, attention-getting aerial vehicle on the masses of human spectators, and he frequently maneuvered his airships for the greatest public impact—though never, *ever*, at the risk to either ship or passengers. His skills as writer and social commentator were put to frequent use in public addresses and in several evocative books about Count Zeppelin and on his own career. He flew his airships through considerable heavy economic weather and understood how to get the best financial terms for his enterprise. All these talents made him a cosmopolitan figure with a worldwide favorable reputation. They probably softened his undeniable characteristics of authoritarian discipline, short-fused aggressiveness, and a sharp but honest sense for business. This entire formidable combination of talent and characteristics was devoted to putting German airships into the skies again between 1919 and 1929.

Eckener spent the years of World War I as commander of the German Naval Airship School at Nordholz. Here he experienced a succession of constantly improving zeppelins from their Friedrichshafen and Berlin factories; vicariously he learned the bitter lessons of the zeppelin in unequal combat

LZ 120 *Bodensee* at Berlin, 1919.
(HAPAG-LLOYD Archives)

with the more rapidly developing airplane.[2] Thus, vastly more knowledgeable than he was in 1914, Eckener returned to Friedrichshafen almost immediately after the armistice. He clearly understood that the airship had no future as a combat weapon, but he was convinced that German nonmilitary zeppelins could lead the way into the immediate promise of long-range commercial aviation.

In Friedrichshafen all was contradiction and improvisation. Airship LZ 114 was almost ready for delivery, but there was no consignee to receive it and no government to pay for it. Thousands of excess wartime workers milled about in a revolutionary mood. Alfred Colsman began thinking of industrial modernization and diversification of the Zeppelin conglomerate, away from combat zeppelins toward readily salable and exportable consumer goods. The prospects for any business, however, were very cloudy in defeated Germany. Thus Eckener's commercial airship conviction won the day. There was a rash suggestion to put LZ 114 across the Atlantic to New York in a great demonstration flight, but Eckener knew that to do so would be psychologically wrong. Instead, he argued for construction of two small pas-

LZ 121 *Nordstern* at Friedrichshafen, 1920. (Papers of Garland Fulton, Naval Historical
Foundation)

senger ships to be inexpensively built from surplus materials on hand. The
first result was LZ 120, the *Bodensee*, operated from August through November
of 1919 by the reactivated DELAG. It was an immediate success with Germans and foreigners because of railway strikes and revolutionary unrest in
much of Germany. LZ 121 was also under construction, scheduled for completion in early 1920 and planned for an international schedule to Stockholm.
Larger vistas still remained in view. All through that year a handful of designers and fliers had theoretically built new airships and abstractly operated
them on simulated North and South American flights. Eckener was on his
way.

The Treaty of Versailles came into force at the beginning of 1920, and it
denied Germany the right to build or fly any airships except the very smallest.
Eckener's zeppelins were grounded, somewhat in retaliation for German airships destroyed by their crews when they were to be delivered to the Allies
as the Imperial Navy had been. The future of the Zeppelin Company was
indeed bleak. Colsman had given Eckener basic support for the zeppelin
venture, but now he increasingly sought to develop other products from
Company resources. In a bright moment it seemed as though an order from
the U.S. Army would save the day—the abortive Hensley contract for

LZ 125. When that contract failed for internal American policy reasons, the darkness really settled in.

The Allied military control commissions were bearing down to dismantle Germany's armaments establishments and surpluses, and their lengthening shadows also fell over Friedrichshafen. Efforts in early 1920 to reactivate the DELAG flights were quashed by Captain Masterman of the Interallied Aeronautical Commission of Control. The same group supervised dismantling of the Schütte-Lanz factories in Mannheim and Berlin and the Zeppelin works in Potsdam. In May 1921 Friedrichshafen had to yield its three remaining airships to the Allies. It seemed merely a question of time until the construction hangars would be razed, as, indeed, the one in nearby Löwenthal had been.

Between 1920 and 1924 Eckener adroitly maneuvered between maintaining the facilities and personnel of Luftschiffbau Zeppelin in Friedrichshafen and seeking to preserve its knowledge and flying skills by transferring them abroad, with whatever preservation of Zeppelin Company rights and interests that might be negotiated. In such a quest Colsman and two others were sent to America for three months in mid-1920. They contacted a variety of possibilities for development of the zeppelin in the United States: the army, the navy, Goodyear, Ford, and banking houses—all to no immediate avail. Plans were in the making with a French consortium. Feelers went out to Czechoslovakia and Japan. For years negotiations dragged on with Spain, culminating in a contract in late 1923 with Trans Aera Zeppelin. General Primo Rivera signed the agreements. Mail contracts were promised for a route between Seville and Buenos Aires. Even King Alfonso was a stockholder. The files of the political archives of the German Foreign Office bulge with paper on the interminable details of these negotiations. In the autumn of 1921 Eckener traveled to Spain and on to Argentina to make his own firsthand observations of weather and potential facilities. In Friedrichshafen they were designing more advanced transocean zeppelins and simulating weekly flights to South America, based on meteorological data regularly transmitted from German ships at sea. Even the British came over. Commander Boothby, representing interests of the Burney Imperial Airship Scheme, came in April 1922, followed by Commander Dennistoun Burney himself (accompanied by Barnes Wallis) in late May of 1923. Few at that time wanted the Germans to go on with zeppelins, but many showed great interest in their designs and flying skills.[3]

By now, of course, LZ 126 (the later ZR 3, *Los Angeles*) was well under way in construction for the U.S. Navy at Friedrichshafen. Eckener no doubt played as much of a role as he could, particularly within Germany, to obtain that contract and get an extension on the life of the condemned Zeppelin Company. It was a curious relationship between the Americans and the Germans. The American supervisory delegation at Friedrichshafen, headed by Comdr. Garland Fulton, attempted to learn every possible detail about construction of the airship taking place there. The delegation felt continually closed off or turned aside by the Germans from any aspects beyond fundamental contractual obligations and broad generalizations. For the Germans, and specifically for Eckener, it was a delicate situation of constant maneuvering with the Americans. He was willing to reveal everything that was contractually and specifically stipulated; for the rest, he held back or concealed the various "secrets" of the Zeppelin Company, pending ultimate decisions that would either rescue the operations in Friedrichshafen or transfer them to another nation with full security for the interests of the German firm.[4]

Here one encounters the name that everyone seems to know, but hardly anyone knows very much about—Mr. Harry Vissering, head of a prosperous Chicago railway supply company. He was one of the many foreigners who traveled on the *Bodensee* in the autumn of 1919, and he became an instant convert to airship travel and a tireless advocate for its further development. He was said to be an intimate of Warren G. Harding and allegedly motivated the president to have America press for the construction of LZ 126. Apparently Eckener and Vissering soon developed a cordial relationship and it is clear that the latter was Goodyear's prime point of contact with Eckener in the formative stages of negotiations that finally led to the creation of Goodyear-Zeppelin in late 1923.[5] It was both an anxious and expectant time for Eckener. Here is how Comdr. Fulton described it in October 1922:

> Vissering is here and is buying champagne for all the Zepps. The "Z" crowd think he is a whiz, and he does do an excellent job in keeping them informed as to what goes on in America. Young (Goodyear) is with Vissering. Goodyear is V's candidate as an American partner for Z. They have been having long sessions with Z, and the result, if any, will come out later, I suppose. . . . V. is also coddling Dornier. He has a scheme of getting D. to develop a commercial plane around some old Curtiss engines. . . . There are rumors of an early and happy conclusion of the Z-Spanish negotiations. Lots of Spanish money. Three sheds to be started at once. A 160,000 (!) cubic meter ship to be started very soon, and so forth. . . . They have had the Spaniards here for nearly a month. . . . With Vissering, Young, Boothby [British], and the Spaniards here, the Zepp have been going around in circles and getting very little work done [on LZ 126]. It looks like much prosperity to them—through very rosy glasses, of course.[6]

The German airship events of 1924 are well known: how Eckener pledged the entire resources of Luftschiffbau Zeppelin to deliver LZ 126 to Lakehurst; how Americans and much of the rest of the world cheered that fortunate flight; how Eckener was lionized in America's great industrial and financial centers; how quickly opinion swung to letting Germany build and fly its airships. All these events were the direct result of Eckener's vision, tenacity, and drive to achieve a place for commercial airships in transocean service at a time when they were the one aircraft feasible for intercontinental travel. In the process Eckener gave tremendous psychological gratification to German national consciousness and pride. The building and flight of LZ 126 gave the

LZ 126, later ZR 3, *Los Angeles*, at Lakehurst, Oct. 15, 1924. (Luftschiffbau Zeppelin)

Germans their first, positive, postwar international image to begin supplanting the Hun-horror stereotypes of Allied wartime propaganda. At last the preeminence of German technology and thoroughness were once again recognized and acclaimed. By his tenacity at home, and his success abroad, Eckener laid the basis for the first revision of the Treaty of Versailles. In May 1926, Germany was permitted to reenter the world of international commercial aviation, including the building and flying of airships. Eckener had played no direct role in these negotiations to lift restrictions on German civil aviation, but his zeppelin feat had contributed significantly to the more fa-

Dr. Hugo Eckener (left) and Lt. Comdr. Charles E. Rosendahl (right) aboard LZ 127, *Graf Zeppelin*, October 1928. (Luftschiffbau Zeppelin)

vorable atmosphere for making these decisions. Thus he overcame the first of his airship opponents, the victorious Allies of 1918, who had intended to deny to Germany any role at all in airship development for the postwar world.

Eckener's second struggle had its roots in the early history of German airship development and touched the most sensitive business interests of the Luft-schiffbau Zeppelin. It involved design improvements by Count Zeppelin's only German rigid airship competitor, Dr. Johann Schütte. This naval architect was the one other important German innovator in rigid airship design. He is almost unknown today except to airship specialists and is totally forgotten in the German public mind. One important reason for Schütte's becoming an aviation nonperson stems from his defeat at Eckener's hands between 1919 and 1924.[7]

Schütte had proposed some crucial design changes to Count Zeppelin after the Echterdingen disaster in 1908. When the old aeronaut rejected these suggestions, Schütte linked his fortunes with industrialist Karl Lanz to build airships incorporating his technological innovations. At the opening of World War I, the German government pressed Schütte and Zeppelin to incorporate each others' best features in their wartime airships. As a result, Zeppelin's aircraft looked, and were built, much more like those of Schütte-Lanz rather than the other way around. It had been agreed that settlement of the patent-exchange and financial obligations of these circumstances would be postponed for resolution until the great victory had been won. As we know, the imperial government that had arranged this technological shotgun wedding was not there to preside at the divorce settlement. At the time of the German collapse, furthermore, Luftschiffbau Zeppelin was completing an airship almost every month, whereas Schütte-Lanz was stalled in technological change-over difficulties. Under these circumstances Eckener gambled that his competitor would never return to business and could be ignored as facing bankruptcy.

Schütte was not giving up so easily. Although the SL factories in Mannheim and Berlin were soon closed down by the Allied military control commissions, Schütte was not ready to cease designing and building newer airships. He was not about to abandon the field to the Zeppelin Company. Like Eckener, he was intent on salvaging his interests for the future; but unlike Eckener, he could not immediately start building a small peacetime airship. His production was in technological transition and the Allies put pressure on him. So he opened his battle on two other fronts: at home he sued the Luftschiffbau Zeppelin and the postwar Berlin government on usurped patent rights and unpaid royalties; abroad he sought to find orders for a new generation of passenger airships, notably in America.

For both parties the litigation became a struggle for life or death, an elemental Darwinian corporate contest for survival of the fittest. Success on

Schütte's part would have meant a crippling invasion of the Zeppelin Company's wartime profits and impairment of its remaining assets. In addition, such success on the part of Schütte would have involved having to take him on in some form of owner or production partnership. Neither prospect was acceptable to Eckener, who was a fighter, not a compromiser. It was no doubt a terrible dilemma for Friedrichshafen. On the one side was the constant Allied threat to close the Zeppelin Company completely; on the other was Schütte's threat to the corporate integrity of the Company; in the center was Eckener's determination to develop the airship as a viable passenger aircraft and to do so for Germany and for his company.

If the ensuing legal brawl was always fought within the limits of acceptable corporate behavior, the ethical dimensions of the conflict did Eckener no great credit. To be sure, there were some gray areas in the patent conflict and in technological changes of design resulting from visual observations of SL ships flying before 1915. During the war, no doubt, Friedrichshafen did make improvement on details as Schütte designs were melded into the zeppelins. From such areas of dispute came a recurring sequence of articles in the aviation press and into wider publicity as well. On both sides the engineers and designers were as partisan in their claims and as vehement in their expression as were the men of business. This inflammation of perceptions and emotional reactions lasted well into the following decade, long after the matters had been legally settled. When Colsman, who had personally been on tolerable terms with Schütte all along, published his memoirs in 1933, there was a final outburst. Schütte held him on the phone for an hour, reprimanding Colsman for his alleged misstatements. Voices rose and tempers flared. At a culminating moment there was Colsman's final vehement word, punctuated by the crash of the receiver on the phone.[8]

For all emotional fireworks, however, there were still the fundamental matters of basic patents and royalty debts to be adjudicated. From the beginning Eckener focused on his larger problem, namely, the efforts of the Allies to forbid his airship construction and flying. In view of this more important struggle, Eckener perceived Schütte, certainly the weaker opponent, as a minor though very irritating factor in his struggles. Eckener's cause was coincidentally enhanced by the fact that Berlin dragged its feet in disputing the debts incurred by the previous imperial government. So time worked to his advantage. With a combination of annoyed disdain and fundamental corporate ruthlessness, he continued to use Schütte's innovations in building LZ 126, Germany's finest airship yet. The combination of legal fees, court costs, time delays, and the imminent completion of the new zeppelin finally took their toll on Schütte. A Zeppelin Company employee wrote a friend in October 1923: "Schütte is having to bury his airship hopes; he's not doing well financially."[9] The in-house monthly survey at Luftschiffbau Zeppelin, reporting on the current status of the litigation, stated in March 1924 that "Schütte appears to be reaching the end of his resources."[10]

The report was not far off the mark. With LZ 126 almost ready to fly in July 1924, and with his American prospects entangled in other legal-financial embroilments, Schütte reached an out-of-court settlement with the German government and with Eckener. Berlin paid him 40,000 gold marks against his claim for wartime millions. He and Eckener agreed to an exchange of all patents, clear of any financial obligations, and to mutual cancellation of all other claims against each other. It was a distasteful settlement for the disadvantaged Schütte to have to accept, but it was the best he could get. Rid of Schütte, Eckener could now fully focus on saving his Company from the Allies, and he was no doubt relieved to know that he would deliver LZ 126 to the Americans with no cloud on its title. He also wanted no further complications for the transfer of his Company's designs and skills to Goodyear-Zeppelin, where Luftschiffbau Zeppelin held a significant minority interest. Eckener had won the struggle for his airship enterprise. He had also cleared the way for an as yet unforeseeable airship future for the benefit of his company and his nation. It had been a hard fight, and it was all "strictly business." Thus Eckener vanquished his second postwar opponent.

Eckener's third struggle of the immediate postwar decade was with the same opponent that had made life miserable for Count Zeppelin, namely, the government bureaucracy in Berlin. Between 1919 and 1924, the Weimar Republic had had to contend with a host of difficulties arising out of the lost war and the German Revolution. By late 1924, however, Berlin had at least two accomplishments to its credit. It had overcome its horrendous postwar inflation by iron fiscal and social discipline, and it had achieved recognition of this feat by obtaining a major international loan to return Germany to the gold standard. It was a remarkable coincidence that LZ 126 arrived in America just as the loan placement (Dawes Plan) was announced as a full success. In the skies and on Wall Street, Germany was flying high. Now the German government moved to restore fully its peacetime relationships with its former enemies. By the summer of 1925, Foreign Minister Gustav Stresemann was well into his complicated negotiations, using British support to lessen Franco-German animosities in order to achieve the famous Locarno Treaties of 1926. Here Eckener's determined thrust toward German airship revival posed a serious psychological difficulty for Stresemann's talks with London and Paris.

What had Eckener been doing? Lionized in America, he had already talked there about passenger airship plans in the context of Goodyear-Zeppelin; but he always had a wary eye on the German future as well. Back in Germany, with the Allies wavering and disagreeing about Friedrichshafen's future, Eckener was fired with enthusiasm to celebrate the twenty-fifth jubilee of Count Zeppelin's first ascent in 1900. He had visited in the spring of 1925 with the famed Swedish explorer, Sven Hedin, and now had a new project in mind.

Airship Notables at Twenty-fifth Anniversary Celebration, Friedrichshafen, 1925; left to right: Dr. Ludwig Dürr, Mayor Schnitzler, Dr. Eckener, Countess Hella Brandenstein-Zeppelin, Alfred Colsman. (Luftschiffbau Zeppelin)

An improved zeppelin was the most likely aircraft to penetrate into the last unknown wastes of the Arctic and central Asia to enhance mankind's knowledge of geography. It could also pioneer transoceanic passenger service. What better opportunity to announce these plans, than at a celebration of Count Zeppelin's accomplishments? And should not the German Foreign Minister himself be there to emphasize the international significance of the occasion? Let Eckener speak for himself:

> I was uncertain about inviting the foreign minister to the jubilee, but decided to ask him personally. It certainly would have given him a favorable opportunity to make some broad political comment in relation to the wonderful reception of LZ 126 in America. I was received [at the Foreign Office] with studied reticence. He promptly began speaking in such unfriendly terms about the 'dubious character' of our planned Zeppelin celebration, about which he had had no prior consultation, that I could only regard him with amazement. And when he then said in obvious ill humor that he would have to

avoid attending the affair, I became so angry that I bluntly retorted, 'Herr Minister, I haven't even invited you!' And with that, of course, the meeting was at an end.[11]

Naturally, Eckener could not have known of the delicate pre–Locarno negotiations which Stresemann then had in hand, but clearly his enthusiasm over the recent impact of the LZ 126 flight in America had quite blotted out any awareness on his part of the too-well-remembered wartime zeppelin raids on London and Paris—a failing that persists in Friedrichshafen to this day.

This episode was characteristic of all Eckener's subsequent relations with Berlin. He had always felt that the government had not fought the Allies hard enough to emphasize and preserve the airship as an aircraft of peaceful commerce. Then, in 1924, the same government that had contracted and paid for LZ 126, had refused any financial guarantee for its safe delivery across the Atlantic. Now its Foreign Office was failing to appreciate what Eckener had done for German aviation and for Germany's image in the still hostile postwar world. Here was a foretaste of several years of acrimony between Friedrichshafen and Berlin.

It had been Eckener's intention to use the pomp, ceremony, and nostalgia of Count Zeppelin's twenty-fifth jubilee as the springboard for his campaign to solicit funds for construction of a new airship. For months Eckener had been organizing a supervisory committee to prepare the ground for his *Zeppelin-Eckener-Spende des deutschen Volkes* (Zeppelin-Eckener-Fund of the German People). This sponsorship list read like a *Who's Who* of contemporary German science, technology, art, literature, finance, and politics—beginning with Lord Mayor of Cologne Dr. Konrad Adenauer. Eckener had tried to get preliminary clearance from various authorities in Berlin and encountered either negative or reserved reactions. The German cabinet discussed the matter on August 10, 1925. Its principal concern was the undoubtedly unfavorable reaction these events would have abroad, and it strongly recommended divorcing the *Spende* announcement from the commemoration of Count Zeppelin.[12] Eckener grudgingly accepted the verdict, but responded with characteristic defensive vigor. His rejoinder read in part:

> As regards alleged unfavorable reactions by the Allies, they should understand that this fund-raising is for purposes of a polar-exploration airship. Even this is just a façade. Actually we are concerned with saving the Luftschiffbau Zeppelin, which after seven years of depression is at the end of its tether. There is the greatest continuing interest in broad circles of the German people for this eminent national and cultural achievement. Prominent men of all parties and diverse social groups have consented to support this effort. This is quite understandable, for the Luftschiffbau Zeppelin is viewed as a national treasure, funded by prewar popular enthusiasm. I believe that a people must *always* be ready and capable of sustaining its spiritual and technological strength, lest it lose confidence in itself and its future.[13]

Funds for the Zeppelin cause. Airship Photograph Sales. Friedrichshafen Hangar, 1935. (Uwe Eckener Archives)

The celebration of the twenty-fifth jubilee was indeed splendid and redolent with nostalgia for Germany's great national symbol—one of few visible signs that had even partially survived the collapse of the empire. Most memorable was a magnificent blue-and-gold-bound commemorative book, celebrating the Count, his peacetime airships, and the recent achievement of LZ 126.[14] All the major officials of the Berlin government who had been invited sent their regrets (or some minor bureaucrat), along with their congratulatory greetings. Foreign Minister Stresemann managed to dispatch a telegram that recalled his own flight in 1909 (with other courageous members of the Reichstag), and expressed hope that airships from Friedrichshafen would benefit the cause of German culture far into the future.[15] In this atmosphere Eckener made his preliminary announcement, that later in the year the German people would have an opportunity—again, as in 1908—to give freely of their hearts and purses for construction of the finest German airship ever.

Early in November the opening guns of the *Spende* boomed. All over Germany subcommittees and individuals sprang into action. All the media were enlisted: magazines, newspapers, newsreel films, even nascent radio. A host of paraphernalia were offered for sale in support of the cause: campaign buttons, pictures, postcards, poster stamps, and other zeppelin kitsch. One of the exhortations cried: "No genuine German will fail to contribute to save the Luftschiffbau Zeppelin, no matter how small his gift. Everyone must give something, so that the unity of our entire nation may be seen to hover in the skies above us! Be Sure to Give! Immediately!"[16]

Eckener and his major aides—Hans Flemming, Hans von Schiller, and Ernst Lehmann—sparked the campaign with an exhausting schedule of speeches and films that took them into every corner of Germany and beyond. If the zeppelin was a symbol of *German* prowess and achievement, then Germans in all of Middle Europe outside of Weimar Germany were to be gathered into the fold. Here was a bond that would transcend the disruptive postwar treaties and give German minorities a sense of cohesiveness with the cultural homeland. So the men from Friedrichshafen were doubly welcome in Austria, and found sympathetic audiences in western Poland, Prague, the Sudentenland, and Hungary—even in distant Romania. *Der Zeppelin* was again an all-German event.

Supposedly this fund-raising drive was meant to emulate the spirit, and to trigger the kind of spontaneous national generosity, that had characterized the gathering of the Zeppelin Fund of 1908. The reality, however, was somewhat different. Germany was now a very poor country, no longer possessed of the exuberant, prewar imperial nationalism. Something more was needed to stimulate the necessarily restricted generosity. Now a small army of zealous solicitors sought to motivate youth groups, veterans, womens' organizations, and pensioners. They moved into schools, churches, unions, businesses, and government offices. On occasion psychological intimidation seemed to supersede spontaneity. That was where the problems with Berlin resurfaced.

On four occasions in late 1925 and early 1926, the full cabinet of the Weimar government discussed the phenomenon of Eckener's call to save the airship works and build a zeppelin for polar exploration. Different ministries had different worries. The foreign office was still negotiating the nascent Locarno treaties and also feared unfavorable repercussions on the delicate negotiations in progress to ease Allied restrictions on German civil aviation in general. The army and the navy were only interested in airplanes and feared that zeppelin nostalgia would divert attention and funds away from their own concealed objectives. The ministries dealing with economics and social welfare felt that the German economy was not yet strong enough to support such a diversion of funds from the mainstream of daily life. Only the ministry of transport and the post office were unreservedly enthusiastic. The minister of finance scored a major point. He predicted that the *Spende* would fall short of its goal, the public would be aroused, the ship would be partially built, and then the Berlin government would be obliged to come to the rescue to get the airship into the skies. In light of these objections, the cabinet denied all support to the *Spende* and prohibited solicitation in all federal offices. Several state governments, notably powerful Prussia, did the same and extended the ban to schools and various state agencies.[17]

To the zeppelin enthusiasts it seemed like a rerun from the recent past: old Count Zeppelin thwarted by resistance and lack of understanding in the hidebound Berlin bureaucracies. Eckener and his zealots redoubled their efforts by fully mobilizing their *Who's Who* of honorific sponsorship. Persis-

Alfred Colsman, 1937. (Colsman Family Archives)

tently they gained the support of all the South German state governments, several central German states, and the City of Hamburg. State rivalries and regional loyalties were manipulated to give full freedom for the collectors of the *Spende* and to bring further pressure on Berlin. *Der Zeppelin* was a powerful emotional rallying point, and by mid–1926 the struggle was over. Berlin spoke its halfhearted blessing and gave permission for fundraising in all federal offices. Even Prussia relaxed its bans. It was a spectacular political victory for Eckener and the *Spende*. They had outflanked Berlin by mobilizing state and regional support for their cause and they had aroused a genuine national enthusiasm for Eckener and the symbolic zeppelin.

And what was the result? Unfortunately, the minister of finance turned out to have been correct in his prediction. Of the seven million marks set as a goal for building and test-flying the later *Graf Zeppelin*, only two and a half million were raised by the campaign—for all of Eckener's tiring campaigns. Two years later, during the month preceding the first transatlantic flight of the *Graf Zeppelin*, a journalist from the prestigious *Vossische Zeitung* interviewed Eckener. He asked him how he viewed the response of the nation to the *Spende* two years before. Eckener's bitter disappointment still rankled. He shot back a derogatory retort and added: "The German people were more interested in throwing their money away on wasteful unessentials than in supporting their Zeppelin heritage."[18] The German finance minister was also correct about the final outcome of the airship venture. Eventually Berlin supplied over a million marks for completion and test-flight of the *Graf Zeppelin*. The rest of the expenses were carried by the financially heavily pressed Zeppelin conglomerate. Thus Eckener finally won his third battle, but only by exhaustive efforts and some embittered disillusionment about the commitment of the German people to the Zeppelin heritage.

Eckener's fourth struggle, this with Alfred Colsman—managing director of the whole Zeppelin conglomerate—had elements both of personal rivalry and of genuinely generic differences about views for the future of the various companies functioning under the Zeppelin Foundation. In the years of Eckener's worldwide and well-deserved popularity, the impression took hold that he alone was the almost lineal descendant of Count Zeppelin—and that this was certainly true in regard to designing, building, and flying zeppelins. In truth, however, as long as the Count lived, Alfred Colsman was his most immediate business representative and, although the old aeronaut was always a pricklish personality to deal with, much of the essential decision making originated with that experienced and talented business executive. It was Colsman who hired Eckener in 1909 as a public relations agent for the DELAG. It was Colsman who sensed Eckener's potential as an airshipman and encouraged him to go for pilot training. It was Colsman who promoted Eckener to head the DELAG, sensing both Eckener's dissatisfaction with his lesser position and his undoubted competencies. When the war came, it was Colsman who had the determining voice in all the business activities of the Zeppelin conglomerate—notably the building of all the wartime airships in Friedrichshafen and Berlin—while Eckener was up north for the duration, supervising the training of the naval airship crews.

Eckener returned to the *Zeppelinstadt* soon after the armistice, charged with ideas to build commercial airships. Early in 1919 he was made head of the Luftschiffbau Zeppelin and vice-chairman of the Zeppelin Foundation, which was headed by an aging nephew of the old Count, Freiherr von Gemmingen. Colsman remained managing director, basically responsible for all the business decisions of the entire conglomerate. It became an uncomfortable situation that invited conflict between the two very sharply etched personalities. In one way Eckener was subordinate to Colsman, if a majority of the board agreed with its managing director; but if the board agreed with its vice-chairman (Eckener), then Colsman could be overruled by the influence of the man nominally subordinate to him. It was a prescription for discord.

From the very outset in 1919 the two men clashed, initially not as personalities, but in their very deeply felt convictions about the survival of the Zeppelin Company. Colsman had little faith in the future of the zeppelin as a commercial aircraft. He had had great success as an enterpriser and, in the dark postarmistice situation of Germany, he tried to preserve the integrity of the company by preparing a new future for it in seeking other, more viable business opportunities. Eckener, on the other hand, was single-mindedly devoted to the airship. He argued that the Luftschiffbau Zeppelin was not just an ordinary business. It had been endowed by the German nation to assure the continuity of Count Zeppelin's airship dreams. With the death of the old aeronaut, it was still the only purpose of this national endowment to devote its resources, in every way possible, to perfecting the zeppelin—now obviously as a commercial aircraft.

These were the two basically irreconcilable positions. Since LZ 120 and 121 were built mostly from remainder wartime airship parts, and since all further construction was prohibited by the Versailles Treaty, the inherent conflict between Eckener and Colsman was temporarily restrained. Eckener had a brief year of airship building and flying. Then came two years of frustrating search, somehow to keep the Zeppelin idea alive abroad or at home. Colsman did lead a three-man delegation to America in mid–1920 to seek either customers for future zeppelins or placement of the airship business in the United States. In the meantime, however, he had been systematically converting one company entity after another to alternative peacetime uses. Luftschiffbau Zeppelin produced light-metal alloys and aluminum consumer goods. Maybach Motors developed a variety of engines for different uses. The hydrogen works manufactured chemicals and industrial gasses. Gear boxes and drivetrains came from the Zahnradfabrik for all sorts of propulsion. The factory that had made the woven outer cover for zeppelin hulls converted to industrial and consumer textiles. Various other alternatives were found; the empty airship hangar at Staaken even became an interim motion picture studio. While Eckener struggled only for his zeppelins, Colsman's competence was effectively at work elsewhere.[19]

After the frustrating years, Eckener's seemingly hopeless cause found reprieve with the American order for LZ 126. This was a far more impressive piece of new business than the dispersed, smaller successes (and some failures) of Colsman's alternatives. Even here, because of the incredible complications of the German inflation, the Luftschiffbau built LZ 126 at a considerable loss—for which, of course, Colsman had to find compensation in the other businesses of the conglomerate. His frustrations over these circumstances finally exploded at a tense meeting of the governing board of the Foundation in August 1924. On that occasion it was revealed that no insurance could be found to cover LZ 126 on her pending delivery flight to Lakehurst. Eckener argued that the Foundation had to pledge all its assets to reimburse the German government, should the flight fail. Colsman, for his part, was not prepared "to bet the Company"—that familiar recurring phenomenon in aviation business history. Eckener, now chairman of the board since Freiherr von Gemmingen's recent death, prevailed and the great risk was undertaken. It was the beginning of the end for Colsman.

For the next five years the daring airship pioneer was pitted against the closely calculating businessman. By now the highly strung personalities of the two men were also becoming engaged in this vigorous conflict. Neither man would tolerate fools of any kind; each put up an energetic defense of his position; and both minced no words in advocacy of their respective interests. Their relationship deteriorated to the point where they could communicate with each other only by formal memoranda.

Outwardly they preserved a façade of mutuality and cooperation in the various Zeppelin enterprises, but their disagreements were at best poorly kept secrets. Colsman received his proper recognition at the twenty-fifth jubilee, even if it was already known that he was quite unsupportive of the *Zeppelin-Eckener-Spende*. He felt that Eckener was pandering to the emotional sentimentality of the German people in general, and specifically tainting the reputation of the Luftschiffbau Zeppelin in his quarrels with government circles. Colsman, therefore, played no role whatsoever in the activities of the *Spende*. Conversely, he had his own set of irritating relations with official Berlin—some of these in matters of heavier-than-air developments. Dornier, for instance, was sought out by the German navy with subsidies to build a huge transport seaplane (the later DO-X); Colsman found these arrangements as compromising free enterprise and consented only with misgivings. He also tried to make "respectable" businessmen of the leaders in the subvention-hungry, emerging Lufthansa. Eckener took no comfort from the fact that Colsman's opposition in either case was derived from business principle, and not from preference for airships over airplanes. Still, in the end, Colsman's successful management of the conglomerate supplied the indispensable additional funds for the *Graf Zeppelin* that neither the *Spende* nor the government could immediately provide.

Eckener triumphed in his struggle with Colsman because he finally won the high ground of psychological influence and personal fame. The transatlantic flight of the *Graf Zeppelin* in October 1928 had all the stuff of drama: great German expectations; a threatening storm at sea (with damage to the airship daringly repaired in flight by the son of the commander); and a rousing welcome in America. There was further drama in May 1929, when the motors of the airship failed en route to America on the eastern coast of Spain and the *Graf Zeppelin* limped back to safety at a French airship base. These events were nothing, however, compared to the epoch-making global flight of August 1929, when Eckener and the zeppelin were acclaimed around the world and returned home to tumultuous welcome in Friedrichshafen and Berlin. Henceforth Colsman's position was untenable. He resigned quietly from the Zeppelin Company in late 1929 and went into retirement—psychologically a broken man, a characteristic fatality of entrepreneurial wars.[20]

There is not the slightest doubt that the golden era of rigid airship development and flying owed almost everything to Dr. Hugo Eckener. It does him no disservice to lay aside the still prevalent image of a lucky, genial, avuncular gentleman, who flew his airships with the greatest of ease. Yes, he had luck; but it was augmented by the infinite preparation and care, the constant attention that he devoted to every detail of airship and flying. Yes, he made a fine public impression. He was, after all, a trained behavioral psychologist and long experienced in public relations. He also understood that one cannot operate an airship with a committee. In that area he was dictatorial, ruthless, and unforgiving of the slightest lapse. These qualities inevitably spilled over into his civilian relationships; and where matters concerned the zeppelin, he was relentless. He drove himself sternly, and he expected the same discipline and unswerving commitment from those working under him. As for being genially avuncular: anyone who did business with him soon had that impression corrected. He understood how to utilize every honest business opportunity; and in business negotiations or conflicts, he gave very little quarter.

With these qualities, and with his steadfast devotion to the prospects of the airship in peaceful commercial enterprise, Eckener defeated the efforts of the victorious Allies to bar Germany from participation in postwar aviation. His unswerving commitment to realize the airship hopes of Count Zeppelin ran roughshod over Johann Schütte and Eckener's opponents in Berlin. It is also clear that he thought of the Zeppelin business and production conglomerate primarily as an airship company, and he vanquished Colsman in those terms.

Yet, how rapidly fortunes changed. For just a very few years Eckener and the Zeppelin Company were a focus of world airship attention. Then came the disasters: R 101, *Akron, Macon,* and *Hindenburg*. The Nazis also arrived, in the service of their political cause, with their Faustian gift—making zeppelins financially possible and commercially profitable. Eckener was kicked upstairs in the DELAG reorganization of 1935, and Propaganda Minister Goebbels tried to make a nonperson of him in 1936. This was a struggle Eckener could not win. Rather than retire or emigrate, he chose to try and ride out the political storm, with Count Zeppelin's dream and heritage still as his lodestar. Just ten years after Colsman's resignation, Eckener's airship dreams and efforts were dead.

Friedrichshafen today venerates the vision of Count Zeppelin and keeps alive the nostalgic memory of Eckener's passenger airships crisscrossing the North and South Atlantic. Industrially, however, it thrives directly by extension on the results of Alfred Colsman's business acumen and managerial talent.

CHAPTER 5 Zeppelin Intermezzos in Detroit, 1920 and 1924

In some ways it was a bittersweet experience for Dr. Hugo Eckener and his flight lieutenants to tour parts of the northern United States after the successful delivery of LZ 126 to Lakehurst on October 15, 1924. It was sweet to demonstrate that the confidence held by the builders and fliers in their zeppelin and in their crew had not been misplaced. It was sweet to hear the orchestra of whistles, auto horns, and other noisemakers that greeted the ship as it flew over New York City in the early evening of its American arrival and flew that triumphal loop around the Statue of Liberty. It was sweet to have the ceremonial photo session with President Coolidge, Secretary of the Navy Wilbur, and other naval dignitaries on the White House lawn. Above all, it was the fulfillment of five years of political and technological struggle to build, and deliver, the first airship specifically designed for transatlantic passenger travel.[1]

Still, it had been bitter to leave Germany, knowing that the ship was sailing into other hands in another country, never to return to the nation of its creation. Eckener had flown LZ 126 during the previous month over every major region of Germany, obviously for trial and correction purposes, but also to give the German people an intimate view of the latest product from the zeppelin factories, which their contributions in 1908 had firmly established. With the triumph of the transatlantic voyage still freshly tasted, it was bitter to stand there in Lakehurst the next day, news cameras clicking, to receive the written receipt from the U.S. Navy, certifying that the ship was properly accounted for and delivered. Finally came the bittersweet journey to Akron, Ohio, to the newly founded Goodyear-Zeppelin Corporation, to make the ultimate arrangements for the transfer of patents and construction expertise. It was good to know that the heritage of Count Zeppelin would survive and thrive in the land that he had visited as a young lieutenant sixty years earlier, but it was bitter to contemplate that the Count's beloved Germany would apparently never see a zeppelin of its own again.

According to the stipulations of the Treaty of Versailles, Germany was to be disarmed to a tiny fraction of its former military, naval, and aerial power. Among those weapons completely denied to postwar Germany was the zeppelin, which after all was still vividly remembered by the citizens of London, Paris, and Antwerp for the devastating psychological impact of those air raids and civilian casualties of 1914–1916. By mid-1924 all the airship installations in Germany had been dismantled by the Interallied Commission of Control, except for the construction facilities at Friedrichshafen. These had survived, thanks to Eckener's indefatigable efforts to preserve them for the ultimate chance of building an airship like LZ 126, and to managing director Alfred Colsman's success in converting a military manufacturing complex to consumer goods production. Some future for consumer goods seemed assured, but what would happen to airship building?

In 1920 the most immediate prospects for even partially salvaging the technology and financial interests of German airship building seemed to lie in their transfer to the United States. Both the Zeppelin Company and Schütte-Lanz sent their most experienced personnel to America that year to reconnoiter the business terrain. Dr. Johann Schütte traveled from Holland. The Zeppelin Company sent a delegation of three experts, led by Colsman. The two competitors crisscrossed each others' routes at various points and were acutely aware of each others' presence—the long siege of lawsuits in Germany had already begun. Both airship builders had similar American targets in their sights: representatives of the U.S. Navy, financial houses in New York, the Goodyear Tire and Rubber Company in Akron. Colsman has left a detailed account of his journey, his contacts, and his discussions. Let him introduce the reasons for seeking out Henry Ford. This was the entry in his travel diary on the day of his arrival in New York City:

27 May 1920 . . . At last, around ten o'clock, after all formalities have been completed, we drive to the Hotel Astor. We are grateful for the expeditious assistance of Lt. Emerson, detailed to our side by Comdr. Weyerbacher. At the hotel we are met by Mr. Lederer, representing the Hamburg-America Line. Shortly, Theodor Knapper of the New York *Herald-Tribune* presents himself, alerted to our arrival by the Navy Department. He seems to represent the activities of Henry Ford, who, he tells us, has a very great interest in airship construction. . . . It turns out that Knapper has contact with [Col. William] Hensley [facilitator of an abortive contract with the Zeppelin Company to build an airship for the U.S. Army in 1919], who is seeking to put us in contact with Mr. Ford in Detroit.

28 May 1920 . . . We decide to notify Goodyear that we have arrived. Tomorrow night plans for travel to Langley Field, where Hensley awaits us; there Sunday and Monday, then to Washington. Visit from Mr. Aldon, Navy reserve officer working with Hensley to pull strings for us and assist in influencing Ford. . . .

14 June 1920 [Excerpt from interim report to Luftschiffbau Zeppelin in Friedrichshafen] . . . [At Lakehurst] the Navy makes every effort to support us. Weyerbacher is completely at our disposal. He is personally absolutely

convinced of the correctness of our proposals and seems to be a good and unselfish advisor. He is convinced that neither Goodyear nor Ford can alone handle the task [of building an airship]. [Late in the war, he told us] Ford offered to build the Navy a rigid airship at his own expense. They rejected the offer, initially probably because they had the ambition to build one of their own, and now probably they realize that they can get along more effectively with us.[2]

How had Henry Ford become interested in possibly manufacturing *airships*?

First one should note some basic characteristics of this remarkable man. Henry Ford was the most symbolic representative of modern industrialization as it developed in the first generation of the automobile era. By 1920 he was already a well-known American folk hero. The Model T, conveyor-belt assembly techniques, and the five-dollar daily wage had given him a very positive worldwide reputation. In more intimate business circles he was also known as a very singular and unorthodox man, with a remarkably wide range of interests and given to unpredictable spontaneous reactions to proposals made in his presence. His close associate, William J. Cameron, liked to say: "Mr. Ford had a twenty-five track mind and there were trains going out and coming in on all tracks at all times."[3] An analyst commented on this phenomenon: "How else does one make sense of Ford's excursions into international politics, racial bigotry, newspaper publishing, fertilizer manufacture, old-fashioned dancing, antique collecting, and the professions of medicine and education."[4]

Other authors have commented on Ford's eclectic ventures into anti-Semitism, negro welfare, medicine, publishing, supermarkets, and railroads.[5] Ford did things very much on impulse, sometimes suddenly ordering significant changes or innovations in an offhand conversation. He also had a great aversion to putting things on record. With this attitude he carried all sorts of data on major decisions in his active mind, never writing long memoranda and barely jotting down a few notes. In this cumulative context he appeared as a modern miracle worker. No wonder that Schütte and Colsman saw in Henry Ford the potential magic key to the solution of their airship dilemmas and, if he could be won, a powerful stimulator for international airship travel.

Ford's involvement with aviation probably began with the major contracts his company received to build Liberty Engines after America entered World War I in 1917. Although only 3,600 engines were completed by the end of the war, the company was just hitting its full production stride when the armistice was concluded, and the Ford production record was by far the best of the five American companies under contract. Ford's involvement with the Liberty Engine was only one of several large-scale, government-related ventures, all intended to use the mass production techniques characteristic of his experience with the automobile. There was the Eagle, an antisubmarine chaser, of which about fifty were completed but only four saw wartime service. There were contracts for both midget and six-ton tanks, of which only experimental models were completed before the war's end. The euphoria emanating from these wartime ventures, with their great opportunities for technological innovation and the promise of multimillion-dollar rewards, may have stimulated Ford's airship enthusiasm.[6]

There is, however, solid evidence of Ford's subsequent interest. In early July 1919, Henry Ford witnessed the arrival, landing, and departure of the British airship R 34 at Mineola, Long Island—the first transatlantic airship crossing.[7] From that time forward, he had various airship building notions. His close collaborator, William B. Mayo, submitted specific plans to the navy department in December 1919. On March 9, 1920, Ford directed Mayo to complete investigations for a one-thousand-foot airship and to prepare for the work, should he find everything favorable. Two days later a news story announced that Ford had offered to build an airship factory in Detroit, estimated to cost one million dollars, to be paid for on acceptance without any guarantee of future orders or amortization of plant. Two weeks later Mayo was in Washington, D.C. to discuss these Ford plans. In mid-April Ford held a news interview to discuss the future of aviation. He expressed his confidence in the passenger airship and thought that Detroit should be a proper inland American point of departure for international airship service. Ford voiced his willingness to build such an airship for the American government.[8] Neither the Schütte nor the Colsman records indicate any specific awareness of these Ford initiatives, but knowledge of them must account for the beeline for Detroit that both German businessmen made in June 1920. Colsman arrived there on June 16, accompanied by two colleagues from Luftschiffbau Zeppelin, W. E. Dörr (a prewar zeppelin captain) and Otto Milatz (head of the Zeppelin Company hangar-construction subsidiary at Berlin-Staaken).

Alfred Colsman's travel journal gives this account of their sojourn in Detroit:

15–16 June 1920. Overnight steamer trip from Cleveland to Detroit, which is crowded with visitors; we are not assured of hotel accommodations until evening. We make telephone contact with [Ernest G.] Liebold, Ford's private secretary. Thereupon an intimate tour of the whole automobile factory. [Here follows Colsman's admiring account of Ford conveyer-belt construction.]

17 June 1920. Invited to be at Liebold's by ten o'clock; we drove in Daniels' [representative of Seiberling accompanying the German trio from Akron to Detroit] car out to the tractor factory of Ford & Son in Dearborn. [There follows another admiring account of tractor assembly.] On the factory grounds we encounter a gentleman without hat or coat, whom I recognize as Ford, since I had seen his picture the day before. His lean, worn features give evidence of the shrewd, intelligent, mechanically gifted man. He gave us a friendly greeting, then disappeared and came again later as we sat in Liebold's office. This idiosyncratic man personally has no office, no chair anywhere in the

factory, much less some comfortable armchair. He is in motion, here and there, using any convenient resting place for the moment. He is well-informed [about airships]. These are things bound to develop in the future, he says, but they are not yet ripe for him. His mission is still to develop mass production. Soon he vanished, with an invitation for us to lunch with his associates, for he had other obligations. At this point I felt that our mission had failed, but his associates had quite different opinions. These gentlemen, upon whose opinions Henry Ford depends, are Liebold, [C. J.] Smith, and [Charles E.] Sorenson, also Mr. Mayo, the leading engineer, who was absent, but will be looking us up in New York in a few days. At lunch we also met a Mr. [Ernest] Kanzler, who was still in Lindau as of 1914. Smith flew last August with the [airship] *Bodensee* to Friedrichshafen and was well informed [on airship matters]. These gentlemen are all very anxious that Ford proceed on this matter and are thus likely to be decisive in its determination. [There follows a further account of various factory installations visited during the afternoon.]

Ford's associates quite evidently consider the airship prospects very favorably and give considerable weight to the diversity and effectiveness of their business enterprise. Discussion of these possibilities in the presence of Daniels was awkward because he must secretly wish that we not reach an agreement with Ford. The prospect of establishing a business association with the great factory layout and production facilities of this energetic man is without doubt of great attraction, but it is quite another question if these are the proper bases on which to found a worldwide airship passenger service. A man like Ford can only do things quite alone by himself. He will not go with the Wall Street people, and they will not go with him. As we parted, Daniels put the question directly to me: will it be Ford or Seiberling? I decided for the latter, because he is not a loner and seeks to establish a broader business relationship.[9]

In a longer letter to the home offices in Friedrichshafen, Colsman elaborated on his Detroit experiences. He identified Ford's senior associates as excellent young men, "mostly of German descent," well versed in manipulation of the press, and usually able to convince their chairman of their points of view. He felt that Seiberling (at this point representing the Goodyear interests) had been uncomfortable about the Detroit visit of the German trio, but that he was accommodating to Ford's intermittent airship interest because a majority of Goodyear's tires were destined for Model T wheels. Colsman emphasized his own preferences by stating that he had made a proposal to Seiberling for delivery of a zeppelin by May 1921, at a lump sum price that included monetary recognition of Zeppelin Company experience and license fees for the first twenty airships to be built at Akron on Zeppelin designs.[10]

The Ford interests, however, had the bit in their teeth. Barely a month later Mayo was off to Europe, primarily to England and Germany, to study the prospects for airships. Upon his departure Mayo stated, "Mr. Ford is thoroughly pleased by the possibilities of long distance aerial travel by dirigibles. It has not been determined definitely that he will undertake their construction, but the decision will rely principally upon my report."[11]

News of Mayo's upcoming trip alluded also to the recent visit of the Zeppelin Company trio in Detroit and their plans to receive him in Friedrichshafen. Any records of that later meeting are lost, but it is known that when he returned from Europe, Mr. Mayo had found an alternative enthusiasm for the all-metal plane he had seen at the Junkers factory in Dessau, Germany. In that direction, of course, Ford would later make aviation history.[12]

With Mayo's generally unenthusiastic report about the prospect for airships, Henry Ford apparently shelved his interest in lighter-than-air transport. Actually, it was Edsel Ford who turned his father's interests more toward airplanes. At any rate, there are no further entries in the Ford Archives Chronological History (as related to dirigibles) until 1925. Franklin D. Roosevelt sent Edsel Ford a honeyed solicitation in April 1921 to be among the first of all prominent Americans to launch the airship plans of the American Investigation Corporation, which was developing its projects on Schütte patents and designs. Young Mr. Ford declined to join. Two years later AIC was adrift in very troubled financial waters. A despairing AIC memorandum for inner circles, entitled "What We Have To Sell," urged the amalgamation of AIC Schütte interests with some others alleged to be in Detroit; these were evaluated as "fundamental and needed by Ford's engineers also working on airship construction."[13] A year later, in 1924, Harry Vissering, Goodyear's and Zeppelin's ever-alert airship agent and advocate, reported on the financial death throes of AIC-Schütte, and concluded, "As to their getting together with the Upson Group in Detroit, I have never been able to see where the Upson Group have had any backing worth-while. Naturally, everyone connected with it would like to make believe that Mr. Ford is back of them, but of this fact I am very much in doubt. As for Upson himself, he has some very impractical ideas concerning airship construction."[14]

Who was Ralph H. Upson, and how did he relate to Ford?

He had joined the tiny aeronautical office at Goodyear in 1911, and went on to achieve national fame as winner (with R.A.D. Preston) of the James Gordon Bennett trophy in international balloon racing. With other records and trophies in hand, he worked on the development of several Goodyear nonrigids between 1917–21. Like Mayo, he had traveled to Germany after the war and was impressed by the all-metal Junkers airplane. Thus he began to think of designing a metal-skinned airship. With Goodyear's commitment to rubberized fabrics for airships, this was not a congenial atmosphere in which Upson could pursue his new interest. In 1920 he met Carl B. Fritsche, who put him in contact with the Detroit automotive world. Late that year he left Goodyear, moved to Detroit, and directed the Aircraft Development Company—an enterprise established by Edsel Ford and Mayo to develop the Metalclad airship.[15]

In retrospect, the interests of Henry Ford in aviation between 1920 and

1925 emerge quite clearly from his own writings of the time and subsequent historical inquiry. He put it quite clearly in his book, *Today and Tomorrow*:

> We have added the making of airplanes to our industries because we are manufacturers of motors and therefore every phase of motor transportation interests us. . . . We are giving more attention at present to the airplane than to the dirigible, but we believe each type has its place in air navigation. The airplane seems to be well fitted for fast express work and the dirigible for the carrying of heavy loads. It is our general thought—although nothing is as yet conclusive—that the dirigibles will take the long main routes of air travel, with the planes acting as feeders. But we are not committed to either type—we want to learn all that we can about both types.[16]

Although these thoughts were published in 1926, after the *Shenandoah* disaster, they accurately indicate the interests and activities of Ford, father and son, between the visit of Alfred Colsman in June 1920 and that of Hugo Eckener in late October 1924.

In 1922, when Ralph Upson and Carl Fritsche were already busily working their way into the intricacies of the Metaclad airship at Grosse Ile, William Bushnell Stout and the Fords came into each others' lives. Both Mayo and Edsel Ford were taken by the all-metal design for aircraft that Stout advocated. He was fully encouraged and was given the requisite financial support to build his prototype airplane. It first flew on April 23, 1924, and opened the way for six remarkable years of Ford aviation development.[17]

For two months thereafter Stout piloted his new plane on short sightseeing flights with passengers and with avid public interest, but under very awkward flight conditions. Detroit had no proper airport. Under this circumstance Stout had to have his plane towed on repeated occasions from his Dearborn factory over to Selfridge Field, an army base twenty-five miles away. He and the Fords observed these conditions with growing dissatisfaction.[18]

As of early July 1924, the Fords had had enough. Promptly a regiment of Fordson tractors appeared on a site adjacent to the engineering laboratories at Dearborn. Dust flew and trees were mowed down on a two hundred sixty acre site. Runways were planned, three hundred feet wide and two-thirds of a mile long. Hangar space, workshops, and service bays were all under construction. "FORD," was spelled out in letters of crushed white stone several hundred feet long; they could be read from a distance two miles up. Henry Ford vowed he would make it the finest airfield in the world.[19]

Into all this activity came Dr. Hugo Eckener and his hosts from Goodyear-Zeppelin in Akron.

The successful transatlantic flight of LZ 126 was only the first phase of a continuing, and wearying, triumphal journey for the zeppelin commander and his flight lieutenants. From Lakehurst on October 16, 1924, it was on to a round of receptions, banquets, and speeches in New York, Washington,

D.C., Cleveland, Akron—and then to Detroit. Captain Ernst A. Lehmann later described these trials of endurance in vivid recollection:

> The major difference between our customs and those of the Americans is simply that over there the guests must entertain the hosts, while of course with us, it is just the opposite. . . . With our tight schedule, Dr. Eckener and I never had time to determine in advance, what each should say, so we always spoke extemporaneously. This was least pleasant for me; interpreting [for Dr. Eckener] was not easy, and then I had to improvise my own comments so as not to repeat what Eckener had already said. After the local chairman's concluding words, there would be a long chain of well-wishers. The people came streaming by. We shook each passing hand until our fingers ached. Then they kept coming back, wanting autographs on their menus.[20]

The airshipmen had already had a tiring social and business schedule in Cleveland and Akron on October 27 and 28, 1924. Lehmann described the continuing journey to Detroit:

> We came home from an exhausting reception at Goodyear Hall at 11:15 in the late evening. At 12:30 A.M. our train left for Detroit. A hasty job of packing and off to the station; passed the night in the jolting sleeper. Arrival in Detroit at 8 in the morning. Received at the station by the inevitable horde of photographers and reporters and the reception committee of the Detroit Aviation Society. We had hoped for a quiet breakfast, but that was not to be. The committee gave us a brief pause in our private hotel rooms, then took us off to a big breakfast reception. At first we were photographed again and again at the hotel entrance, then we were released for breakfast with the avidly eager newsmen. An hour later we were off by car to visit the Packard Motor factory, together with some new aviation engines. Thereupon followed a tour of the Ford Motor factory under the guidance of Mayo, Ford's chief engineer, who attached himself to me for the rest of the day. After lunch at the Detroit Athletic Club, with the usual speeches, the cars brought us out to Dearborn. Mr. Ford, whom many consider the world's richest man, received Eckener, Mayo, and me in his private office. The others had to wait nearly an hour, while he conversed with us. I like the old gentleman very much; he really has a fine, distinguished face. Afterwards Mayo invited me to come again to Detroit, at Ford's express desire, to consult on the erection of an airship mooring mast that he wants to give to the city of Detroit. In larger company we then took a tour of the aviation workshops under Ford's personal supervision. By now it was time for the dinner to be given in our honor by the Detroit Aviation Society. Again there was a lot of speech-making, ending with more questions from the guests. At 9 in the evening we transferred to the local German club "Harmonia," whose members received us with yet another dinner and a melodious men's octet. Mercifully, they also had beer for us, an excellent homebrew, so that we survived until 11 o'clock. Then came another round of hearty handshaking at departure, and we were off to take the night express to Chicago.[21]

The German airship visitors, led by Dr. Hugo Eckener, included Lehmann, Hans Flemming, and Hans von Schiller—all later airship captains in their own right. Their American hosts from Akron were President Paul W. Litchfield of the Goodyear Company, his talented publicity man Hugh Allen, and

Luftschiffbau Zeppelin officers in Detroit, Oct. 29, 1924; left to right: Capt. Ernst Lehmann, Dr. Hugo Eckener, Capt. Hans Flemming, Capt. Hans von Schiller. (Von Schiller Archives)

Harry Vissering—that invaluable facilitator of German and American airship interests in the early 1920s. Their Detroit hosts included President of the Detroit Aviation Society Harold E. Emmons; President of the Detroit Board of Commerce Jefferson B. Webb; wartime ace, Capt. Eddie Rickenbacker; and well-known motor advertising executive, E. LeRoy Pelletier. With these and others in the group, the Germans first met Col. Jesse G. Vincent, designer of the aircraft engines of the *Shenandoah*, who was working on more advanced types at the Packard Motor Company. It was an auspicious beginning for a day steeped in aviation technology and in celebration of the German airshipmen—and it was properly commemorated with the obligatory group photograph.[22]

Edsel Ford and William B. Mayo came into their own as hosts during the afternoon. In Dearborn they took the party to the new airport under construction; visited William B. Stout in his workshops, where the first American all-metal airplanes were being built; and met Upson and Fritsche in their offices at work on designs for America's only all-metal airship—to eventuate in 1929 as ZMC-2, the navy's single Metalclad airship.[23] Then it was time to meet the motor master himself, Mr. Henry Ford.

Out of this meeting came, quite spontaneously and unexpectedly it seems, the only positive result of the airshipmens' visit and a monument to Ford's characteristically unpredictable behavior—the airship mooring mast at Ford Airport. Ford was known to be an avid reader of Ralph Waldo Emerson. He had marked certain passages that strongly appealed to him: "Only in our easy, simple, spontaneous actions are we strong. . . . We love characters in proportion as they are impulsive and spontaneous. . . . " These sentiments

German airshipmen visiting Henry Ford; left to right: Lehmann, Eckener, von Schiller, Ford. (Luftschiffbau Zeppelin)

reappeared in one of Ford's own notebooks: "The only way to get happiness is to pursue it. . . . Happiness is in the pursuing. . . . Our spontaneous action is always the best. . . . You have got to keep doing and doing."[24]

Time and again in his long career Henry Ford made major decisions on conversational impulse. The career advancement and survival of the men around the motor magnate depended on their success in anticipating his intuitive impulses, literally trying to read his mind and to foresee his behavior. Given these circumstances, there is little reason to doubt the validity of the little personality vignette that appeared in the *Detroit Free Press* after the airshipmen had departed:

They Shall not Pass! Henry Ford is going to have a mooring mast, so that any flying ships that pass in the night or day, may stop to see him.

"You know, I've never been up," said Mr. Ford to Dr. Eckener, as the two trudged around the Dearborn grounds on Thursday, "but I'd be willing to go up in yours."

"Not possible," said the ZR III pilot. "We couldn't bring it here. You have no mooring mast."

"Bill," directed Ford, promptly turning to William B. Mayo, his chief engineer, "write at once to the Navy Department and find out what a mast will cost."

"I already have," smiled Mayo.

"That's thinking ahead," Ford complimented. "Let's get it here right off and we'll have something for Eckener to hitch to!"

The Zeppelin chief smiled broadly.[25]

Late that evening Dr. Eckener and his airshipmen vanished in the night, westward toward another exhausting day in Chicago. Never did an airship under their command ever come to Detroit to accept the hospitality of the mooring mast, the seed for whose creation had been planted the previous afternoon.

Henry Ford personally dedicated the new Ford Airport at Dearborn on January 15, 1925. With sweeping generosity he invited all fliers—army, navy, marine, airmail, commercial, and private—to make use of his private airfield. He referred to the mooring mast under construction and announced that it would be ready in late summer to receive America's premier airship, the *Shenandoah* (Daughter of the stars).[26] Almost at that moment he had in hand a letter from Admiral Count Erich von Zeppelin (ret.), nephew of the airship inventor, inquiring about possible employment for his brother, Count Ferdinand, who until recently had been a director of the Zeppelin Company subsidiary in Staaken, Germany, near Berlin. But there would be no place for the count with Ford, either in Detroit or abroad, neither as an airship builder nor as a motor engineer.[27] Later it was rumored in the press and recorded in the Ford archival aviation summary that Ford was proposing to build a metal airship for the American government—a contract that would eventuate in 1926 for construction of the Metalclad ZMC-2.[28]

It would be several years before all the necessary construction at Ford airport was fully completed. Four million dollars would be spent on two massive paved runways, modern flight control equipment, and spacious passenger accommodation—the largest and most modern airport in the United States.[29] The mooring mast was meant to add a further dimension of anticipated transoceanic travel by airship, directly from Detroit. It was completed in early July of 1925, the tallest airship mooring in the world—two hundred and ten feet high, its three legs deeply anchored in concrete, seventy-one feet apart. A five-passenger elevator ran up the first one hundred seventy-six feet; a covered stairway led upward from there to the operating platform.[30] There it stood gleaming new, awaiting the arrival of the *Shenandoah*, already the subject of several preparatory communications from the U.S. Navy. An unknown lieutenant commander, named Charles E. Rosendahl, was sent soon thereafter to Detroit to make arrangements for the *Shenandoah's* visit in late summer. His heroic actions with a section of the disintegrating airship in the early morning of September 3, 1925, brought him instant national recognition and opened the way for his career as America's premier airshipman.[31]

The great privately built mast had cost nearly four hundred thousand dollars, but it seemed to be as ill-fated as the first visitor it had expected. Ernest G. Liebold later commented that it never was right, it leaked when it rained, and they were always having to send men over to fix something.[32] Much later historian Hepburn Walker, Jr. wrote:

U.S. Army semirigid, RS 1 at Ford mast, Dearborn, Mich., Sept. 18, 1926. (From the Collections of Henry Ford Museum and Deerfield Village, No. 3697-189)

The Ford high mast was unique in that it included a moveable feature permitting the nose cone of the airship to be hauled down, together with the entire dirigible, so that the ship would just clear the ground, as with the later stub masts. A nearly vertical downward track was included, which could swing the entire 360 degrees around the structure of the mast itself.

Theoretically, a side gust would result in the ship swinging into the wind and the track was intended to ride around the mast to the lee side. *BUT*, an airship in a side gust has a tendency to sail ahead, the same as a sailboat. This would not be a problem when the ship was moored to a fixed point at the top of a mast. The ship's nose would be restrained from moving ahead and the airship would revolve with the wind like a weathervane.

An airship moored at any point below the top of the Ford mast would have been jeopardized. A side gust would likely swing the vertical track and nose cone forward around the mast, while the airship itself would weathervane with the wind. The result could well be a major accident, as the airship would likely be entangled with the mast and suffer severe structural damage.[33]

In the autumn of 1926, two aerial visitors finally arrived. First was the army semirigid RS-1, a lumbering, ugly vehicle and the largest of its kind in the world. On September 18, in a dark early-morning overcast, Mr. Ford was atop the mast to welcome the disembarking airship commander. Of course, it was not Dr. Eckener, and Ford did not venture aboard, much less "go up."[34] Circumstances were brighter five weeks later, when Dr. Eckener's ship, now called the *Los Angeles*, arrived to spend a brilliant autumn day at the

Airship ZR 3, *Los Angeles*, at Ford mast, Oct. 15, 1926. (Henry Ford Museum, Edison Institute. No. 3826-189)

Goodyear airship *Pilgrim*, 1925;
left to right: Capt. Ernst Lehmann, blimp pilot James Staley,
Comdr. Jacob Klein, Paul W.
Litchfield. (Goodyear Archives)

mast. Thousands of cars converged upon the airport to visit the gleaming, sunlit silver rigid. Ford personnel and other dignitaries went through the ship from bow to stern, though Mr. Ford himself was apparently not there to enjoy the occasion. Late in the afternoon of October 15, the ship departed, given extra helium from reserves placed at the mast the year before in anticipation of servicing the *Shenandoah*.[35] No other airship ever graced the mast again, though it made contact with the spacial future on October 23, 1934, when Dr. Jean Picard and his wife used it to step into the gondola of their stratospheric balloon in search of a record-breaking ascent.[36]

During the later 1920s Mr. Ford made aviation history with his sponsorship of America's first commercial airline and the building of the Ford Trimotor, which gave the nation's infant airline business its first effective commercial airplanes. Meanwhile, at Grosse Ile, Upson and Fritsche were working on their second design for a metal airship. In late 1925, Ernst Lehmann wrote Goodyear's Litchfield an apprehensive memorandum, worrying about political pressures favoring "the Detroit Group," which was allegedly seeking "to shatter our prestige."[37] He need not have feared for Goodyear-Zeppelin which had its own advantages of preference in the U.S. Navy for its planned giant rigids. Michigan politics, however, did assist Ford in obtaining a government contract for building the ZMC-2. This unusual experimental ship did honorable naval service between 1929 and 1938, but never established itself as a viable alternative to the *Akron* or *Macon*.[38]

On October 13, 1928, as Dr. Hugo Eckener was flying the *Graf Zeppelin* across the North Atlantic on its maiden voyage, the *New York Times* carried a story reminding its readers of Eckener's visit to Detroit with Henry Ford in 1924. It was anticipated that the *Graf* would visit Detroit on a brief extra swing to the Great Lakes, thus realizing Ford's long-delayed anticipation.[39] A week later William B. Mayo was visiting the *Graf* in the hangar at Lakehurst, and rumors were rife that Ford would help finance the establishment of transatlantic mail and passenger service. Plans were still tenuous about the projected midwestern flight, for the *Graf* was undergoing serious repairs and was anxious to return to Germany. Would Mr. Ford be aboard for the potential tour? "He is a great man," Dr. Eckener said, "and I should like to have him for a passenger; but he is very busy and I don't know whether he will have time to go. Besides, it is doubtful if we can tie up to his mast in Dearborn."[40]

That wrote *finis* to the Zeppelin intermezzos in Detroit except for a few subsequent courtesy visits by Zeppelin personnel. Ford was now fully into all-metal planes, Eckener was securely focused on Goodyear-Zeppelin, and the city of Akron aspired to become the inland terminal for transatlantic airship flights.

CHAPTER 6 The Political Origins of the Airship *Graf Zeppelin*, 1924–1928

Great technological constructions generally have three kinds of origins: one in engineering design, another in financial feasibility studies, and the third in dimensions of political ambition and manipulation. The rigid airship, with its unique, attention-attracting size passing serenely through the lower skies, was particularly an object of political maneuver. The *Graf Zeppelin* had already matured as a design in a succession of engineering studies in Friedrichshafen in the earlier 1920s, though its financial feasibility was very much clouded at that time. Politically, however, it would be conceived in the unlikely joining of the interests of four men: a pretentious former German foreign minister; two world-famous Scandinavian explorers of Inner Asia and the North Pole; and a very concerned German zeppelin commander.

Even as LZ 126 was still en route over the North Atlantic toward Lakehurst in mid-October 1924, the American press was speculating on the future of zeppelin building in Germany. France insisted that the Luftschiffbau Zeppelin be dismantled in accordance with the Treaty of Versailles, now that the so-called reparations airship was arriving in America. Colonel William N. Hensley, commandant at Mitchell Field and author of an abortive U.S. Army-Zeppelin contract in 1919, stated that he was a great supporter of airships and that destruction of the Friedrichshafen factories would set back the prospects of passenger aviation by fifty long years. Mr. C. G. Grey, editor of Britain's most prestigious aviation magazine was quoted:

> I want to say that we have a great admiration for the Zeppelin commanders and crews who bombed London in the performance of their duty. . . . I can say for the aeronautical people in England that the destruction of the plant would be a crime against civilization. The Zeppelin people know everything there is to be known about airship construction.

This essay is the expanded and revised version of a paper given at the meeting of the Pacific Coast Branch of the American Historical Association, at San Diego, Calif., Aug. 19, 1976.

Presumably the Germans would continue to do it more successfully than either the Americans or the British.[1]

The political tone for the occasion was already set by German Foreign Minister Gustav Stresemann, who telegraphed his congratulations to Commander Hugo Eckener in these words, "Greeting and thanks to the conqueror of the skies, who has by this memorable transoceanic flight achieved the highest possible success of technology and science, and thus has fostered Germany's renown and visibility in the world." Missing from the message was a second sentence originally prepared for transmission, but then judiciously suppressed for reasons of possible unfavorable political repercussions, "German foreign policy will always consider it an obligation of honor to Germany's air pioneers to liberate German aviation from the shackles that still constrain it."[2]

Into this pattern of conflicting enthusiasm and apprehension came a quite unexpected communication from the German embassy in Stockholm. Counselor Wipert von Blücher notified the foreign office of a visit by Dr. Sven Hedin, famous explorer and president of the Royal Swedish Academy of Sciences. The roving Swede was enthusiastic about using a zeppelin to retrace Marco Polo's central Asian route to Peking. Though Blücher felt that all this

Dr. Sven Hedin, 1925. (Universitetsbibliotek, Stockholm)

smacked rather too much of Jules Verne, he felt he should report it to Berlin. Could Germany possibly derive leverage in the zeppelin situation through this query from a distinguished scientist in a prominent nation that had remained neutral in the recent war? No doubt the matter should be kept strictly confidential.[3]

Very soon there were further developments. Sven Hedin and Dr. Svante Arrhenius had brought the matter before a meeting at the Swedish Academy. The discussion was vigorous. Arrhenius argued that demolition of the Zeppelin works would deny the world of science an instrument of demonstrable technological superiority in extending the frontiers of knowledge, notably in the sciences of geography and cartography. He proposed a petition to the heads of the Allied governments for retention of the construction facility. Hedin relinquished the chair to argue that such a step by the Swedes alone would hardly be effective; other academies in other neutral nations must be drawn into a concerted international effort. Several draft resolutions were proposed. Finally, a special Committee of Five was appointed to draw up a resolution for consideration at the next academy meeting.[4]

Counselor Blücher was liberally supplied with information from these supposedly confidential academy deliberations. In his continuing reports he stressed the need for scrupulous secrecy and emphasized that the reputation of the Swedish Academy would remove any suspicion of politics in the matter. Yet almost in the same breath he stressed how the action might be politically manipulated to Germany's advantage and urged that the Zeppelin Company, and others, be prepared for what was to come, so that the anticipated favorable action of the prestigious academy would not be an exercise in futility. By now German Ambassador Hans von Rosenberg (Foreign Minister of Germany in the Cuno Cabinet, November 1922–August 1923) had returned from a trip abroad and taken the reins of the affair in his own hands. He urged forthright action to enlist the Zeppelin Company in support of its Swedish savior. Meanwhile, top secrecy was essential. He, too, was taken with Hedin's rhapsodic anticipation of areas not traversed since Noah had sailed over them in the ark—from Syria to Baluchistan and the sources of the Ganges, over the trans–Himalaya to the headwaters of the Yangtse-Kiang, and finally on to Peking—all recorded with the best of scientific instruments and reels of motion picture film. Germany's image would soar the world over and become known in the most remote hut of central Asia. Could Berlin, in strict confidentiality, contact the Zeppelin people for available airship plans and tentative operational data? The very pro–German Swedish explorer and the ambitious German ambassador nicely reinforced each other, while the Zeppelin Company was quite unaware of these activities in Sweden.[5]

In mid-November of 1924 the members of the Swedish Academy voted to send a circular to the other academies in all of the European nations that had been neutral in World War I. The academy's message stressed the function of the zeppelin as "an extremely valuable resource" for geographic and cartographic research and deplored that "certain generally known circumstances place serious obstacles in the way of building and development of this means of communication in the future." Could other academies join together with Sweden, indicate their views, and suggest common action "to promote the general interests of scientific research?"[6]

Rosenberg telegraphed the good news to Berlin and pressed for some appreciative official response to the Swedes. He advocated several actions. First, the foreign office should develop sympathetic commentary in the German press, emphasizing the nonpolitical nature of this Swedish scientific appeal. Second, he urged immediate and energetic distribution of the news, especially in America, and then publication of a selection of positive reactions to the Swedish appeal. Third, he suggested that the results of these activities be judiciously funneled to the Swedish press office in Berlin. Finally, he proposed that the Zeppelin Company telegraph its thanks to the Swedish Academy, and he suggested that it would be a most chivalrous gesture if the Company would baptize its construction hangar as the "Gustav-Adolf-Halle"—an act of generosity that the Swedes would appreciate. Such naming would bring a cachet of international recognition that might further deter the hovering Allied demolition party.[7]

These ham-fisted suggestions found no immediate response in Berlin; indeed, the foreign office was extremely cool in its several sparse replies to the ambassador's enthusiasm. Later in November Blücher complained that no appreciation was forthcoming from Berlin and that Hedin, pro–German that he was, had worked very hard to induce a strong response from the members of the academy. The embassy had, after all, encouraged Hedin to initiate the international scientific effort. Berlin responded that the German press had exhausted itself on zeppelin enthusiasm, that Reichstag elections were looming, and that Eckener was just under way returning from America.[8]

The embassy in Stockholm continued to complain that so little was happening in Germany to further the cause of rescuing airship building there. Blücher confessed that Hedin had had his hands full in overriding the objections of the pro–Allied members of the academy. Still, most of them were willing to see the appeal to the other politically neutral academies carried through to fruition. All the more were they now surprised at the evident lack of German response, when they were prepared to be of such service to German science and technology. The embassy advised that the natural disposition of the Swedes inclined toward an inferiority complex; therefore their psyches must be caressed in order to maintain their enthusiasm for things important to Germany. Fortunately, the report concluded, the Swedish-German Association (*Svensk-Tyska Forening*), whose patron was the queen of Sweden, and which had a major influence on Swedish intellectual-political attitudes, was planning to invite Dr. Hugo Eckener to address the membership at a formal banquet in March 1925. The ambassador, wrote Blücher, had been rebuffed on his suggestion to baptize the construction hangar in Friedrichshafen; now one must make *certain* that Dr. Eckener get the privileged invitation *and* that he accept it![9]

At the end of November Eckener arrived in Germany from America. Cautiously briefed on the Swedish situation, he expressed his delight to Berlin and promised to respond at once to the initiative of the Swedish Academy. He professed great interest in Hedin's plans. Such a voyage of exploration was entirely feasible. Design and operations staffs at the Luftschiffbau Zeppelin would take the task in hand promptly. Finally, he would be delighted to visit Stockholm in mid-March of 1925.[10]

Meanwhile, back at the Swedish Academy, responses were only slowly coming in. When they had all arrived by early January of 1925, they made poor reading for the adherents of the German airship cause. This was the gist of their contents:

> Denmark: yes, geographic and cartographic research should be fostered, but the proposal would encounter great difficulties. Copenhagen would await the suggestions of others.
>
> Finland: of course it was a matter of great concern. A joint resolution should be sent to the Committee on Intellectual Cooperation at the League of Nations. Helsingfors looked forward to further information and to participating in a joint resolution.
>
> Netherlands: favored the removal of limitations to air travel, but stated that "the obstacles mentioned in your circular are caused by the Treaty of Versailles, hence have a political character." Amsterdam would take no action whatsoever.
>
> Norway: the scientific society relied entirely upon the expertise of famed Polar explorer, Fridtjof Nansen. He favored the airship for arctic exploration but felt that the obstacles were all of a political nature and that scientific academies should not become embroiled in such controversies.
>
> Spain: affirmed the importance of airships, but saw serious difficulties in organizing an international rescue effort. Madrid would limit its involvement to casting a vote whenever a final proposal materialized.
>
> Switzerland: found that the Swedish circular posed questions that were not fundamentally scientific but perhaps somewhat political. Therefore Bern had no specific response, especially since Stockholm had made no specific proposals.[11]

As these replies were coming in, the exchange between the Swedish and other academies became generally known and the news was heard in the slowly continuing deliberations by the Allied governments. They were disagreeing among themselves about the future of German airships. The Americans urged that the Germans be permitted to resume their development and flying. England and Italy wavered. France alone remained resolutely opposed. Outside of the Allied deliberations three elements were at work. First was the general enthusiasm in much of the western world for airship flying, together with specific praise for Eckener and German expertise. Second was the secret manipulation of the situation by the German ambassador to Sweden and his staff, and the hitherto ambivalent response from Berlin. Third was Hedin's sponsorship for Germany through the Swedish Academy and other neutral scientific societies. Into this configuration now came a fourth element that would inflame and confound the German involvement with the situation. It would irritate Hugo Eckener beyond belief. It would force the German government to take a position on the issue and eventually commit that government to supply funds to complete the new airship that Eckener would succeed in conjuring up out of the whole set of unusual circumstances. That fourth element was the unexpected appearance of Capt. Walter Bruns, chairman of the German section of Aeroarctic, an international committee of scientists seeking to foster polar exploration by air.

Aeroarctic was established shortly after the war by the distinguished Norwegian polar explorer, Fridtjof Nansen. As its founder and first president he gave the society great credibility, thanks also to his postwar work on behalf of refugee and famine relief.[12] Capt. Bruns was an experienced German army airship commander with several dozen flights to his credit. His German section of Aeroarctic included a major part of all the international members, among them geographer Albrecht Penck and Hugo Hergesell, Count Zeppelin's old and loyal scientific advocate. In November 1924 Bruns had met Hedin and impressed him very favorably. The captain had also lectured persuasively in Norway and Finland on a proposed transpolar flight from Murmansk to Alaska. Ambassador Rosenberg reported to Berlin his alarm over these events. He concluded:

> I would appreciate learning if you have any more specific knowledge of Bruns' enterprise and of his relations with the Zeppelin Company. His plans for financing his operation are quite mysterious. Should he proceed, he will detract from the goodwill we have earned from Eckener's feat and he will cast a shadow on the whole airship idea if his project is not financially and organizationally sound. Furthermore, it is tactically most awkward that he proposes to have his airship built not in Germany but abroad. The recent initiative of the Swedish Academy was predicated on the assumption that the Friedrichshafen works were to be saved for future construction of exploration airships. That argument will be destroyed if some German competitor like Bruns toys with the possibility of building the airships outside Germany.[13]

This communication signaled great difficulties to come. The appearance of Aeroarctic had had one initial advantage: its prestigious Norwegian president, who had won the Nobel Peace Prize in 1922, could conceivably assist the German airship cause with the Allies. Still, how was the chairman of its German section to be handled, with his notion of having the airship built abroad? Before long it would be revealed that Bruns had been in contact with Johann Schütte since 1922, that Schütte had designed a polar airship for that group, and that Schütte would seek to build it abroad. That, of course, would bring Eckener promptly to his feet in vehement opposition to Aeroarctic as a whole. The German government would become enmeshed in the embroglio. On the one hand, it would continue seeking a general civil aviation agreement with the Allies and specifically would hope to use Nansen's influence by way of his interest in the polar airship scheme; on the other hand,

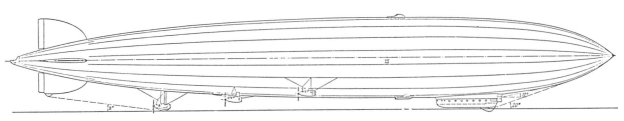

Projected SL airship for polar exploration, 1925.

Schütte airship (proposed) for polar exploration, 1925. (*Der Luftschiffbau Schütte-Lanz, 1909–1925*, p. 73)

it would seek to mediate between Aeroarctic and Eckener, bringing the scientific prestige of the German section and its hopes for an international airship expedition into some consonance with the agitation at Friedrichshafen. The next four years of German airship development would periodically and emphatically be punctuated by reverberations from this internal conflict.

During December the various players in this complicated game began to establish and clarify their positions. Capt. Bruns held a news interview announcing his polar airship plans, asserting his commanding role, and implying Nansen's support. It was the first of his escalating series of "loose-cannon" pronouncements.[14] Simultaneously Eckener was notified by the foreign office of Aeroarctic's activities. The airshipman responded in studied detail that he was aware of Bruns, that the idea of polar airship exploration had originated with Count Zeppelin and his scientific advisers in 1909, and that therefore the Zeppelin Company and its experienced personnel had an indisputable, unique moral and practical claim to sponsor and carry out such a project. Eckener concluded that any notion of Germans seeking to build an airship abroad would seriously jeopardize Germany's case with the Allies for regaining her right to build and fly airships at home.[15] From Stockholm, Rosenberg reported his efforts at "damage control," seeking to bring Eckener and Sven Hedin into direct contact, while springing the naive Swedish acacademician from the trap he had fallen into with Bruns.[16] Finally, the Berlin foreign office was intimately in touch with Eckener to smooth the riled waters at home and in Scandinavia.[17]

Early in March 1925 Eckener gave several lectures in Stockholm. He established a cordial rapport with Sven Hedin and other scientists. The Bruns specter was banished from Sweden.[18] Not so from Berlin, however. Eckener was pressed to compromise with Aeroarctic; he would do so only if the Zeppelin enterprise had a commanding role. Aeroarctic turned to the German ministry of transport for approval and funding. Now it was revealed that Schütte was the alternative builder, that there were construction contacts in Denmark, and that even Russia was anxious to be involved. At this point the ministry of transport made four conditions to which it would hold for all the ensuing years of controversy: (1) the airship must be built in Germany; (2) the Zeppelin Company must play a major role in the project; (3) the airship must be primarily a vehicle for polar exploration, and (4) Aeroarctic and Eckener must reach some workable agreement.[19]

Throughout the spring and summer the jockeying and posturing continued. Eckener, Bruns, and others met only to disagree. Hedin and other academicians quarreled about destinations for the proposed airship exploration: the North Pole, Tibet, or the Upper Amazon? A major foreign office official met Nansen unofficially in Geneva to enlist his influence with the Allied airship conferees in support of a "scientific" airship. Bruns held further disastrous press conferences. Blücher in Stockholm wrung his hands over all the dirty German linen being washed in public. In late June the ministry of transport presided at an armistice between Eckener and Aeroarctic. Documents give the details unemotionally.[20] More interesting is Eckener's report to Hedin:

> We have come to an agreement on the terms I proposed. Luftschiffbau Zeppelin will get the funding, will build the ship, and take all the leadership responsibility. It will make the ship available to the Aeroarctic for two polar flights, of course with our experienced flight crews. For the rest, our company can make use of the ship as it sees fit. The ministry agrees, so do the professors, and little boy Bruns will appropriately be relegated to some menial task with the ship's crew. . . . In August, right after the vacations, we will launch our campaign to raise the funds. I hope to have success here, even though business conditions are presently quite unfavorable.[21]

Meanwhile, with all the German news about airships—those zeppelins that had rained death and destruction on London and Paris—in the background, Foreign Minister Stresemann was quietly and successfully pursuing his negotiations with Britain and France that would produce the Locarno Treaties in the autumn of 1925. On another track of negotiations with the Allies, the deliberations about airship building in Germany were broadening into the larger issue of freedom for all German civil aviation. Nansen, taking his cues from Bruns and from the unofficial conversation with the German foreign office delegate, suggested that Aeroarctic should petition the Allies for immediate permission to build the airship for polar exploration. Doubtless Eckener knew little about Stresemann's delicate negotiations and no doubt cared less about the German-Allied aviation conversations. Hearing of Nansen's proposal, however, he simply exploded. In a letter to Hedin he vented his anger on the knaves of Aeroarctic: Bruns was still falsely proclaiming that he would lead the expedition; Dr. Bleistein (Schütte's man!) was still trying to save something of his boss's lost cause. Eckener concluded:

> I will postpone my final judgment of the Society [Aeroarctic]. For now I shall direct all my energies towards raising the funds for our airship. I will not wait for some permission from the Allies to begin construction. In fact, for basic psychological reasons, and considering the political impasse at home, I will move to raise the funds from the German people themselves, on the natural assumption that the Entente simply *cannot* deny us Germans the right to build

an airship for purely scientific purposes. It would hobble and cast shame upon our whole enterprise if we went trotting off to the Entente for permission. I can do quite well with out the indispensability of that "Study Society" and of Mr. Bruns seeking Allied permission through Professor Nansen. I will not submit to that kind of argument, but will start my own campaigning forthwith. The committees for solicitation are being formed, and in the middle of August, when everything is ready, we will step forward to appeal to the German people.[22]

The twenty-fifth jubilee of the first ascent of Count Zeppelin in the summer of 1900, was celebrated with great festivities in Friedrichshafen on August 21–22, 1925. The widely read *Vossische Zeitung* of Berlin devoted a long, front-page leader to the celebrations, reporting among other things:

We took a stroll through the construction hangars. Empty were the workshops, empty the gigantic hangar where a year ago the silver giant LZ 126 swayed to and fro. If there is any degree of reason still left in the world, life will be pulsating in these hangars again very shortly, as it is here that the giant North Pole zeppelin will have to be built. Dr. Eckener's firm resolve is to go to the North Pole, despite Germanophobe Amundsen's objections.

Later Eckener gave a long formal address, which included a very emotional condemnation of Allied policies at the making of the Treaty of Versailles. He concluded:

I am therefore certain that, for the sake of cultural advancement, for the benefit of the world at large, all this needless harassing and tormenting of airship building will soon be dropped. I believe the Entente will not refuse its consent, when it is approached for permission to construct a large exploration airship in Germany. That is why we have formulated our plans to realize Count Zeppelin's final great idea and to dispatch a scientific expedition to the polar regions by airship.

The zeppelin commander did leave a small loophole for alternative use of the airship: "It goes without saying, and I am not denying it, that such a polar expedition will give us something more than scientific information. We will obviously get experience and proof of the suitability of the zeppelin airship for long-distance voyages in all climates." Eckener concluded with his announcement of the imminent opening of a campaign for subscriptions to build the new airship specifically for polar exploration.[23]

Thus Eckener struck out on his own to raise the necessary funds to build his airship. Aeroarctic and the German government were pushed aside. The Allied prohibitions were ignored, if not openly and contemptuously challenged. The nationwide canvasing for the *Zeppelin-Eckener-Spende* subsequently raised considerable difficulties with the Berlin government, though not for reasons related to the Aeroarctic problem. After some initial successes, the campaign lagged in meeting its intermediate financial goals. In compensation the exhausted Zeppelin canvasers increasingly stressed the old Count's unique accomplishments and appealed to German cultural nationalism. In that process all sight of the great original objective was lost—to explore the polar regions by airship. Ultimately the campaign fell short by two-thirds of its seven-million-mark goal. The *Graf Zeppelin* was subsequently built by adding nearly three million marks of Company funds to the two and a half million laboriously culled from the German people in fifteen months of arduous campaigning. An additional sum would have to come from the German government, and here Eckener would again come face-to-face with Aeroarctic.

Even before the celebration of Count Zeppelin's twenty-fifth jubilee in late August 1925, there had been preliminary rumblings of Eckener's fundraising intentions. Professor Kohlschütter of Aeroarctic was appalled. He felt that this action would destroy everything that Nansen was working to achieve; the distinguished Norwegian would not lend his name to an obvious German nationalist revival.[24] Hedin promptly wrote his friend Eckener, wishing him success for his financial campaign, but stating politely that this action had the effect of a German bull in the Scandinavian china shop. Hedin reported that he had conferred with Nansen, found him indignant, and told Eckener there was danger that the Norwegian would transfer his project to Moscow, where he enjoyed great respect for his efforts in Russian famine relief. Could Eckener reach some new accord with Aeroarctic?[25] Only the German embassy in Stockholm was optimistic: now that fundraising was under way, the government must push to make it all successful. Should the embassy seek to solicit funds from Germans living in Sweden?[26]

Thenceforth it was on-again, off-again between Eckener and Aeroarctic. In September the airshipman told Hedin that he would put *his* new airship at the disposal of Nansen for two exploration flights in 1927.[27] Several long Aeroarctic memoranda to the foreign ministry in late 1925 underlined the continuing chasm between Eckener's nationalist objectives and those of the international scientific community.[28] At this point there follows a gap of almost a year in the documentation. It should be noted, however, that in late May of 1926, the Allies gave Germany full freedom of civil aviation, including unrestricted authorization to build and fly airships of any size. In late November of 1926 another "complete breakdown" occurred in the relations of Eckener with Aeroarctic. Nansen's plans were "ruined" because the airshipman "totally disagreed" with them and refused to "loan" his airship for their purposes. Why? Because Nansen had failed to move the Allies to cancel the airship restrictions. Now that the Entente had done so for other reasons, a *German* airship could be built, flown by *Germans* and with *German* scientists aboard. Dr. Eckener declared further that Aeroarctic had canceled its own order for an airship at the Zeppelin works. For his part, he wanted absolutely nothing more to do with that Society.[29]

Meanwhile, the arctic air had been humming with the vibrations of aircraft motors. During the summer of 1925, Roald Amundsen and Lincoln Ellsworth arrived in Spitzbergen by flying boat. In May 1926 Comdr. Richard E. Byrd and Floyd Bennett crossed the pole by Fokker monoplane. Soon they were followed by Amundsen, Ellsworth, and Gen. Umberto Nobile in the Italian-built semirigid *Norge* which was flying over the pole from Kings Bay to Alaska. Nansen and Aeroarctic continued planning for their own, more elaborate arctic expedition, which required a more sophisticated airship than the limited capabilities of an Italian semirigid could provide. At a larger conference of government and Aeroarctic officials at Berlin in late September 1927 [probably with Eckener's participation: the documentation is unclear], the conferees agreed that a German airship would be supplied for Nansen's project. It was further understood that in return for a government subsidy to assure completion of its airship, the Zeppelin Company would place it at the disposal of Aeroarctic for two flights in 1929. Furthermore, Nansen promised to launch a vigorous publicity campaign on behalf of the venture, a task the German government could not tactfully accomplish in its own right. Finally, the officials agreed to review progress on this project the following spring.[30]

Promptly, in April 1928, Nansen sent a reminder to the German foreign office. With Nobile's second polar airship voyage about to begin in the new semirigid *Italia*, Nansen urgently inquired about availability of the German airship. Probably he knew that LZ 127 was in its final stage of completion at Friedrichshafen, and he may have felt that the polar aerial scene was becoming crowded. He indicated that he would be in America in mid-May and there hoped to persuade the U.S. Navy to place the dirigible mooring tender *Patoka* at his disposal off the coast of Alaska at Nome. He also indicated the upcoming Aeroarctic scientific congress scheduled for late June in Leningrad, where he hoped to actualize an earlier Soviet promise to provide a mooring mast on northern Russian soil. Now, asked Nansen, where do we stand with that German zeppelin?[31]

An office memorandum prepared for the foreign minister gave a detailed chronology of the government-Eckener-Aeroarctic airship muddle. As for Eckener, the report stated that he had apparently never been sympathetic to having his airship used for polar trips. As long as the *Spende* was going well, he had ignored the question whenever possible. When it essentially failed, he had had to turn to the ministry of transport to bail him out. He received 400,000 marks from the 1927 budget, and for 1928 the Reichstag had voted him an additional 700,000 marks. If Aeroarctic could demonstrate that it had the required financing for its project as of January 1, 1929, the government would hold Eckener to its terms.[32]

The airshipman was still having other problems: how would he fund the costs of his maiden voyage to America? Aeroarctic was no better off in seeking several million marks to finance its polar expedition. In August 1928 Aeroarctic notified the German foreign office that it could not meet its 1929 deadline. Eckener put together his own funding from a combination of sources: news and film royalties, petroleum company gifts, fees for carrying stamp collectors'

Collectors' mail to finance *Graf Zeppelin* polar flight, 1931. (Lee Payne)

mail, and additional Company monies. His flight to America in mid-October was a sensational success. Now Eckener could move into command of the situation, assuaging the German government and dictating to Aeroarctic. Yet another conference of the principals was held at the German ministry of transport in late November of 1928. Eckener renewed his previous commitment to Aeroarctic with a promise to make the *Graf Zeppelin* available for a gratis transpolar flight in the late spring of 1930. Aeroarctic would be responsible for financing all other costs of the expedition. The expedition would begin and end at Friedrichshafen. To smoothen future relationships, Eckener was appointed to the board of directors of the German section of Aeroarctic and procedures were established to arbitrate any future disagreements.[33] The next move was up to Nansen and the scientists.

Time passed. The new zeppelin flew several times across the North Atlantic. It visited the Holy Land. It flew around the world. It made a pioneering triangular flight to South and North America. The *Graf Zeppelin* was flying in every climate except that of the arctic. The problem was that, with the deepening world depression, Aeroarctic could not raise the millions of marks to finance the expedition. In the midst of these disappointments, Nansen suddenly died in May 1930.

Shortly thereafter Eckener was elected as international president of Aeroarctic. While he was busy all that summer with European flights, he was now carefully preparing for his own version of a polar expedition. Bruns had been maneuvered out as head of the German section, though he was still

Dr. Eckener as president of Aeroarctic, 1930. (Lufthansa Archives)

consulted by Eckener—if only to prevent his making precipitous press announcements.[34] As always, Eckener juggled precariously with several possibilities of financing, which the world depression made just as difficult for him as it had for Nansen. Initially he had support from the Hearst press and various filmmakers to stage a sensational meeting of the *Graf Zeppelin* and Sir Hubert Wilkins in a submarine at the North Pole. When these plans failed and that support diminished, Eckener had to cut his cloth to fit other dimensions. The insurance essential for the trip required that the *Graf Zeppelin* fly no farther than just inside the Arctic Circle. Given this limitation, where could a scientific expedition go? Here Nansen's earlier Russian contacts fortuitously yielded fruit. With major Soviet participation a moderate schedule of scientific studies was prepared northeastward along the Russian arctic perimeter and to Franz Josef Land. These studies included investigation of earth magnetism as related to air navigation; general meteorological observations; and cartographic research of the virtually unknown north Siberian sea frontier. Worldwide press and film publicity for the "polar" flight of the *Graf Zeppelin* brought positive light into the deepening shadows of the depression. Still, the expensive expedition went no farther into the arctic than Count Zeppelin had gone by sea to Spitzbergen twenty years before.[35]

For almost seven years the "polar" dimensions of German airship building and flying had echoed through the German and international scene. Where stood the players in the drama as of the summer of 1931? Ambassador von Rosenberg was still in Stockholm representing his nation's interests. Sven Hedin and Eckener had ceased communicating in 1926. The Swedish explorer had shifted his interest to Junkers monoplanes and with Lufthansa support was charting central Asian routes to the Far East, subsequently followed by his greatest expeditions into Mongolia, the Gobi Desert, and western China. When he later published his review of all the significant Germans he had ever known, he forgot to mention Eckener. However, one member of the Royal Swedish Academy of Sciences did participate in the 1931 expedition. The German government and foreign office had long since had to grapple with far weightier political and financial problems at home and abroad. Aeroarctic had its brief, restricted week of accomplishment as the airshipman's directed instrument. Thereafter, its purpose achieved, it lapsed into obscurity. Only the airshipman fully succeeded.

Hugo Eckener attained his objective. The work of his hero, Count Zeppelin, was carried on in a peaceful alternative to its original purpose as an instrument of war. Eckener did not initiate the intrigues of Rosenberg and Hedin; but once aware of them, he artfully turned them to his own advantage. Far less delicate were his confrontations with the Allies, with his opponents at Aeroarctic, and with government offices in Berlin. He met their objections with a populist appeal to the German public. While that venture was a financial failure, it was a psychopolitical success. In the process, the "airship for scientific polar exploration" became the bait that caught the crucial million marks from the German government which Eckener needed to complete the *Graf Zeppelin*. Finally, time and circumstances eroded the substance of Aeroarctic, so that in keeping his promise to it and to Berlin, Eckener could further his efforts to develop the commercial airship. Events, personality, and luck all combined to give Hugo Eckener his success.

CHAPTER 7 **France Perceives the Zeppelins, 1924–1937**

With the defeat of Germany sealed by the Treaty of Versailles, France moved after 1919 to become the greatest military air power of Europe, and achieved her objective by the early 1930s. All over the Western industrial world these were years of rapid advance in aircraft design and competition by size, speed, range, and payload. Within a decade after Versailles, England, Germany, and the United States had all scored major successes in commercial aviation. France alone lagged behind in the civilian sector. Then in 1929, Germany astonished the world by flying a commercial zeppelin around the globe, a distance of 21,000 miles in twelve days with only three intermediate landings. The shadow of the Teutonic colossus, symbolized in the zeppelin, deepened its impact upon the French psyche.[1]

During the interwar years the rigid airship held a powerful and unique fascination for individuals and masses the world over. Particularly until 1935 it appeared that airships alone had the nonstop range and payload capacity that would make regular transoceanic flight operationally and financially feasible—provided that hazards of structural fragility and flammable lifting gas could be overcome. After several spectacular airship disasters in the early 1930s, Germany alone was visibly successful. And when the Nazis came to power they systematically manipulated the zeppelins for maximum political propaganda effect at home and abroad.[2]

Zeppelins provoked mostly negative associations in the French mind. Even though France received the very latest and finest zeppelins as war reparations in 1920–21, the airship stirred few hearts there. The heroic efforts of Comdr. Jean du Plessis de Grenédan to make airships a factor in French naval re-

This is a slightly enhanced version of an article originally published with the coauthorship of Stephen V. Gallup. Both authors wish to acknowledge the invaluable aid of Mlle. Marie de Montlaur, Service des Archives, French Ministry of Foreign Affairs. Reprinted by permission of the coauthor and the *South Atlantic Quarterly*, vol. 78, no. 1 (1979), pp. 107–21.

connaissance were fatal and fruitless.[3] *Le Zeppelin* was the peculiar instrument of *le boche:* It has bombed Paris; it could spy on France during overflights; it could become a commercial competitor and propaganda threat. Above all, its prohibition in 1920 by the Versailles Treaty and its subsequent commercial revival in 1926 (over energetic French protests, but within the Locarno Accords) was symbolic of German threats to the postwar French security system.

The French had already received a rude shock when the great construction complex of Luftschiffbau Zeppelin at Friedrichshafen was not dismantled after the war and was given a new lease on life by building of a "commercial" airship as reparations for the United States. The delivery flight of that airship to America in October 1924, under the command of Dr. Hugo Eckener, was hailed as a cultural triumph in Germany and an aviation wonder abroad. On October 16, 1924, *Le Figaro* wondered how long the zeppelin would remain peaceful, commented on German exultation as "*revanche morale,*" and feared that the exploit would heighten German prestige to the detriment of France. Subsequently a long report from the French minister of war dealt with the German aviation challenge, including references to the dangers of a German overseas thrust by zeppelin to eastern South America.[4]

Between 1925 and 1928 the indefatigable Dr. Eckener raised two and one-half million marks by public subscription, constructed a new long-range transoceanic airship (the *Graf Zeppelin*), and flew it southwestward over France to the Mediterranean and on to America with worldwide attention. Overflight permission was given grudgingly, for Paul Tirard, French high commissioner of the occupied Rhineland, had already protested against "experimental" airship flights over his domain. He viewed these actions as deliberately provocative, "a new symptom of the policy presently followed by certain elements seeking to create incidents . . . [to bring further pressure to bear on France] to withdraw from the occupied territories."[5] The successful zeppelin flight ignited a Franco-German newspaper war. *L'Echo de Paris* made a pun on the "Gaffe" Zeppelin, while *Le Matin* belittled the whole accomplishment. The German press viewed such comments as signs of irrepressible jealousy. Newspapers in Hamburg headlined, PARIS, FULL OF HATE AS ALWAYS! *La Liberté* rejoined ironically that German officers no doubt had convinced themselves that the citizens of Montélimar, a city under the *Graf* overflight, had great confidence in Locarno, having forgotten the terrible memories of war. The "peace" zeppelin was seen as a mirror image of the "war" zeppelin; its thirteen passengers [sic] could be replaced by thirteen bombs, thus transforming the dove into a bird of prey. The *Hamburgischer Correspondent* set the tone for German reactions: "Can we Germans forget the musical accompaniment of the French press to our departing zeppelin? They complained when it flew over the Rhineland and blamed us for lack of tact in ostensibly using the zeppelin for propaganda. Of course, all French policy from the occupation of the Ruhr to recent military maneuvers in the Eiffel mountains, from court martials in occupied territory to espionage in German industry,

French caption reads: "How goes it? . . . Any delay? . . . Yes, captain, twelve years late." (French newspaper cartoon, spring 1930) (Uwe Eckener Archives)

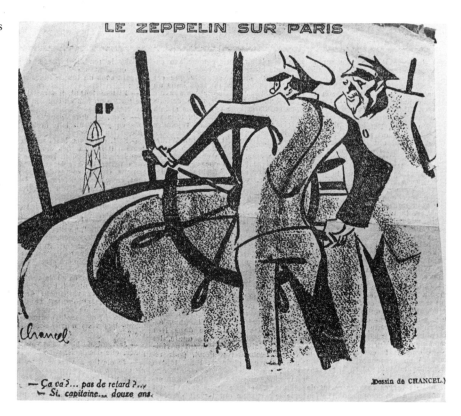

LE ZEPPELIN SUR PARIS

— Ça va ?... pas de retard ?...
— Si, capitaine... douze ans.

(Dessin de CHANCEL.)

have always been full of tact!" As newspapers exchanged verbal salvos, French diplomats from posts in Europe reported in detail on the public enthusiasm which the maiden flight of the *Graf Zeppelin* had stimulated in their areas on behalf of Germany.[6]

The German airship signified even more to the French than a propaganda stunt, a threat to peace, or an instrument of leverage in diplomacy. After the *Graf*'s successful return to Germany, Ambassador Pierre de Margerie reported form Berlin on intensive negotiations under way to coordinate Zeppelin Company and Lufthansa maneuvers to obtain air routes to Latin America. He quoted the *Vossische Zeitung* on the poor image of France in comparable efforts: the French line Aéropostale was in a "pitiful" operational state; accidents were numerous, French planes were second-rate and there were rumors that Paris would demand reliable German Junkers craft as reparations in order to put the French South Atlantic enterprise on its feet. The German challenge was real, and the stakes were high in commerce and political prestige. The *Graf Zeppelin* indicated that France now had a serious competitor, despite the initial French advantage secured by the aviation prohibitions of Versailles.[7]

Early in 1929 Germany requested permission to fly over French territory, as well as Syria, on a test flight of the *Graf* to the eastern Mediterranean area.

As usual, the foreign minister checked with the air, navy, and war ministries. The minister of war objected that several "forbidden" areas were near the proposed itinerary and that there was no way to assure that photography would not occur. He gave his assent only on condition that the zeppelin fly at night over France and not pass north of a line Pontarlier, Lons-le-Saunier and Chalon-sur-Saône. As for Syria, he added, "permit me to remind you of the serious repercussions that a dirigible flying German flags might have upon our influence in this country, especially in view of the important role that German supervision played there during the war." Briand agreed to the minister's conditions, but the Germans balked at the night-flying over unfamiliar hilly ground. They promised to secure all photographic equipment. They also requested permission to carry drop-mail for France, but the minister of posts was negative; he feared the mail would fall into hostile hands and be destroyed because of the nationality of the fliers. The flight passed without incident, while French Mediterranean consular officials en route reported on public enthusiasm over the airship passage.[8]

The next test flight took the *Graf* to the Iberian Peninsula. The German request gave a detailed itinerary over France, a promise to secure photographic equipment, and an invitation for two French engineers to make the trip. French objections were raised on grounds that with reparations negotiations still hanging fire, Frenchmen aboard a German zeppelin would cause political "inconveniences." The flight had other political repercussions. The French consul at Tangier wrote that the *Graf* had made a great impression on the natives, hardly to the benefit of France. From Lisbon the French ambassador reported with some satisfaction that a very belated request by the *Graf* to overfly the Portuguese capital found the Portuguese foreign office miffed by German bad manners. From inside France came the sharpest reaction. M. Schneider, director of the great armament works at Le Creusot, complained that the ship had flown slowly just 200 meters above his factories and created great disquiet. The French press made the most of the story. Briand then checked on the matter carefully and found that all photographic equipment had indeed been secured and that the ship had, in fact, passed at 700 meters height and at normal speed. This was not the only time that ground observers in France would mistake the height and speed of the passing airship. The following years saw numerous apprehensive complaints that the zeppelin was a spy ship that took pictures of military objectives.[9]

Whether flying southwestward or westward, German airships required permission to overfly France. The terrain was far more favorable geographically and meteorologically than alpine Switzerland. The airship could conserve lifting power by flying at lower altitudes (greater payload), and the route over France was obviously more direct to the Americas. These facts were not lost on French officials. When Germany requested further permission for overflight en route to New York, the minister of war sent Briand several notes demanding much more prudence in granting such requests. The ship should fly only at night; and if there were one more irregularity, permits should be denied altogether.[10] Briand responded that he was satisfied that the Germans were up to no chicanery, that the unscheduled flight over Le Creusot was caused by adverse weather. He further urged accommodation because Paris was negotiating with Berlin for extension of air routes through Germany into Scandinavia: "We are asking more of our neighbors than we are offering them. We have, therefore, every interest to avoid giving them the impression of being negatively disposed in their regard." The minister of war agreed, but he urged Briand to inform the Germans not to make any false moves that might arouse public opinion, which was "properly sensitive to the aerial threat."[11]

These interministerial negotiations caused a day's delay in the departure of the *Graf Zeppelin* for America in mid-May of 1929. At an impromptu German press conference Eckener was reported to have said, "This is the third time the French have made a mess (*Schweinerei*) for me." Other German papers played up alleged petty French jealousy of German technological achievement.[12] *L'Action Française* (May 17, 1929) responded in kind, referring to alleged German violations in photographing Le Creusot. It condemned Eckener's reference to *la belle France*, a term used supposedly only by German revanchists; all this was evidence that Germany was undermining the spirit of Locarno. On the left, *Le Populaire*, organ of the Socialist party, took a different view: "It has taken eight days for the French government to consent to the overall flight with infinitely bad grace. This chauvinistic absurdity is beyond all limits, a shabby action far from honoring its authors."[13] Again an airship overflight was the cause of a public row, the French afraid of German aerial surveillance, the Germans accusing the French of jealousy and bad faith. Briand, the great compromiser, tried to allay the fears in the cabinet which the minister of war had aroused with his demands for stringent control of zeppelin passage.

Dramatically the atmosphere changed within a few days. The *Graf Zeppelin* developed serious engine trouble and had to turn back. Eckener got permission to land in France and barely managed to limp into the base at Cuers Pierrefeu, a surviving remnant of Du Plessis de Grenédan's great hopes for airships in France. The German airship, crew, and passengers were received with cordiality and friendly messages from Paris. Eckener responded with a gracious speech of thanks. The illwill that had poisoned the press was dissipated; most German newspapers praised the French for their aid. Late in May, Briand wrote in his report to the ministers of air, navy, and war, "The recognition which German public opinion gives . . . the French Government brings a sentimental note into the relations between the two countries which (though we should not exaggerate it) undermines those hostile [German] elements that are against detente."[14] On May 29, *Le Figaro* drew a cautious balance:

Zeppelins are masterpieces of aeronautical architecture. As such they deserve the deepest and most sincere admiration. In favorable circumstances they are capable of marvelous exploits. Their passage thru the sky is an event of touching beauty. But they are monsters and, practically speaking, they are alarming. They need a vast amount of open space to land without difficulty, huge hangars to house them, and crowds of men to handle them on departure and arrival. We can only compare them to colossi with feet of clay.

On the same day Jules Cambon, in the twilight of his life, wrote a long piece in *Le Figaro* in praise of the cooperation and goodwill engendered by the near tragedy. Ambassador de Margerie also thought the incident augured well for Franco-German relations, though his views had a tinge of malicious joy. German public opinion was impressed with French help, but the crippling of the airship was a blow to German nationalist pride which was "severe but deserved. . . . The failure of the zeppelin has thus worked wholly to our benefit."[15]

The era of good feeling continued for the rest of the year. In the summer of 1929 the *Graf* made its spectacular round-the-world flight. The French foreign office gave routine clearance. Adverse wind conditions forced Eckener to fly directly over Paris. Polite greetings were exchanged between him and French air authorities. The press made no fuss. *Le Figaro* gave more space than others as the airship proceeded around the world. But while praising the feat, the press suggested that the zeppelin was too big, vulnerable, and fragile to be a viable transport for the future. The French ambassador in America was less sanguine. He reported at length on the enthusiastic receptions in New York and Washington, "where German interests are so numerous and so powerfully well organized." He took comfort from a Philadelphia paper which argued that, once the novelty had worn off, the public would become uninterested in sending postcards, typewriters, and candy at such great expense. When the *Graf* returned to Friedrichshafen, it was an occasion for great celebration. The French consul in Stuttgart was invited to various festivities and treated with great friendliness. He reported that everyone praised France for her aid the previous May, and he expressed confidence in the peaceful character of the zeppelin flight program.[16]

In the spring of 1930 the Germans again requested overflight permits to Spain and to England; Paris was on the itinerary of the second. This would be the last time a zeppelin ever flew over the Ile de France. After the flight the papers were full of commentary and photographs. From right to left the Parisian press was at it again. *L'Action Française* featured a letter from the sixteenth section of the League of Patriots, denouncing the slow passage of the airship as "deliberate provocation" and "a propaganda weapon." *Le Temps* expressed its displeasure indirectly, reporting how the *Graf* had incurred British displeasure by hovering over London's Wembley Stadium and diverting attention from the crucial English soccer finals. *L'Humanité* took *La Liberté* to task for doctoring photos of the zeppelin to make it appear that no one in Paris was watching, then concluded: "of course the commercial airship could tomorrow become an engine of war; but at the moment, when capitalism everywhere is arming and overarming, the zeppelin, despite its great size, is really insignificant [*une petite chose*]."[17]

For French interests in South America, however, it was certainly not to be *une petite chose*. By the late 1920s Paris had established a firm aviation foothold there. As of 1930 Latin American commercial airspace had been divided up between Pan American Airways, Imperial Airways, and Aéropostale. Germany and Italy had been left out. Planes of the Aéropostale flew to Dakar, fast ships took the mail across the South Atlantic to Brazil, and other French planes carried it on to Argentina, Chile, and Peru. "Aéropostale became a flying ambassador; its regional offices, its airfields and its stations were French havens where our fervent friends met."[18] Heavy government subsidies supported the venture. Pilot Jean Mermoz, the French Lindbergh, attempted a daring but abortive Natal-Dakar flight in 1930, boosting hopes of early regular all-air service from Paris to Rio and Buenos Aires. At this point the depression and the zeppelin sounded the death knell for French supremacy in the area.

The failure of Mermoz's flight came just a month after the *Graf* flew majestically nonstop from Spain to Brazil on the first leg of a triangular trip that carried it on to America and back to Germany. The French ambassador in Rio cautioned Paris not to attempt any further aviation spectaculars, unless they could be certain of success (as the Germans appeared to be). Half a year later he reported French interests on the defensive. True, Aéropostale had established an "important and durable" influence, but a new German competitor in connection with the zeppelin interests (the Brazilian-sponsored airline Syndicato Condor) was making serious inroads into French business. The economic sacrifices of the French government to keep Aéropostale in operation were fully justified. Without them France would lose her position as *maîtresse* of the area.[19]

Against this background of financial difficulties and German airship competition, Aéropostale became a subject of controversy in the French National Assembly, as the government proposed to take over the almost bankrupt company and merge it with others in a more viable commercial aviation venture. Debates were heated as interests and personalities clashed, but there was general agreement on one theme: French prestige was at stake.[20] During the year 1931 argument continued as subsidies dwindled and business declined—but only for the French. Simultaneously Dr. Eckener was visiting in Paris to get French cooperation for regular German airship service to Brazil in the form of a general convention on overflight arrangements and French mail contracts. Aéropostale counterattacked in the French press. The German airshipman returned home empty-handed, except for continued French willingness to grant permits for test flights, one at a time. In 1932 there were

LZ 127, *Graf Zeppelin*, awaiting departure to Brazil, 1932. (Luftschiffbau Zeppelin)

nine such South American round-trips amounting virtually to regular service. In the fall of 1932 Eckener spent several weeks in Rio negotiating with authorities for construction of a modern airship base and Brazilian financial support. The French ambassador was pessimistic: Brazil enjoyed pitting the foreign aviation interests against each other; the Brazilians were enthusiastic about the airship; and the prospect of a second airship in service would make the French position impossible. At year's end the French chargé in Lima complained that the Lufthansa-Zeppelin-Condor combine had a virtual monopoly of air service between Europe and South America. A few months later, in June 1933, the French commercial attaché in Rio echoed that France must respond soon or "the immense financial effort, . . . the huge subsidies and precious lives lost to create the first rapid connection with South America—all will have been spent in vain."[21]

Aéropostale finally went bankrupt in May 1934, and the new Air France took its place; but the great French head start was lost. From Peru, Chile, Paraguay, Uruguay, Argentina, and Brazil the French diplomats complained repeatedly that the highly visible zeppelin (even when it did not visit most of those countries), and its Syndicato Condor affiliate, now commanded the attention in the area that had once been a prestigious French commercial domain. Characteristic was ambassador François Gentile's report from Montevideo that indicated great enthusiasm there. In Paraguay the press was talking of nothing but the zeppelin. Everywhere the airship was portrayed as a symbol of friendship and fraternity among peoples, but without mentioning what terrible instruments of death the zeppelins had been during the war. The flight of the airship over Montevideo was the signal for launching a strong German propaganda offensive in Uruguay. French prestige was declining throughout southern Latin America.[22]

Meanwhile, back at the foreign office, new initiatives were directed toward the point of origin of competition—the question of overflights. With the development of regular German airship service in spring 1933, the French foreign and air ministers agreed that France should demand negotiation of a special air convention with Germany, obviously to put limits on further German air expansion and gain concessions to safeguard French interests. Their efforts moved only slowly toward fruition and with resistance from other sources. The minister of the navy complained that the zeppelin had flown low over port installations at Casablanca and that such overflights should be prohibited in the future. M. Saint-Léger, secretary general of the foreign office, wrote a long report on the *Graf* (June 30, 1933), raising the old problems of spying, damage to French commercial interests, and need for German concessions. Now the Nazis were in power, and French sensitivities were even greater. The prefect of Nîmes (Gard) complained that the *Graf* had flown low over the city, where "the population was much disturbed because of the nationality of the airship with its swastikas and the low altitude of its maneuvers." Late in 1933 a long study from the ministry of the interior showed that whatever goodwill had existed after the forced landing at Cuers in 1929 was now dissipated; on seven of nine trips, usually down the Rhône Valley, the airship was accused of flying low and slowly for the purpose of military reconnaissance.[23]

In early December 1933, the under secretaries of war, air, navy, interior, foreign affairs, and colonies had a long conference about the dilemma which the zeppelin posed for France. Could the French ban zeppelin flights altogether? No, for France was dependent upon Germany for access to northern central Europe. World opinion would find such action unfair, and German reprisals would be painful. The minister of war still worried about photography, finding the airship a more effective instrument than the airplane. The minister of colonies reported that in view of German interests in Morocco the "natives" were dangerously impressionable. Could France try for a hard bargain with Germany? No, that would be dangerous because Germany could always alternatively work out a combination of better advantages with Italy, Spain, and the British in Gambia. At length it was decided to reduce German

LZ 127, *Graf Zeppelin*, at Recife, Brazil, 1935. (Lufthansa Archives)

overflights to two very closely defined corridors in southern France, away from militarily sensitive areas, in return for a new French route in central Europe. Agreements would also be sought on sharing of air routes and payloads on the South American run. These decisions set the tone for French policy for the rest of the airship era.[24]

The whole issue, however, still remained very sensitive. The report of M. Poincaré, French air attaché at Berlin in the mid-1930s, are a rich and voluminous source of information and attitudes on the matter. One of his first dispatches dealt with the Nazi propagandistic exploitation of the South American run. A Professor Matschoss had made the trip to Brazil and on his return spoke of the country as "a veritable German colony." Poincaré underlined the numbers of Germans in Brazil, the close ties between Nazi ideology and the Brazilian-Germans, and the leverage this situation gave Berlin in its negotiations with Rio.[25]

The Franco-German air negotiations dragged on for nearly a year and a half. The interval was punctuated with various technical successes, competitive propaganda outbursts, and tragedy. The Reich was perfecting a combined airplane-seaplane service with a catapult seaplane mothership in the mid-South Atlantic, and Germans waxed proud. About that time the French began nonstop flights, Dakar to Natal, with Mermoz piloting the *Arc-en-*

Ciel. The French press was ecstatic. Then the *Arc-en-Ciel* was grounded for several weeks, giving the Germans a chance to vaunt the "superior safety" of the *Graf* and make fun of premature French celebration. Later, in 1936, Mermoz lost his life in a flight between Dakar and Brazil; all France mourned the death of its Lindbergh.[26] At long last the Franco-German negotiations were completed. In the words of the Zeppelin representative there:

> The one day that we had originally anticipated for the negotiations extended into nearly a week. We went back and forth on issues of prestige, flying dates for French and German aircraft, rates, characteristics of competition, etc. Some of our sessions were very dramatic. Frequently I had to call the offices and ministries in Berlin for further instructions. We were prepared to send the *Graf Zeppelin* on its first trip (in 1935) in a detour around France. But at the last minute we finally did make a treaty.[27]

In fact, the French achieved the goals they had set a year and a half before at the meeting of the under secretaries: itineraries of the zeppelin were severely restricted and France got very favorable concessions for the limited over-flights.[28]

Soon after the long negotiations over the South American route had been resolved a new problem arose. The *Hindenburg* was now ready for service. In February 1936 the German ambassador requested a new route for the North American service across the Ile de France and Normandy. At the subsequent interministerial council meeting (war, navy, air force, interior, foreign office, and air) only Marcel Déat for the air ministry favored the request. The other five ministers expressed concern for national security, despite Déat's observation that the Germans probably already had more than enough photographs of northern French terrain. Only the two previously established narrow southern corridors were made available. The German request to permit the new airship to use the standard corridor on its maiden voyage to Brazil was still unanswered when Hitler broke the Locarno Treaties and marched into the Rhineland. Subsequently the *Hindenburg* had to make an inconvenient detour down the Rhine, westward over Holland, then out along the English Channel. It was, however, permitted to use the standard southern

Olympic display, Condor-Zeppe-
lin offices, Rio de Janeiro, 1936.
(Luftschiffbau Zeppelin)

Opel "Olympia" auto sent to
Brazil by LZ 129, *Hindenburg*,
spring 1936. (Luftschiffbau
Zeppelin)

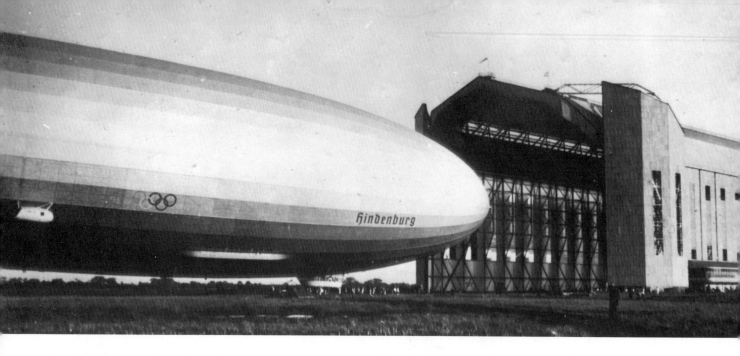

Hindenburg at Santa Cruz airport, Rio de Janeiro, April 1937.
(Lufthansa Archives)

route on its return. French defense ministries reacted more nervously than
ever and noted how the swastikas passing overhead were detrimental to
French public morale.[29]

In the summer of 1936 the two zeppelins made twenty-nine highly visible
round-trips to the Americas, eighteen of them through the restricted French
corridors to Brazil, ten along the Rhine and English Channel carefully avoiding France while en route to New York. At the air ministry, M. Déat (and
later, M. Cot) felt that France was missing a great opportunity to tie France
into the apparently highly successful transatlantic service by not encouraging
the airships to stop at Orly and thus in fact to make Paris the central continental point of arrival and departure. But from Berlin, M. Poincaré reported
ominous Nazi progress and "certain victory in this struggle for conquest of
Atlantic hegemony": six airships by 1940 and fast catapult seaplane service in
both hemispheres—all of which made French prospects appear "singularly
difficult."[30] The Germans were on the threshold of a spectacular commercial
aviation triumph.

Then the element of the spectacular was indeed realized, but in a way
hardly anticipated by the Germans. The explosion of the *Hindenburg* on its
first North American flight in 1937 put an end to the era of airships and their
continuing powerful psychological impact upon the masses beneath them.[31]
Though the archives are silent on the matter, it seems likely that there was
a collective sigh of relief when the zeppelins no longer flew over France. For
a decade the "colossus," the "monster" had catalyzed French distrust and fear
of the Germans. It had demonstrated to Europeans, Americans, and Asians
that Germany was preeminent in the genius and dedication of its airship
builders and fliers. The impressive zeppelins had passed over urban sophis-
ticates and primitive tribesmen, affecting all who saw them. Trade went with
the flag, and it was the *Graf* which most visibly spearheaded the German

180

drive to return to economic power in South America, inevitably at the expense of France.

Finally, as the archives show again and again, *les zeppelins* brought back bitter memories to the French of the Great War. After 1927 no year went by without complaints that the airships were spying on French military installations and by implication thumbing their noses at the Treaty of Versailles and diminishing French prestige. Such reactions came not only from officials but from men in the street who often wrote angry letters to the government. The ministers of the Front Populaire, elected in 1936, were just as apprehensive as their predecessors in the Center-Right governments of the earlier 1930s. As the zeppelins with their vivid swastikas became flying billboards for triumphant national socialism, French public reaction became even stronger. Though the Franco-German air agreement of 1935 appeared to settle the question of overflights, the appearance of the *Hindenburg* and her expected successors saw the French firmly resisting any further facilitation of German triumphs.

In 1929, just after the triumphal global flight of the *Graf* and near the height of Franco-German postwar detente, Hugo Eckener discussed the great prospects of transatlantic airship travel with a visitor and then commented soberly: "If only the French would trust us. . . ."[32] Cosmopolitan though he had become, neither Eckener nor his achievement could escape their intimate identification with aroused German pride and nationalism. Indeed, the tremendous popular impact of zeppelin successes gave many Germans a sense of psychological compensation for the humiliation of Versailles. Inevitably the French perceived the situation in quite the opposite sense. The zeppelin frequently overhead vividly symbolized the resurgence of Germany and her challenge to the postwar European hegemony of France. Quite directly the zeppelin overshadowed French aviation technology and was the most visible instrument of declining French commercial influence in South America. Seldom has a single technological accomplishment, however brief the duration of its impact, had such widespread popular influence and invited such political manipulation and concern. How could the French be expected to trust *les zeppelins*?

CHAPTER 8 Politics, Personality, and Technology:
Airships in the Manipulations of
Dr. Hugo Eckener and
Lord Thomson, 1919–1930

It always has been evident that energetic and determined individuals project their personalities in decisive and formative ways through enterprises and agencies. The thrusts of such personalities can vary from impact upon limited business or professional enterprises up and through the social structure to leadership and policy making in government. Such efforts are sometimes accompanied by an individual's fascination with leverage or devices that in themselves produce rewarding ego-satisfaction, while also being instruments in attaining wider influence and power. The lives and careers of Dr. Hugo Eckener and Lord Thomson illustrate two such personalities, each galvanized by the same technological device in order (1) to seek the realization of the potentialities of the device in itself and (2) to bring that successful result to bear upon a larger issue of national policy. Eckener and Thomson worked with similar technology but under very different national and political circumstances. The German achieved worldwide acclaim in his time; the Englishman perished on the very threshold of anticipated success. What factors would seem to account for these tragically opposite results of Anglo-German airship competition in the 1920s?

Let us begin with two disclaimers. First, the word *manipulation* as herein used does not imply fraudulent or improper behavior on the part of these men, but it does emphasize the very active propagation of their causes and their use of shrewd and skillful management therein. Both were convinced that the immediate future of their respective nations was intimately tied to the far-ranging airship. Eckener saw it as an immediate postwar opportunity to give defeated Germans a new claim to worldwide endeavor and to give Germany a new peaceful image among nations. Shortly thereafter Thomson

This essay was originally published in the *Aerospace Historian*, (Sept. 1981), pp. 165–72. Reprinted with permission from *Aerospace Historian*, © 1981 by the Air Force Historical Foundation. No additional copies may be made without the express permission of the author and of the editor of *Aerospace Historian*.

pressed his idea to strengthen the weakening bonds of empire and to let Britain rule the air as it had earlier ruled the waves. These were serious ventures and they were diligently pursued by both of these men.

Second, this study does not presume to be an exercise in psychohistory. It does intend to deal with interrelated aspects of character, personality, and actions that inevitably impinge upon the boundaries of psychological interpretation. If in that process Eckener appears as something less than a dazzling hero figure and Thomson as something more than a determined *hazardeur*, it is to provide a clearer understanding of the ways these men expressed their personalities in pressing airship technology upon the policies and imaginations of their respective peoples.[1]

At the end of World War I the airship appeared to hold great promise for commercial exploitation; indeed, it seemed to be the only vehicle of promise for long-distance and especially transoceanic flight. In 1919, for instance, air service opened between London and Paris with planes carrying four passengers and barely spanning the distance of 250 miles. At that same time, the British rigid airship R 34 crossed the North Atlantic nonstop for 3,000 miles with 30 men aboard, plus 28 tons of fuel and ballast; and it returned to England the next week under the same specifications. That event alone influenced planning for transoceanic commercial aviation for the next decade.[2]

Psychologically, the image of the airship was firmly engraved upon people's minds, though its impact varied from nation to nation. For Germans, *der Zeppelin* was a unique Teutonic achievement, unmatched in any other nation, that had apparently proved itself in peace and war. Although British airmen had successfully countered the zeppelins by 1917, the English public had a strong impression of the zeppelin as a barbarous instrument of Hun terror. When England in 1924 embarked upon its revised airship building program, much emphasis was placed upon its unique British and quite unGerman qualities. But no matter what their national emphases, the airships in the skies of the 1920s aroused a hitherto unequaled display of public amazement, excitement, and fascination—a phenomenon sometimes then described as "zeppelin fever."[3]

Politically, therefore, as of 1919, the airship was a focus of international attention and expectation. The British and the Americans, though discounting the airship as a tactical instrument of war, continued their interest in it as a naval reconnaissance vehicle. Soon the British focused their entire interest upon its peacetime uses. The victorious Allies, of course, sought to exclude the Germans from any kind of further use of zeppelins and imposed prohibitions upon them. At stake here was really the future commercial development of the airship, and thus the Allies tried to eliminate the most successful builder and only prewar commercial operator from competition. The Germans obviously viewed this action as one of the many humiliations of the Versailles Treaty and would respond enthusiastically to one man's dogged efforts to retain for Germans the facilities to build and fly their zeppelins.

Thus the stage was set for Dr. Eckener and Lord Thomson to bring their personalities and efforts to bear upon their respective nations' attitudes and policies.

Hugo Eckener was born into a comfortable bourgeois family in the North German seaport city of Flensburg in 1868. Seven years later, Christopher Birdwood Thomson began his life in India in a noted British military family. Each child enjoyed stable family relationships and attended the best schools in his respective social milieu. By the time they entered advanced education, each had developed characteristics that would identify him throughout the rest of his life. Eckener was probably more introspective, probing in reactions to his fellowman and experiences, forthright in speech and action, and demanding of himself and his associates. Though he spent much of his later life in groups and crowds, Eckener was not basically a gregarious person. Early in life he learned to sail and enjoyed contesting sea and weather in a self-reinforcing communion with nature. Thomson was more of an extrovert. Social graces came easily to him. His high spirits commended him to his fellowmen and let him take circumstances in his stride. He worked well with groups on the playing field and in personal relationships. He would come to enjoy politics and self-projection. In their younger years, both men developed well defined belletristic dimensions: for Eckener his love of music and art would become a welcome refuge from the pressures of public responsibilities; for Thomson his love of literature, languages, and music would become an asset in making the most of positive circumstances and a source of strength in contesting the less favorable ones. In either case, these were men who aggressively moved to confront situations and to reshape them in their own notions of the future.

The next fifteen years found Eckener with no decisive career direction, while Thomson developed a splendid record with the Royal Engineers. Eckener took a degree in experimental psychology with Wundt, dabbled in journalism, became interested in social-economic questions, and moved to Friedrichshafen in southern Germany to study and write. He continued to do journalistic pieces on odd and interesting topics, including the curious efforts of a retired cavalry general who was trying to fly an elongated balloon within a rigid metal framework. Thomson saw considerable action in South Africa, came to the favorable attention of Lord Kitchener, and continued his rapid rise through various African postings. By the time Thomson returned to England in 1907, to a prestigious military instructional post, Eckener had experienced his conversion from journalist critic of the airship to becoming a participating advocate of the technology. It would be another fifteen years before Thomson sparked his own enthusiasm for airships.[4]

Once Eckener had found his cause—the challenge of flying and perfecting the zeppelin—he gave it all of the remarkable energy and drive of the rest of his active life. Until the war, he worked his way up through various managerial and operational levels of the Zeppelin Company. Soon after the war began, he became commander of the naval airship flying school at Nordholz on the North Sea. From there came the data and experience that matured his confidence in the airship and his determination that Germany should continue to lead in its development. The war, of course, proved the unfitness of the zeppelin for combat, and thus Eckener moved to make it the major vehicle for peacetime air travel.

While most Germans staggered under the psychological impact of the loss of the war and the overthrow of the conservative order, Eckener promptly turned with single-minded resolve to preserve the construction company of the recently deceased Count Zeppelin, to retain a nucleus of fliers, and to put passenger ships into the skies as soon as possible. Here he combined his passion for the technology with the conviction that thereby Germany could gain a new kind of international recognition to compensate for her massive defeat. The ink was hardly dry on the Treaty of Versailles in August 1919 when the first postwar zeppelin was already flying and a sistership was under construction. Belatedly, the Allies moved to shut down the construction and ground the airship, but Eckener had the bit in his teeth. Others in the company were prepared to give up airship building and flying, but Eckener pressed them to keep the technology alive by delaying dismantling of the works, by seeking to move construction abroad, and finally by contracting to build a reparations airship for the U.S. Navy. That gave him his great opportunity: he built the finest airship ever and flew it across the Atlantic for delivery in October 1924. The zeppelin, Germany, and Eckener became an international sensation.[5]

From this success Eckener maneuvered internationally and within Germany to build the first larger ship for transatlantic service. As we recall the great popular enthusiasm of the later 1920s for all aspects of aviation, it is easy to overlook the formidable obstacles that Eckener faced. Building an airship cost millions of dollars when planes could be built for thousands. Eckener had no commanding government position and no government funds on which to draw. His factory stood under the threat of destruction according to provisions of the Treaty of Versailles; his company had limited financial resources. Still, with a combination of iron will, shrewd psychological insight, and some luck, he achieved his objective. Less than five years later his ship (the *Graf Zeppelin*) opened the age of transoceanic air travel by circling the globe—21,000 miles with three intermediate landings.

At the moment of Eckener's first transatlantic triumph in 1924, Thomson was head of the air ministry in Britain's first Labour government. At the outbreak of the 1914 war he had been stationed in the Balkan Peninsula. In 1915–16 he was military attaché in Romania where he once narrowly escaped death in a zeppelin raid on Bucharest. Subsequently he served in Palestine, then with the Allied Supreme War Council, and finally with the British delegation to the peace conference. His disillusionment with the postwar settlement and the policies of the government produced a change in his life almost as dramatic as Eckener's in 1906: Thomson gave up an assured career with the British establishment and joined the opposition Labour party. His friends and former associates thought him mad as he lived in restricted circumstances and lost elections in 1919, 1922, and 1923. His genuine belief in moderate socialism had been slowly maturing. In addition, he was caught up in the British aviation enthusiasm of the early 1920s and became a firm believer in the commercial potential of the airship.

Though Thomson himself became an airship enthusiast, Englishmen generally were not so convinced. With the terrors of the wartime zeppelin raids in recent memory, there was nothing in England comparable to the German pride in airships. However, the British navy and air ministry did experiment variously with captured German zeppelins and new ships built to German designs. Between 1919 and 1921 the British public witnessed a series of accidents that culminated in the loss of a great new dirigible, R 38, built for America. The best of the British airship experts also perished with this ship. At that time, all of the naval and most of the air officials wanted out.

The surviving airship believers wanted a new beginning; after all, even then the best airplane still could only carry a dozen passengers less than 500 miles. In three years of seemingly interminable conferences, two basic decisions were finally made: (1) Britain would abandon the whole ill-starred legacy of copying German zeppelins and would launch a new program of design and engineering based on fundamental research and step-by-step experimentation; (2) this program would be government-financed and focused on commercial airships to strengthen the ties of empire.[6]

Comdr. Dennistoun Burney, an engineer with the Vickers armaments firm and inventor of the minesweeping paravane, spearheaded various projects to improve, to combine, or to rescue the British airship venture. He was the major civilian in that enterprise and was ably supported by Barnes Wallis, who had designed an original airship (the R 80) that was not completed until after the war and hardly had a chance to prove its worth. Burney's Imperial Airship Scheme was well advanced in consultations with the British air minister, Sir Samuel Hoare, when the Conservative government fell in January 1924.

At this point Thomson, the airship enthusiast, came onto the scene. Soon elevated to a peer, he took the name of Britain's most important airship station and became Lord Thomson of Cardington. He adopted the goals of the Burney project, but he completely changed its implementation. Two fundamentally new ships were to be designed and built—the largest ever, for 100 passengers and tons of cargo. One, in continuity of the Burney scheme, was contracted with Vickers; the other would be built by the Royal Airship Works at Cardington in a "blend of State and private enterprise designed to bring out the best in both without a monopoly in either."[7] Here was injected

The *Graf Zeppelin* visits Cardington, spring 1930. (York University Archives)

a political influence that probably contributed significantly to the ultimate British airship disaster. The Labour government could not endanger its Liberal support by full nationalization of the airship building program. So it compromised instead with a competitive venture that pitched capitalism against socialism and produced quite unanticipated technological and bureaucratic disadvantages that dogged the government ship, the R 101, to the very last. Although Lord Thomson would be out of office between November 1924 and June 1929, these decisions determined official British airship policies until the disaster of October 1930 which would also claim Thomson's life.

Meanwhile, in Germany, citizen Eckener pursued his single-minded purpose. While the Allied powers were delaying and quarreling among themselves about dismantling the Zeppelin works, Eckener in mid-1925 commemorated the twenty-fifth jubilee of the old Count's first flight by launching a nationwide appeal for public contributions to build the new ship. He capitalized psychologically on nostalgia for old times, upon the precedent of public financial support for Count Zeppelin in dark days of disaster in 1908, and on the widespread public enthusiasm for Germany's new postwar image in the skies.[8] Progress was not easy. When Stresemann first heard of the project (just as his sensitive Locarno negotiations were getting under way) and he told Eckener he probably could not attend the function, the airshipman told the foreign minister he had not been invited.[9] That was the clue for Eckener's whole relationship with the Weimar government. No less than four times in 1925–26 Eckener's enterprise came up for discussion by the full cabinet in Berlin. Prussia and other states forbade official collecting in their areas; the foreign ministry was appalled; General von Seeckt and the Reichswehr had very different policies for the future of German aviation.[10] Eckener was undeterred. For more than a year he and other Zeppeliners conducted a marathon speaking tour and collection campaign up and down Germany, in Austria, and among German minorities in central Europe. Everywhere he advanced the airship as the symbol of German cultural renascence. As of mid-1926 he had won: by fortunate circumstance the Allies removed their punitive aircraft restrictions and the government finally assented to official fundraising throughout Germany, though complaining that it would inevitably be forced to make up for any shortfall. The objectors were right. The campaign *did* fall short and Berlin was ultimately forced to provide subventions to complete a project it had never approved. Thus was shown the remarkable interconnection between a determined man, a highly visible and attractive technology, and a broad public sense of psychological compensation for the humiliations of Versailles.[11]

The qualities of Lord Thomson's personal involvement with airships were very different from those of Eckener. Visionaries though both men were, Thomson had nothing comparable to the decades of Eckener's intimate experience with construction and flying; he only had traveled twice in an airship as a passenger before his final, fatal flight. But he did have enthusiastic conviction about the potential of the vehicle. He had boundless confidence in the abilities of subordinate teams of designers and engineers to produce a new, perfected breed of airships. He believed that the socialist (Cardington) ship would be better because it could draw upon greater resources, conduct more experiments, and contain more innovations. Technologically this circumstance would become a major flaw. In airplanes (small units at small cost) experimentation, and changes resulting therefrom, could move progressively from one prototype to the next, each unit discrete and individually tested. But the government airship (with dimensions of an ocean liner and costing millions) was a single prototype subject to constant experiment and change in various details while in the process of construction. Although individual aspects (diesel motors, new gas cell fittings, etc.) were tested separately, there was no way of knowing how all these things would work together when the ship finally took to the skies. In all fairness, it should be indicated that the designers and engineers as a group were almost as naively assured as Thomson was. Finally, the air minister had full confidence in the ability of Britain's airshipmen who, in all truth, had only a small fraction of the accumulated experience and wisdom of the Germans. Over all these aspects Thomson would preside like the conductor of the orchestra; but unlike Sir Thomas Beecham, he was only partially familiar with the score and did not effectively react to the disharmony evident at rehearsals.

The role of government and the character of public opinion also were different in England. There was full continuity and commitment of official sponsorship for the Imperial Airship Scheme through the Conservative and Labour governments from 1924 to 1930. The British people, however, had nothing like the mass psychological involvement of the Germans. Government leaders, especially the air minister, thus came increasingly under pressure to demonstrate the viability of their project as the years wore on. And wear they did from one delay to another: changes in design, strikes, problems in construction, and more strikes. Year after year the fulfillment was postponed. Public opinion and parliament became restive and skeptical as ever-rising costs followed delays and, worst of all, the Germans appeared to be winning the competition for long-distance airship triumphs.[12]

Thomson was out of office from 1925 until 1929. He spent these years avidly watching and propagating the cause of airships in speaking tours and publications.[13] When he returned as air minister for the second Labour government in 1929, he was under pressure to bring the program to an early effective culmination. Inevitably there were the elements of personal conviction, his political ambition, and his commitment to scoring successes for socialism. The significance of these factors was intensified by the German accomplishments of their global zeppelin flight in 1929 and the first service to South America in May 1930. At that point both British airships had flown only in trials, and the government ship had to be sent back to Cardington for major rebuilding because it could not conceivably make the projected flight to India in its original design.

There were additional pressures. Because the two ships were experimental prototypes, there had to be plans for additional ships and expanded ground service facilities. Where would the money come from? How could the program and its political freight be rescued? Thomson seemed to find the answer in the Imperial Conference scheduled for mid-October of 1930. Previous Imperial Conferences had been intimately involved in planning the airship services. Canada, India, and Egypt already had built facilities. It was time that the members of the empire should further assist to realize the imperial project.[14]

It was Lord Thomson's only choice. Discounting the exaggerated personal ambition attributed to him, there was still the fact that everything he had stood and campaigned for in the past decade was at stake: imperial communication by airship, socialist principles of enterprise, and his personal identification with these two causes. In full confidence that they could do their

R 101 at Cardington mast prior to departure, Oct. 4, 1930. (Quadrant House, No. 10291)

work effectively, he gave the builders at Cardington their deadline for late September. When notified of further delays, he responded: "I must insist on the programme for the Indian flight being adhered to, for I have made my plans accordingly."[15] And they were adhered to, including departure into the teeth of an autumn storm. On the night of 4–5 October, Lord Thomson, the cream of Britain's airship personnel, and the whole Imperial Airship Scheme perished in the explosion of R 101 on a hillside in northern France. When the funeral cortege and accompanying military units somberly moved among a million watching citizens in London a few days later, it was the greatest public peacetime pageant since the coronation of George V in 1910. And close behind the coffins walked Dr. Hugo Eckener with his small delegation of Zeppeliners.

Unlike as their personalities were, Eckener and Thomson had in common their resolute confidence in the practicality of the airship and a vision of its future in the service of their nations and international amity. They differed in their degrees of knowledge of the technology and the finesse of airship flying. They also contrasted in the circumstances and character of their political manipulation.

In every respect Eckener was always on much surer ground than Thomson because he knew and understood intimately both the technology and its operation. After a few early adverse experiences with each, he never accepted *any* engineering or operational aspect on faith. Everything had to be tried, checked, and (if possible) proven in advance of application. He had an astute

The two patriarchs of R 101 prior to departure, Oct. 4, 1930: Lt. Col. V. C. Richmond, Asst. Dir. Airship Development, and Lord Thomson, Secretary of State for Air. Both were lost in the disaster. (Joe Binks, G. Chamberlain Archives)

understanding of mass psychology and reasonably understood the German psyche and character. He had a healthy skepticism, indeed disdain, of bureaucracy and public servants. He never hesitated to accept even a rough fight with politicians or businessmen whom he considered less astute than himself. But he was *enormously* respectful of the forces of weather and what he knew to be the safety parameters of airship flying. For all his vision, he regarded his objectives and dealt with individuals and circumstances as a solidly prag-

R 101 funeral cortege, London, Oct. 11, 1930. (G. Chamberlain Archives)

matic realist. He seldom took a chance, but when he sensed an advantage in his struggles, he could press it to the point of ruthlessness. His last opponents were the Nazis, and they overcame him only by the cumulative pressure of circumstances and by finally giving airships the support they required at *their* price.

Thomson was equally a man of character but of very different accomplishments and style. He had the training of a military engineer, but for all his enthusiasm for airships, he had no pragmatic knowledge of their construction or any experience in their operation. He understood the need for better meteorological training in England and pressed for it at the air ministry, but he was quite innocent in his psychic relationship with the forces of weather. Thomson was a man probably born to command in a characteristic British establishment pattern. His socialist convictions hardly changed his social manner; indeed, it was the persistence of his style, his connections, and his establishment know-how that made him such an asset to that government of working men who had to get along with a British society whose patterns of behavior they would not then change. In his relations with the British public, Thomson was most often the patient persuader, convinced that the people could and would acquire "the habit of the air." He was concerned that Britain seize the moment of aviation opportunity and apprehensive lest she miss it. He remained confident that England's best aeronautical brains could provide all the requisite solutions.[16] In councils and in Parliament he struggled with gradually diminishing success. When he saw circumstances closing in upon him, he did with quiet resolution and a kind of self-certain innocence, what he thought was required of him as a leader to see the project through. It was no pose when he had earlier replied to a question about the possible hazard of airship R 101, "She's as safe as a house—except for the millionth chance."[17]

Eckener and Thomson each operated by the dictates of his personality, experience, and style. The crucial difference was that British technology had not caught up with that of the Germans, that English workmanship was poorer, that Thomson had too much trust in his experts, and that he apparently felt that the vision and the program would be lost if he did not move decisively in the autumn of 1930. Eckener would later be defeated, but Thomson was trapped by circumstances and his interpretation of them.

What matters now is that we have here the first instance of twentieth-century aerotechnology and politics interlocked in government-industrial enterprise. In that relatively more primitive technological era there was greater room for the play of personalities. More recently the space programs of the 1960s and the equally international SST competition of the 1970s have given far greater dimensions to the thrust of technological visionaries, to political ambition, and to the exploitation of technology in the competition for national prestige. In the absence of most documentation, we can only sense the patterns of these current interrelationships. In the case of Eckener, Thomson, and the airships, however, the interplay of politics, personality, and technology has become clear. Possibly it can serve as some model for the study of more recent phenomena.

CHAPTER 9   F. W. (Willy) von Meister: Portrait of an Airship Businessman

F. W. (Willy) von Meister, 1975.
(Von Meister Family Archives)

"You couldn't *miss* me in a crowded room with 200 people!"

In his full and richly harmonious voice Willy von Meister was telling me over the phone to Newark airport how I should find him at the Suburban Hotel in Summit when the airport bus dropped me there. He arrived a few minutes after I did and even in the empty reception hall, he made a distinct impression with his height of six and a half feet and the slightly more than two hundred pounds that he carried gracefully. His courtly manner, gracious without a hint of self-consciousness, marked him as a man of fine upbringing and sophisticated social experience. At age seventy he appeared in the prime of life, with his clear eyes, full face, and carefully groomed grey-silver hair. Needless to say, he was impeccably dressed.

I had known of F. W. von Meister since 1930 when, as a high school senior, I had sent a group of letters to his offices for dispatch from various points of the first triangle Pan American flight of the *Graf Zeppelin*. He directed the New York establishment of the Luftschiffbau Zeppelin, arranging for all aspects of planning and servicing the airship flights—except for booking passengers, which was handled by the Hamburg-America Steamship Company (HAPAG), which had processed the zeppelin passenger details of the DELAG since 1909. It was a fine bit of luck when I had learned in Washington the year before that he was still living near New York and a great source of airship information. So I had written to him in May 1973, hoping to visit him later that summer. Now I was sitting with him in his car, driving through the New Jersey countryside toward his home in Peapack. We had exchanged the necessary preliminaries and inevitably came to the most dramatic question—the destruction of the *Hindenburg*.

"Well, I'll tell you how I saw it, Professor. . . ." He stretched his left arm out so that his hand rested just above the air condition vent on the dashboard and let the cold air circulate up into his jacket sleeve. "I was there at Lakehurst with Rosendahl, watching the airship come in at about dusk. It had been raining and the air was heavy with humidity. The ship was doing an 'American' (or high) landing. This involved attaining static equilibrium at about a hundred feet, dropping lines forward, having these picked up by the landing party and brought over to the stub mooring mast. There the lines would be attached to a winch that would then draw the ship down to the field. As the ship slowly circled the field, there was a ripple along the top of the outer cover midship toward the tail, then a momentary sag. The ship dropped ballast and leveled out. There was another ripple, a sag, a ballast drop and ship leveling. By now the ship was almost directly over head. We were facing in a westerly direction. Rosie was at my right looking left, upward across my line of vision, toward the bow of the *Hindenburg* as the first lines were being dropped. I happened to be looking upward to the right toward the tail. Suddenly there was an orange-yellow light at the top of the ship, just forward of the upper vertical fin. The flare plunged downward, apparently along the vertical gas shaft to about the center of the hull. For the tiniest moment it gave off a glow like a lantern being lit. Immediately there followed an upward, outward explosion and billowing of flame. All this occurred in fractions of a second."

"Later, with the report of the investigation commissions, I was convinced by Professor Dieckmann's theory of an electrostatic origin of the fire. He had conducted tests which showed the new kind of 'dope' applied to the outer covering of the ship had produced a dielectric constant different by several orders of magnitude from materials previously used. My own impression of the origin of the fire was confirmed by the surviving crewman, who had been stationed inside the hull, near the bottom of the lower vertical fin. He had described his looking up and seeing the 'lantern lighted' and the subsequent sequence of events."

By now Willy was maneuvering in the parking lot of a restaurant in Peapack. We entered the premises. He was cordially greeted by the maître d' who led us to a table in a quiet corner. A single rose in a slender vase set off the white table linen, gleaming silver, and sparkling crystal. During the leisurely lunch we talked about various things. I particularly recall Willy recounting his family history and early contact with the zeppelin business.

"My mother was born in London in 1871 of American parents. They had come to England in 1860 from Charleston and had never returned to the States. She 'came out,' as they say, in the early 1890s and moved in quite a London social whirl. Here she met my father, Wilhelm von Meister, at that point with the German embassy and later prefect at Homburg, a spa near Wiesbaden frequented by the German aristocracy and important international businessmen."

"She married my father in 1900. She was a charming woman, very gifted socially. She soon found acceptance and welcome at the home of the German dowager empress, the eldest daughter of Queen Victoria and mother of Kaiser Wilhelm II. This contact opened into the imperial court and my parents were soon frequent guests when the kaiser came to Homburg. Shortly before I was born in 1903, the crown prince asked to become my godfather. Soon after my birth, when the kaiser was again in Homburg, he also asked to be my godfather. My mother was in some embarrassment as she explained to him that there was already one imperial godfather in view. 'That's no problem,' said the kaiser with a sovereign gesture, 'we'll endow this young man with *two* imperial godfathers; that should double his chances in our empire!' "[1]

"By the time I had graduated from the *Gymnasium* in 1920, the empire had ceased to exist and my godfathers were exiled in Holland. I went to university, majoring in mechanical engineering. As you perhaps know, my grandfather von Meister had been a technical man (a chemist) and together with two others had established the large dye industry of Farbwerke Hoechst. When I graduated from Darmstadt Technical University in early 1924, the future in Germany was very bleak. We had just come through the horrendous inflation and I saw few prospects there."

"My uncle, Walter vom Rath, was then head of the Farbwerke. I could have started there, but he thought the future was not very bright. About that time my parents entertained a visiting American. He strongly encouraged me to seek my fortune in America. I left Germany in late February of 1924 and went to work in the Star-Durant auto agency in Newark. That summer I returned home for a visit and went down to Friedrichshafen; my uncle had some connection with the Zeppelin Company there. I met an engineer at Maybach Motors and got the notion of opening an agency in the New York area to sell the expensively fashionable Maybach cars and creating a market for Maybach engines in the boat business. One day at the Kurgarten Hotel I also first met Garland Fulton, who was then head of the American mission there overseeing construction of the reparations airship LZ 126. It was the beginning of a lifelong friendship. I returned to America late that summer with an agency-dealership for Maybach engines and parts. When LZ 126 had completed her spectacular transatlantic flight in October, I went to Lakehurst and got a contract to service the Maybach engines in the airship, now named *Los Angeles*. Two of my men worked much of their time on these motors until they were later replaced by American engines."

After lunch we drove out of the little town of Peapack into a countryside of low rolling hills. Soon we entered a green valley, then turned off, up a gentle forested hillside. After a broad turn through the woods we approached the garage of a spacious two-story home built into the hillside. Willy pressed a button on a small instrument, the garage door began to lift, and he turned to me with a cordial smile. "Welcome to 'Pushbutton Paradise'," he said.

In the garage we left the car, got the luggage, and started for the interior basement door. I dropped my suitcase to admire a slightly water-stained rectangular picture on the wall. Eighteen inches high and nearly three feet long, it was a full picture of LZ 130, sistership of the *Hindenburg*, with cutaway views of the interior at several points. A bold caption at the upper left read: The LZ 130 IS GERMANY'S BID—for aerial passenger traffic on the North Atlantic in the summer of 1938. It came from an article in *Fortune* magazine (July 1938), dramatizing competition of the flying-boat plans of Boeing, Douglas, Consolidated, and Sikorsky *vs.* the zeppelin, between America and Europe. Into the house we went: utility area, recreation room, and a long hallway lined with bookcases. On one wall hung a handsome watercolor of the *Hindenburg* over a hazy New York cityscape. Up the stairs we went into an entrance hall that opened on a spacious living room overlooking the valley, seemingly carried on the tops of the trees. Willy pointed toward the bedroom wing of the comfortable home and I settled in.

I was still dozing when Willy knocked on the door to announce that "aahftanoon tea" would soon be served. He had not yet appeared when I came to the living room and that gave me an opportunity to examine it more closely than one politely should. It was a veritable museum! Handsome baroque and Biedermeier secretaries and cupboards were spaced along the interior walls, offset by comfortable chairs and couches in colorful slipcovers. The walls displayed several large family oil portraits and a bold coat of arms of the Colloredo-Mansfelds, the family of Willy's deceased wife. Here also—and in other rooms of the house—were tinted eighteenth- and nineteenth-century prints of towns and castled landscapes. The artistic taste of the family was reflected in the handsome china displayed in the cupboards—Dresden, Meissen, Royal Prussian Porcelain Works and a brilliant collection of Viennese Augarten porcelain figurines. Older and newer styles blended easily in this hospitable room above the treetops.

Miss Gusla, an attractive young woman who managed the household, brought in the silver tea service and placed it on a low table near the fireplace. Willy came in and courteously thanked "Fräulein Gusla"—this was a bilingual house. He settled into an ample comfortable armchair, which he later identified as "the throne." We began talking again, sometimes English, sometimes German. He was a fascinating raconteur as he spoke in his cultivated resonant voice, with diction more English than American and a trace of Continental accent. His lively narrative developed a further dimension with interpretative movements of his head and hands at dramatic moments, when his gift of lingual mimicry put one in the presence of a tight-lipped Prussian, a talkative south German, or a drawling midwesterner. Occasionally his right hand would caress a large red plush frog with two staring black button eyes squatting at the front of the right arm of his chair.

We began to talk of the various people he had known in the airship years. Of course he began with Hugo Eckener. "I first met the doctor the evening the *Graf Zeppelin* landed at Lakehurst after its dramatic maiden flight across the North Atlantic [October 12–15, 1928]. The excitement there was incredible. The zeppelin had already brought traffic to a standstill when it passed over New York City that afternoon. Tens of thousands of people converged on the Naval Airship Station. Traffic was in a terrible snarl for miles around. Inside the station it wasn't much better. Officials, naval people, friends, and hundreds of reporters jammed the area outside the hangar where the ship was berthed. Hugh Allen, the head of Goodyear publicity, was supposed to have made arrangements to handle the passengers and their luggage, the mails, and so on. Well, it was a terrible mess. American immigration officials were making all kinds of unnecessary difficulties, and customs officials were no better.

"I was near enough and saw at one point that Dr. Eckener was having great difficulties in making himself understood. I asked him if I could help him with interpreting or anything else. He seemed quite relieved at the prospect and immediately put me to work. First we straightened out the immigration formalities. Then we found a place for the twenty passengers away from the crowds. I supervised unloading and moving of the baggage through customs. Only then could I turn to the real purpose of my trip—to inquire if any assistance was needed for engine maintenance. They had had a rough trip, including a very dangerous situation when the cover tore on one of the horizontal stabilizers and Dr. Eckener's son, Knut, really risked his life crawling out over the exposed surface and making some emergency repairs. I established contact for facilitating various services for the zeppelin. It was long after midnight before the most necessary things were done. Then Dr. Eckener sought me out to thank me for my help and asked if I could continue to assist him."

"That was the beginning of a wonderful association and a great friendship that lasted over the decades until he died in 1954. The next day I was in New York City, where he and his officers were given one of those great, traditional ticker tape parades through lower Manhattan and then up Fifth Avenue. I didn't go along for that because there were a lot of things to do in the city, but I was there for the great banquet that evening at the Waldorf-Astoria. After that things happened in a whirl. We went to Washington, where we were received by President Coolidge, then up to Capitol Hill for a round of meetings, and on to some of the embassy circuit. It wasn't all socializing for Dr. Eckener. Wherever possible, with officials of the Navy and State Department, with congressmen and senators, Eckener was pressing with his plans for transatlantic zeppelin service. It was the same thing when I went on west with him, to Akron, Cleveland, and Detroit. In Ohio we talked in detail with Goodyear-Zeppelin, in which Dr. Eckener's German firm had a 25 percent interest. In Detroit we saw Henry Ford, Walter Chrysler, and the General Motors people—always talking air transportation, motors, and business prospects. Dr. Eckener was an old hand at dealing in such situations; but you can imagine what an impression it all made on me, a very young man, just past my twenty-fifth birthday!"

"In the evening of October 27, as I was driving Dr. Eckener back to Lakehurst, he invited me to join him on the return flight of the *Graf Zeppelin* to Germany. Well, I accepted with great appreciation and so I had that wonderful experience." [Several years later Willy wrote: "Just got back from a trip to Europe last week. I went over on the Concorde—first flight of British Airways from Dulles to Heathrow. The flight time was 3 hours and 38 minutes! This, compared to 71 hours, 58 minutes with the *Graf Zeppelin* from Lakehurst to Friedrichshafen in 1928, is quite a major improvement."]

Willy recalled little detail about the work in his office in preparation for the *Graf Zeppelin* global flight of August 1929. Still, he had a vivid recollection of his sojourn in Los Angeles late that month to assist Eckener and the airship during its thirty-hour stopover at Mines Field.[2] "I went out there by the fastest possible way on the new rail-air service begun that year by Transcontinental Air Transport: TAT—'Take a Train!' Out there I met [Lt. Comdr. T. G. W.] Tex Settle, who represented the navy that was supplying extra hydrogen and a ground crew of several hundred sailors. This was just one of the examples of early American-German cooperation in developing joint experience in flying and handling airships. Every time a zeppelin came to America, or flew from there, at least one American airship officer was aboard to learn from German experience. I was also looking forward to meeting my friend from Lakehurst, Lt. Comdr. Rosendahl, who was flying on the zeppelin around the world as the American observer aboard."

"Tex Settle and I stayed close to the radio that last day of the long Pacific crossing, getting hourly position reports from the airship. Here we got a wonderful example of Dr. Eckener's use of psychology in airship flying— you know, he had a Ph.D. in psychology from Leipzig University in the early 1890s. Well, we noticed as the reports came in during that day that the zeppelin was not making its usual speed. It did not arrive over San Francisco until late that summer afternoon. Nor did they arrive at Los Angeles until long after midnight. Early the next morning, as I drove in to the Biltmore with Dr. Eckener, I asked him: 'What slowed you down up there along the northwest coast? Did you have some kind of motor trouble?' He turned to me. I saw that knowing smile on his face. 'But my dear Mr. von Meister,' he said, 'when for the first time in world history an airship flies across the Pacific, should it not arrive at sunset over the Golden Gate?' His calculation was entirely correct. The *Graf Zeppelin* got a tumultuous reception in San Francisco!"

Willy rejoined Eckener in New York. The commander sent his ship back to Germany, while he stayed behind for several months for intensive negotiations in Manhattan, Washington, and Akron. Willy was involved in most of these efforts and deliberations. These weeks were a climax of commercial airship expectations. With the stock market crash of October 1929, financial potentialities began to wane. Goodyear-Zeppelin had just dedicated its new Airship Dock in Akron and began building the first of its two naval dirigibles. Simultaneously the company began a long process of pressing for legislation in the congress to provide federal subsidies for commercial airship construction and operations comparable to existing merchant marine support. Yet, there was trouble ahead. Pan American Airways would rapidly control the airways of the Caribbean and expand down the east coast of South America. Juan Trippe was an experienced infighter on the Washington political scene. He was by then committed to flying boats and was already eyeing the North Atlantic and the Pacific for future air service. The commercial airship was thus faced with a formidable technological, business, and political opponent at the very moment it needed smooth financial and political flying.

In May–June 1930 the *Graf Zeppelin* made another spectacular flight in a broad triangle from Germany to Brazil to Lakehurst, and back to Friedrichshafen. Hopes for airship travel soared. All summer long the *Graf* made further newsworthy flights to the North Cape, all around central Europe, and to Russia. Then came a shattering blow to airship prospects. The British airship R 101 crashed in early October on the first leg of a widely publicized flight to India. Among the victims was Lord Thomson, the British air minister, and with him died Britain's plans for a network of airship lines to link the empire more closely together.

In this connection Willy recalled a significant experience:

"Dr. Eckener was, of course, proud of the zeppelin achievement as a German accomplishment. Still, he always stressed the airship role in terms of a peaceful international future. Through Goodyear he was tied in with American developments; and he also had a strong, positive interest in the British airship plans. England's R 101 was designed with nets around the gas cells to relieve the structure from the expansive stress of the cells pushing against the hull framework. When the airship was in flight the cells swayed inside the structure and developed leaks where they chafed against the girders."

"Through the 'grapevine' this trouble came to the attention of Dr. Eckener and/or his engineers. I was just visiting him in Friedrichshafen. He told me that he was worried about the safety of Lord Thomson's flight to India. Since I had told him that I was stopping off in London to spend a couple of weeks with my mother, he asked me if I had any connections that would help making contact with Lord Thomson. I told him I would try. He explained to me his basic point of view that commercial airship development could only progress if it were an internationally successful venture and that he was anxious to help the British overcome the problems of their cell placement in R 101. He told me that if I could see Lord Thomson very privately, would I please convey the following message to him: Dr. Eckener would send two or three of his top engineers for a confidential visit to England, with no publicity about their trip, but with the intention of consulting with the British engineers about alleviating the problem of the swaying cells."

"Through the connections my mother had in London it was easy for me to arrange an appointment with the British air minister. It was on a cool day in late April, and there was a cheerful blaze in the fireplace of the paneled and comfortably furnished office of Lord Thomson. He was extremely cor-

Willy von Meister in 1929 with J. C. Davidson [Union Carbide Corp.] and Dr. Hugo Eckener. (Von Meister Family Archives)

dial. I was alone with him and explained to him what I have just told you. He replied that this was a very kind and interesting gesture of Dr. Eckener's, that he would consider it, and give me his reply in a few days. Soon he called me back and told me that his engineers were convinced they had resolved the problem by installing pads on the edges of the structure to prevent further chafing of the cells. He thanked Dr. Eckener very much for his offer and indicated that R 101 would proceed to India as scheduled."

That account raised the question of helium for use in airships outside the United States. Nonflammable helium was available nowhere else in the world, and American legislation in 1927 forbade any appreciable export because it was considered a vital natural resource necessary for naval airship scouting. Yet Eckener apparently had some hopes of getting the legislation amended to benefit foreign commercial airships. About a month after the R 101 disaster he announced in an address to the American Chamber of Commerce in Berlin that the next zeppelin would be designed to fly with helium. This meant scrapping LZ 128, already partially under construction, but constricted by the dimensions of the old hangar in Friedrichshafen. Plans were now for a much larger hangar to permit building of a *Hindenburg*, with which it would be possible to shift from hydrogen to helium when the opportunity came.

I asked Willy how tenaciously Eckener had tried to get helium from America. He thought several moments and then said: "I recall that Dr. Eckener spoke of exchanging German airship experience and even a fully operable airship for American helium in early 1930s. I know he talked very privately with the secretary of the navy, with naval airshipmen, and with the Goodyear people; but there was no effective follow-up. This was a very political issue. Politics meant publicity and Dr. Eckener shunned publicity in the helium matter, feeling that it would adversely affect the zeppelin operation getting under way between Germany and Brazil. Probably Litchfield and others at Goodyear-Zeppelin tried to help him. With the *Hindenburg* about to fly in 1935–36, Eckener was under constant pressure about helium; but he couldn't publicly press for it, lest it undermine confidence in the airship. Nor could he publicly voice doubts because that would jeopardize the whole new North Atlantic service."

"Late in the fall of 1936, I met with some officials and Capt. Ernst Lehmann at the air ministry in Berlin. At that time I was special representative of the Deutsche Zeppelin-Reederei in New York and vice president of the newly established American Zeppelin Transport, Inc. I was trying to arrange for training of American airshipmen in 1937 by placing two or three of them on each flight of the *Hindenburg* and her anticipated sistership. 'What can you offer in compensation?' Lehmann asked me. I replied that we would pay the regular passenger fare and in addition would make every effort (with the backing of the U.S. Navy, the National City Bank of New York, Goodyear in Akron, and others) to secure helium for the DZR ships. Lehmann replied with a touch of arrogance: 'That is really no inducement; we have been operating our commercial service with hydrogen very successfully for years.' I responded, 'My dear Lehmann, I sincerely hope you will not have cause to regret your opinion.' The *Hindenburg* disaster occurred the following May and Lehmann lost his life there."

Politics were always a factor and frequently a problem in Eckener's airship career. He had successfully kept the equipment and hangars of the Luft-schiffbau Zeppelin intact during the early postwar era of Allied determination to remove the zeppelin from Germany. When Eckener raised funds for con-struction of the *Graf* in 1925–27, he had encountered considerable opposition from some Berlin government circles. Already in 1932 he had his first major encounter with the Nazis, when he refused to make the zeppelin field and hangar available for a regional Nazi rally. Willy recalled:

"There was other trouble when Dr. Eckener prepared to fly the *Graf* to the Chicago World's Fair in late October 1933. The German embassy in Washington received threats of anti–Nazi sabotage to the ship, which had carried the official swastika markings on the port side of the vertical tail fins since July of that year. I had to contact officials in Chicago about that. Instead of trying to land near the fair, as was originally planned, we stopped at a more remote site. On landing we were immediately surrounded by a cordon of dozens of armed deputies. A large midwesterner strode up to me and introduced himself as the sheriff of Cook County. 'Mr. von Meister,' he drawled, 'I'm here to protect you and your ship against any attack!' [Willy's mimicry of the midwestern accent was fabulous.] All this was very disagreeable to Dr. Eckener, who knew how many Chicagoans had originally come from his own country. On departure he took the *Graf* on a long, low circular clockwise flight around the edge of the city, showing inwardly the traditional red-white-black colors on the starboard side of the fins. He later said to me: 'Did you think I wanted to show my friends the swastika?' "

"On our return to Lakehurst and Washington, we had a call from the White House, inviting Dr. Eckener to 'tea with Mrs. Roosevelt.' The caller said he would indicate later when precisely we should arrive. The next message came to the effect that 'tea' would be served at 10 A.M. I was bewildered. When we arrived at the White House, we were promptly brought to the Oval Office. There was no sign of Mrs. Roosevelt. The president greeted us cordially, saying he hoped we would understand this strange arrangement. On this basis he could receive us *without* having to invite the German ambassador!"

"Dr. Eckener clearly expressed his anti–Nazi views privately, though his public actions also indicated where he stood. He refused to be aboard either ship when the two zeppelins were requisitioned for a three-day propaganda flight up and down Germany in late March of 1936 to drum up enthusiasm for the Rhineland plebiscite. Politics also played a role in various thoughts of the Zeppelin people in 1935–36 to shift the focus of international airship flying from Germany to then-Republican Spain. Private negotiations were well advanced to make Seville the hub of western airship service. Here the lines would converge from the United Sates, from Brazil and Argentina, and from the Far East (by way of a Dutch line from Java through India). Lufthansa would then fly the passengers from Seville to various capitals in Europe. The plans made for better operational efficiency: avoiding the worst weather on the North Atlantic route; shortening the distance to South America; and eliminating the leg between southern Spain and Germany, with its extra weather problems. The plan would have taken the zeppelins out from under direct Nazi operational surveillance and also avoided the continual irritations with the French. I don't know if the Nazis would have finally agreed to this major shift; but we Americans, the Dutch, and the Spaniards had some high financial cards to play in the game. Of course, with the Spanish revolution in July 1936, it was all washed up."

Willy recalled another dimension of Eckener's political sensitivity. "He had an important relationship with the *New York Times*. Mr. Otto Kahn had been an old classmate of my father's in Germany. He helped me a lot in my early years in New York and through him I met Mr. Adolph Ochs of the *Times*. I believe I introduced Dr. Eckener to Ochs in 1929, but at that time the zeppelin people had their exclusive news relationship with the Hearst press. Dr. Eckener again met Ochs in June 1930, at the time of the first zeppelin tricontinental flight. Thereafter he always stopped at the *Times* offices whenever he came to America, to meet with the editorial staff for long off-the-record briefings on the political situation in Germany. When Dr.

Eckener had his run-in with Goebbels in March–April 1936, and the Nazi propaganda minister had him blacklisted in the German press, I called Mr. Findley at the *Times* to ask if something couldn't be published on Dr. Eckener's behalf. The response was very cool. 'Mr. von Meister,' said Findley, 'the columns and particularly the editorial pages of the *Times* are not open to outside influence.' The next day, however, there was a strong editorial on Dr. Eckener's behalf that was widely echoed in other papers. The day after *that* I had a call from Mr. Herbert Scholz at the German embassy in Washington: 'Willy, what did you arrange with the New York papers about Eckener?' "[3]

"After the *Hindenburg* disaster Dr. Eckener and I visited President Roosevelt again to see if he could give us any help with influencing a change in the American helium export prohibition. Subsequently we went up to the Hill and lunched with some members of the Senate Armed Services Committee. Later we appeared before the House Military Affairs Committee. Dr. Eckener responded very openly to any questions of the members, but I was astonished at the depth of anti-German feeling there and the sharp queries about the German political situation. A couple of years later, just after the Nazi annexation of Austria, Dr. Eckener met my father-in-law, who was quite enthusiastic about the event. The old commander's comment to him was directly to the point: 'Count Colloredo, it is apparently not clear to you that we are being ruled by a gang of criminals. . . .' "

By now it was very late in the afternoon. We heard a motorcycle charging up the road through the trees to the house. A few moments later the front door burst open, and a very young man wearing a large motorcycle helmet strode into the room. "Take off your helmet," Willy said, "and meet Professor Meyer." Turning to me, he explained, "This is my youngest son, Seppi, who, you see, keeps us all alert." At that point I excused myself, for father and son had things to discuss.

Fräulein Gusla served dinner in a spacious dining room. Wide windows overlooked the surrounding treetops and various shades of evening played upon the nearby hillsides. We spent the dinner hour telling each other about our families and all sorts of small talk.

Later in the evening Willy asked me to join him in his study and we opened another chapter of his life with the airships. "I was never a stamp collector; but when the zeppelins began carrying mail in 1929, I started this collection of zeppelin letters." He showed me a very representative group of covers from all the major flights, including scarce items from Canada and Central America. These were all jumbled together in a large box. I urged him to preserve them more carefully and safely, for with their various American, German, and South American zeppelin stamps they constituted a collection of considerable value. Other information indicated to me what a major role Willy had played in negotiating the several postal contracts for carrying American mails on the global flight of 1929, the Pan-American flight of 1930 (with its now very valuable set of three special American zeppelin stamps), the polar flight of 1931, the Chicago visit of 1933, the transatlantic mails with the *Hindenburg* in 1936.

Though he could remember little about the various details of these negotiations, he recalled aspects of the general situation. "At the time of the global flight in 1929 it was clear to me that collectors needed more information to better serve their interests. There was a tendency for stamp dealers to keep news of the upcoming flights to themselves, so as to have an advantage in mailing covers on their own account, then offering them later for sale at higher prices. I felt that collectors should have access to all the possible information about upcoming flights. I left all that in the very capable hands of my office assistant, Mr. K. H. Royter. He handled all the arrangements for the flights from 1931 through 1937. We actually handled mails through our Madison Avenue offices, and thousands of collectors took advantage of our services, since we placed advertisements in various papers and stamp magazines. We also mailed letters on our own account and sold them afterwards to collectors for basic postage. This service applied only to German and Brazilian mails, so you will probably find a lot of letters in collections today addressed either to Hans Royter or to me. Of course, this wasn't pure altruism, because we depended heavily on collectors' mail to help finance the costs of the flights. But I think everybody profited."[4] We spent some further time in collectors' shop talk. Then we heard Seppi returning from an evening foray on his motorcycle, and it was time for me to retire.

We had breakfast the next morning in a nook off the kitchen. Willy had been up betimes and arranged an assortment of papers and books on the large dining room table. He took me into the morning sunlit room and made a small gesture with his arm: "There you are, Professor. That's about all I've been able to find. I hope it will be useful. Now you must excuse me for the rest of the morning."

I spent the time till lunch examining the material. I had already seen about two-thirds of the items: books, pamphlets, magazine and newspaper articles, copies of some letters to government offices, and various items of zeppelin memorabilia. Yet, the new items were more important than the familiar ones. There was a statistical listing of all the flights of the *Graf Zeppelin* and *Hindenburg* with all sorts of basic performance data. Directly from von Meister's offices was his year-end report of 1936 to Capt. Lehmann of some major and many minor improvements that had to be made in passenger service and other aspects of operation on the *Hindenburg* for the coming season of 1937. His office also produced a thirty-page background study indicating how DZR-AZT should move in developing American-German airship service from 1938 onward. Involved were such matters as leasing a German-built ship until Goodyear could build its own ships again, demonstrating how inflation by helium would minimally affect airship performance, and showing how relatively small American government subsidies of commercial aviation

LZ 129, *Hindenburg*, at Lakehurst, summer 1936. (John D.
Archbold)

Willy von Meister assisting at
Hindenburg passenger embarca-
tion. Lakehurst, summer 1936.
(Luftschiffbau Zeppelin)

LZ 129, *Hindenburg*, departing
hangar, Frankfurt/M., summer
1936. (Lufthansa Archives)

had been compared to those of the European nations. A small program indicated details on the *Hindenburg* VIP flight of October 9, 1936, which von
Meister had arranged together with Esso Marketers—its guest list represented
the elite of American commercial aviation and business-financial firms. There
was a two-inch pile of written sheets, the handwritten draft copy of Dr.
Eckener's memoirs, largely composed at "Pushbutton Paradise" when he was
a prolonged guest there in 1947. Later Willy and I compared the manuscript
with the printed volume; the texts were identical. Finally, there was a strange
object: a darkened aluminum disk, five inches in diameter apparently "commemorating" the *Hindenburg* disaster. The obverse bore the inscription
6.V.1937 superimposed on smoke clouds rising from the burning airship
descending on to the word "Lakehurst." The reverse showed an eagle in
soaring flight over a small swastika and a bold inscription *"Nun erst recht"*—
which translates unidiomatically into "now with renewed vigor." Willy could
not recall the source from which the plaque had come; but two years later

207

I would read in a letter Eckener had written his wife in mid-May, just after returning from the investigation at Lakehurst and reporting to the air ministry in Berlin, that Göring had used almost those very words.

Then it was time for lunch. Fräulein Gusla set the table to serve a good *Mittagessen*. We chatted amiably about various things. Willy turned to make a point. "You know, Professor," he began—and stopped. He made an impatient gesture: "I think it's silly to go on with this 'professor' business. Now why don't you call me Willy?" And so we became friends and before much longer had slipped into the familiar *du* when speaking German.

I spent part of the afternoon reading Gordon Vaeth's book on the *Graf Zeppelin* which he had written with considerable assistance from Willy about fifteen years before. At tea time I pressed Willy again with more questions, this time about the various business arrangements with Goodyear, in the New York financial community, and with Germany. As time will, it had worn away most of the detail, but some essentials remained:

"Harry Vissering, a Chicago railroad equipment manufacturer, was really the key figure in establishing the American-German airship connection. After the Allies had got their share of the postwar distribution of remaining German zeppelins, he felt America had been left out. Asserting that 'We want our airship!' he had pressed hard on the issue. He was a good friend of President Harding and through Harding got some pressure on Washington agencies. Goodyear, of course, was in the blimp business and Vissering got Paul Litchfield in Akron interested. He acted as liaison between Litchfield and Eckener. That combination brought about the reparations contract for airship LZ 126 and establishment of the Goodyear-Zeppelin Company in 1923."

"Goodyear-Zeppelin, from Dr. Eckener's point of view, was oriented toward commercial aviation, but the tremendous investment required to establish a zeppelin construction business obviously led Goodyear to seek military-naval contracts. These resulted in the building of the *Akron* and the *Macon* as naval units. Goodyear, of course, wanted to build commercial airships from these naval prototypes."

"Dr. Eckener was always uncomfortable about this aspect of his relations with Goodyear. He had staked his whole personality and career on the notion of the airship as a vehicle of commerce, a symbol of peaceful international relations and goodwill. Of course, he was technologically vitally interested in the advances in design and operation which these American ships represented. After all, they were designed by a top engineer (Dr. Karl Arnstein) who came from Luftschiffbau Zeppelin to Akron in late 1924 with twelve other specialists. But Dr. Eckener had had enough of war."

"That potential use of airships for naval-military purposes had a fateful influence on the whole airship story. Goodyear had a public relations man named Hugh Allen, who was very successful in his work. He preached a lot about the helium monopoly as 'God's great gift to American defense.' This meant that our naval airships had a preeminent advantage in any conflict. I think Goodyear pushed very hard in the mid–1920s to get the restrictive national helium legislation. It really backfired on us in the 1930s, after the navy had lost their ships. If we could only have flown the *Hindenburg* with helium."

"At first Dr. Eckener had to play ball with Goodyear pretty much the way they wanted the game. By 1935, however, both Goodyear and the American naval airshipmen were utterly dependent on German airship policies and successes. What the zeppelins did would make or break the whole airship future. Well, not exactly. Flying boats and land planes were developing rapidly. I am convinced, though, that if we had been able to get helium—and if the war had not come—the airship would have been competitive until the early 1950s. Then the speed and convenience of transatlantic airline schedules would have closed us out, just as they eliminated the oceanliners in the later 1960s. But it was a wonderful way to travel."

"That was certainly proved to our guests on the VIP flight in the early autumn of 1936. We had chartered a Pullman car train from Pennsylvania Station for our seventy-two guests to depart at about midnight from New York City. The train was shunted on to the Lakehurst Air Station siding— a few hundred feet from the mooring mast where the *Hindenburg* was stationed. Shortly after sunrise our guests were transferred by limousine from the sleeping cars to the *Hindenburg* entrance stairs below the passenger quarters. There was a heavy ground fog which made it practically impossible to see the airship from the railroad siding. The size of the ship visibly surprised many of our guests as they came aboard."

"The navigation officers had placed maps on the dining room tables—the dining room was located a few steps above the port promenade deck. Several of the guests studied the maps on which the navigator had marked the route of our trip over the autumn colors of New England. I was explaining the route just as the hatches were being closed and heard the faint signals indicating our departure. A few minutes later Nelson Rockefeller looked at his watch and asked me, 'When are we taking off?' I replied, 'But we have been in flight for several minutes.' He exclaimed, 'I don't believe it!' and rushed to the promenade deck windows. And then he saw that we were above the fog, now patchy, and moving above the shore below."

"At lunch Admiral William H. Standley, chief of naval operations, was sitting next to Dr. Eckener after demitasse was served. Other guests at the table had left to see the landscape. Dr. Eckener and I (the interpreter) sat alone at the table talking about airships and their operation. The Admiral asked Dr. Eckener confidentially for his frank opinion on the military usefulness of rigid airships for the U.S. Navy. After what seemed like several minutes Dr. Eckener looked Admiral Standley straight in the eye and shook his head no, not in view of the capability of modern airplanes. Admiral Standley seemed greatly pleased at this answer, which confirmed his own thinking. He expressed his gratitude to Dr. Eckener for his frankness and confirmed that this exchange would remain confidential. Eckener was an honest man and never compromised with his conscience."

"As we were returning we received a radio message that Lakehurst was again engulfed in ground fog and that it had been necessary to cancel flights of the two American Airlines DC-3 planes that had been scheduled to take some of our guests back to Newark, which was then New York City's commercial airport. I made a public announcement of the cancellation and that our guests would be returning to New York by special train. I also added that shortly after our arrival the *Hindenburg* would depart on schedule for the next trip to Germany. Immediately after my announcement Capt. Eddie Rickenbacker (of Eastern Airlines) came up to me and said I must have surely arranged for that airplane cancellation to demonstrate the superiority of the airship vs. the airplane!"

In the course of my two-day visit with him, Willy and I talked of many other things about the zeppelin era. He was planning to begin writing his memoirs in the autumn of 1978. In early July, however, he was killed in an automobile accident. Friends and airship buffs everywhere thus suffered the untimely loss of one of the most important and knowledgeable personalities of the commercial airship era.

CHAPTER 10

Problems of Helium and Spy Flights:
The Brief Career of LZ 130

Almost eight years before *Graf Zeppelin II* first took to the skies on September
14, 1938, the decision had been made that it and the earlier sistership, the ill-
fated *Hindenburg*, should be designed to fly with helium. The shocking loss
of Britain's R 101 on October 5, 1930, prompted Dr. Hugo Eckener to cancel
his intention to build further direct descendants from the design of the spectacularly successful *Graf Zeppelin* (LZ 127), which was too small to fly any
major distance with helium. The specifications and initial construction for
LZ 128 were then scrapped and plans were launched for a new generation
of helium zeppelins. These new intentions involved two major expenditures
and one worrisome conundrum. The first necessary expenditure was to build
an enlarged construction hangar to accommodate an airship more than one-
third greater in diameter than LZ 127. Here Count Zeppelin's loyal old supporter came to the rescue. The state of Württemburg supplied two million
marks to build a new hangar during 1929–30, alongside the venerable construction site of many of the earlier zeppelins, from LZ 74 to LZ 127. Second,
while the much greater expenses of building LZ 129 and LZ 130 were largely
borne by the Zeppelin Company, significant financial infusions came from
the Nazi government by way of some public works funds and from nearly a
million marks annually in operating subsidies for the South American flight
program. The remaining conundrum lay in the questionable availability of
indispensable helium from the United States.

Laws were passed by the U.S. Congress in 1925–27, fortifying the nation's
natural monopoly of the world's helium supply by prohibiting its export
except in minute quantities for scientific research.[1] Proponents of this measure, including the Goodyear Company, argued that it gave America a unique
dimension of national defense with airships scouting for the nation's battle
fleets. The years between the loss of R 101, the commissioning of the *Akron*
in October 1931, and the loss of the *Macon* in February 1935, saw LZ 129
nine-tenths completed in Friedrichshafen. Much German opinion has it that

Eckener made numerous efforts during that time, whenever visiting the United States, to convince American authorities to make helium available for the new generation of zeppelins, but that his appeals were firmly rejected by the Americans.[2]

Actually, the situation appears to be far less cut and dried. There is no doubt that Eckener was fundamentally concerned for the safety of his airship operations—otherwise he would not have built his new zeppelins to fly with helium. Still, there is a remarkable ambiguity about the forcefulness of his search for the essential nonflammable gas. No doubt he raised the question with various American officials close to the scene: Presidents Hoover and Roosevelt; Comdrs. Fulton, Rosendahl, Settle and other important navy personnel; some members of the congress and some top bureau officials; Vissering, Litchfield, and lobbyists Harpham and Knowles of the Goodyear Company; and, of course, with his American representative, Willy von Meister. Most likely he was informed that the American helium legislation was very firm in its exclusive intent, but that under Section 4 of the Helium Act he could make application to designated authorities for export permission. To date there has appeared no document recording a formal application for helium by Eckener, or by any other German authorities, prior to May 6, 1937. Furthermore, it is remarkable that none of these individuals with whom Eckener had official or more intimate contact, who were still living and were interviewed between 1972 and 1985, could specifically recall any legal or formal steps that Eckener had ever taken to procure American helium before the destruction of the *Hindenburg*.

These ambiguities are understandable in light of the events of their time. Since the first *Graf Zeppelin* was in a sense still an experimental airship, and since it could not be adapted to long-distance flight with helium in any case, its operation with hydrogen could be justified. While the *Hindenburg* slowly took shape between 1930 and 1936, world economic conditions changed radically for the worse, as did German politics. Foreign exchange was initially rationed by the Weimar Republic in 1932 and was rigidly controlled by the Nazis from 1933 onward. Helium, if it were to become available, would be considerably more expensive than hydrogen readily produced in Germany. By 1933 the Zeppelin Company was at its financial nadir and the Reich hoarded its foreign exchange for only the most essential imports, many of these armaments-related. Meanwhile the *Graf* was sturdily flying and its crews were acquiring ever-greater skill and familiarity with hydrogen—and therewith increasing confidence in their expertise at airship handling. Between 1934 and 1936, as LZ 129 was nearing completion, there were continuing experiments to accommodate this airship to some combination of hydrogen and helium: more sophisticated systems of water recovery to save valving the expensive helium and projects to place a hydrogen inner cell suspended within a proposed helium outer cell.[3] Nazi arrogance about various German technological feats reinforced the quietly growing assurance of the zeppelin fliers and buttressed Berlin's aversion to spend *valuta* for unnecessary imports. Finally, by supplanting the DELAG with DZR in 1935, Eckener had been kicked upstairs and removed from most of his influence in the operation of the airships.

All through the summer of 1936, as the *Hindenburg* and the *Graf* plied their trade across the Atlantic to the Americas, zeppelin enthusiasm rose and records fell. Now there were plans to increase cabin space on the *Hindenburg* for twenty-two additional passengers, thus exceeding her capabilities under helium operation. At that time Willy von Meister found Capt. Lehmann disinterested in helium. In October the DZR issued a very positive summary on the year's airship operations—for the first time ever approaching profitability—and expressed robust confidence for the 1937 season.[4] Concurrently there was also an in-house document for restricted circulation, appropriately designated as airship futurism, but still seriously outlining prospects for the next decade: thirty-six to forty airships operating worldwide by 1945, many of them German; others in joint service with America, Britain, Holland, and possibly even France and Italy. Germany would build a majority of them; some would be constructed at Cardington and Akron. A German airship academy in Frankfurt would supply the officers and crews for all these new liners in their frequent flights to the Americas, South Africa, and the Far East, together with weekly round-the-world service.[5] In neither document was there any mention of potential competition by flying boats—or even a whisper about helium.

A more sober account, but no less quietly confident, recorded the minutes of a conference at the Reich air ministry on November 20, 1936. Present were major representatives from the ministry, the Luftwaffe, the foreign office, the Zeppelin Company, and the DZR. Based on the excellent results of 1936, discussion involved plans to charter German airships to America or Britain, to expand terminal facilities at Frankfurt (a new double hangar, with a subsequent revolving hangar in prospect) to convert the *Graf* to a training ship upon the arrival of LZ 130 the following August, and anticipating LZ 131 and LZ 132 in 1938 and 1939. The protocol concluded:

> Senior Councillor Fisch once again urgently emphasized that under all circumstances helium must be obtained for the new airships. Dr. Eckener and Dr. Dürr declared that, given the great expense of helium and corresponding greater expense of building larger airships, there would also be a diminution of their operational cost-effectiveness. The builders would maintain continuing further contact with the air ministry on this issue.[6]

Almost to the day six months later, Hugo Eckener was again at the air ministry, this time to give some preliminary judgment about the *Hindenburg* disaster and to make amends for a hurried and well-publicized comment the day before that it was likely not an accident. En route to America with Germany's investigation commission, he wrote his wife about the Berlin meeting:

Nazi commemorative medallion on loss of *Hindenburg* as of May 6, 1937. Original is five inches in diameter. (Obverse) (Von Meister Family Archives)

Nazi commemorative *Hindenburg* medallion. (Reverse) (Von Meister Family Archives)

At the air ministry I first saw [General Erhard] Milch, who promptly took me to see Göring. Dürr had also arrived and went with us. Göring let us give him our opinions and then said, "I was never much for airships, but now we *have* to persist with them." I recommended that we temporarily suspend flights of the *Graf Zeppelin* until we had a better understanding of the catastrophe, and that was accepted.

We then had a long talk with Councillor Fisch about the radio broadcast I had to make over the entire German network, and in English by shortwave to the United States, counteracting my comments in Graz about the possibilities of sabotage. Well, they already considered that possibility in the U.S.A. four years ago [Chicago flight 1933] and certainly the British think it plausible.

No matter what the circumstance, we must now get helium. I sincerely regret that because of the great difficulties in obtaining it heretofore, I let myself go on using hydrogen, although we had already designed the *Hindenburg* for helium. Now the situation forces us to get it—and the Reich will foot the bill.[7]

Upon his arrival in America the next day, Eckener was quoted by the *New York Times* reporter as saying that he had never previously asked the United States for helium.[8]

Meanwhile, air minister Göring further expressed his newly won support for airships with a celebratory proclamation to the "Men of German Aviation"—and to the general German public. Once again, as in 1908, a zeppelin disaster had become a focus of public attention. This time, however, the upsurge of public sympathy was abetted as a calculated Nazi propaganda ploy. Göring praised the zeppelin as Germany's unique contribution to world aviation and memorialized the victims of the disaster: "Now with renewed vigor (*Nun erst recht*) we will utilize all our experience to reestablish air service between Germany and the United States with complete safety and forever." In the spirit of Count Zeppelin, Göring concluded, he was accelerating completion of LZ 130 at Friedrichshafen, further to bind the nations of the world together in peace.[9] His optimism was catching. For a third time in German airship history the purse of the common man opened to raise funds for a new zeppelin. Thousands of marks appeared within several days in the Reich. Germans abroad and foreign airship enthusiasts sent contributions to Reich embassies in Rio de Janeiro, Mexico City, and Washington, D.C. This politically unsponsored fountainhead of popular expression met a prompt nullifying reply from Nazi authorities. Just as the German victims of the disaster were about to be memorialized in a nationally broadcast ceremony from Bremen, the security offices of the Reich interior ministry issued an edict, which read in part, "As long as the Reich government has not authorized nationwide solicitation, all these [spontaneous] activities must forthwith cease. An [official] campaign is not likely, since the airship *Hindenburg* was fully insured."[10] Among other things, the Nazi authorities did not want Hugo Eckener to have the slightest possible leverage to enhance his own popular image.

With the emotional broadcast account of the Lakehurst catastrophe ringing in their ears, and newsreel images of the burning *Hindenburg* before their eyes, most Americans and their congressmen pressed to have the restrictive helium legislation amended so that transatlantic airship service could be resumed. The loss of the *Akron* and *Macon* stilled any remaining arguments that helium was vital for American national defense. A few voices were heard, warning that Nazi Germany might employ airships for some ultimate military purpose or to divert the inert gas to some other military use; but popular sympathy for change in the helium law far outweighed these cautions. While DZR in the Reich boasted that Germans by the score had already prepaid passage on future zeppelin flights, AZT in America made a survey of public opinion about airship travel and found two-thirds of the sample still favorable.[11] The small minority of rigid airshipmen in American naval aviation, of course, enthusiastically favored helium for Germany. Flight with the zeppelins was the only opportunity they would have to maintain their skills until America again built rigid airships. Goodyear, needless to say, worked overtime in Washington for passage of the new law. With this American effort, in early September 1937, Congress amended the Helium Act, which President Roosevelt promptly signed.[12]

Once helium was available, the Zeppelin Company turned to convert LZ 130 to its new limitations. Not only did the inert gas cause a 7 percent loss in buoyancy, it also required about six tons of additional operating equipment. Most of the savings in weight had to come off the net payload of the airship. This adjustment was made by cutting the passengers to forty and the crew by ten; by eliminating structural and equipment weight; and by somewhat reducing reserves in fuel, water, and passengers' supplies. Beer in its heavy bottles was a casualty here, though spirits and the famed wines of the Rhine and Mosel would still be dispensed in moderate quantity. The directors of AZT carefully calculated the financial future of their own venture. They found it reasonably promising, given favorable mail contracts, a 75 percent load factor, and possible governmental subsidies.[13] In Germany financing was a secondary problem, for as Eckener had written his wife, the Reich would foot the bill.

Through the autumn of 1937 and the early winter of 1938, events moved constructively toward resumption of transatlantic airship service the following summer. DZR negotiated a contract for eighteen million cubic feet of helium to cover the initial inflation and subsequent replenishment after every flight of LZ 130. Willy von Meister was overwhelmed with details of procuring helium, arranging for its shipment via Houston or Galveston, getting another lease from the navy for Lakehurst facilities, and securing new mail contracts. The Germans built helium storage and purification facilities in Frankfurt and prepared thousands of flasks for gas shipment from America. A specially converted German freighter was already waiting for the gas at the Texas port.

Cutaway representation of
LZ 130, *Graf Zeppelin II*, 1938–
39. (Luftschiffbau Zeppelin and
John M. Mellberg)

Then, on March 12, 1938, the Nazis invaded Austria and annexed the country
to Germany. American-German relations reached a new low.

While the National Munitions Control Board had earlier approved the
sale of helium to Germany, the secretary of the interior had not yet signed
the contract for the sale. Harold L. Ickes was now adamantly opposed. Possibly the president now also basically disapproved, but could let his cabinet
officer take the heat for the decision. And heat there was, as the state department and the navy argued with Ickes not to complicate America's foreign
relations or to deprive her airshipmen of continuing opportunities to practice
their craft. Neither the war or navy departments found any military usefulness
for helium, but Ickes was relentless in his opposition.[14] On April 29 the
American ambassador to Germany cabled the state department:

> In a conversation last night Göring raised the matter of helium. He spoke with
> deep emotion and bluntness. . . . He said, "I cannot understand what leads a
> nation to earn the enmity of another over such a little thing." He declared to
> me with considerable solemnity that as Chief of the Air Service he gave his
> word of honor that the helium would not be used for war purposes, indeed it
> would be too stupid to contemplate putting an airship into war service which
> could be shot down so readily. Germany, however, could not accept a control
> of its word of honor. If it was impossible to get helium, the German people

would not forget America's attitude, but it would not give up thereby the use of airships and would continue them with hydrogen.[15]

Shortly thereafter Eckener himself arrived in Washington, personally to plead the airship case. Earlier he had sent a cable to the president and now he faced the irascible secretary. Goodyear lobbyist Thomas A. Knowles brought him to the interior department on May 14. Knowles subsequently filed a confidential report, recalling his memory of Eckener's words about the confrontation. Eckener bluntly indicated that the American as well as German commercial airship future was at stake. Ickes said he was sorry but that he could do nothing. The crucial point was the possible military use of helium to the detriment of the United States. Ickes and Eckener went round and round:

> The doctor evidently asked the secretary how this helium could be used for military purposes. The secretary stated that German zeppelins could be used to bomb London. The doctor replied that this was impossible under the present status of aerial warfare and pointed out that the warships would be blown up in their sheds within ten hours of the opening of hostilities. He told Secretary Ickes about the raid on the airship plant in Friedrichshafen which took place almost immediately after the declaration of war in 1914 as an example of how quickly airship facilities could be attacked. [Actually, the air strike occurred three months after World War I began and was totally ineffective.] Secretary Ickes's reply seemed to be that the Germans would not have their airships in the sheds, but would have sneaked them away and perhaps have them out scouting over the oceans for weeks at a time. Dr. Eckener apparently decried such use under European conditions and considered this along with bombing as impossible uses of the airship. . . . Much of the argument seemed to be on this "could"-"would" in basis with Secretary Ickes taking the position that as long as anything was within the realm of possibility the helium must be refused.[16]

The old curmudgeon has left an account of the meeting in his *Secret Diary*. He indicated his high regard for Eckener personally but stated that he had to observe the law. He could not accept the airshipsman's conviction that the zeppelin would never again see military use. Ickes was certain that Hitler would authorize any action, regardless of assurances or promises Eckener might have given. Toward the end of the meeting the zeppelin captain asked if helium might be made available in a year or two; if so, he was prepared to undertake training flights with hydrogen in the interim. Ickes responded that congress might change the law or that he might be replaced by another secretary with different views. It was poor consolation.[17]

Eckener thus returned empty-handed to Friedrichshafen, where other impulses gave stimulus to airship flight. As of early June 1938, DZR director Issel and Capt. von Schiller had applied to the Reich air minister for permission to fly LZ 130 with hydrogen. They argued for the favorable propaganda effect of resumed flights, but they were most seriously interested in restoring the morale of the builders in Friedrichshafen and the fliers at Frankfurt by opening a schedule of test flights for LZ 130 and edging toward

Electronic surveillance team aboard LZ 130, summer 1939; left to right: Dr. Erich Hilligardt, Capt. Albert Sammt, Dr. Ernst Breuning. (Verlag Pestalozzi)

World War I spy basket renovated for use in LZ 130 electronic surveillance, 1939. (Verlag Pestalozzi)

beginning the construction of LZ 131.[18] In the immediate offing was also a long-planned celebration of the centennial of Count Zeppelin's birth, and for that the promise of an imminent resumption of airship operation was essential. The Nazis gave the celebration a special propaganda spin with a distinguished international guest list and the obligatory commemorative postage stamps. The Zeppelin Company opened its spacious new museum and featured the publication of Eckener's authoritative, laudatory biography of the Count. With special tours for the guests through LZ 130 in the construction hangar, the air was charged with anticipation that a new chapter of zeppelin history was still likely to open.

The airshipmen were chafing at the bit after all the frustrating delays and controversy about helium. There was more than just the understandable enthusiasm to put their grounded ship back into the skies. LZ 130 had undergone significant internal reconstruction to reduce weight in preparation for flight with helium. Now they were anxious to reassert the role of the airship in flight and to prepare for resumption of international schedules when helium finally did become available. Several research plans also required attention. Most important was Professor Dieckmann's project for intensive study of electrostatic charges for their possible bearing on the *Hindenburg* disaster. Newly installed equipment to condense engine exhaust for water ballast needed testing. Among other projects in view were possible experiments with swiveling propellers driven electrically from power sources inside the airship. All in all, the airshipmen of various specialties had a busy schedule of work in view. An opening would soon beckon to them, but hardly in ways anticipated at the Zeppelin centennial or by most of them individually.

A window of opportunity appeared for noncombatant military use of the airship. Since the turn of the century, when electricity had become the prime transmitter of energy, there had been sporadic scientific observations on wireless waves reflecting and deflecting from metallic objects some distance away. During the early 1930s, a German naval scientist had found a way to detect objects at a distance under water by bouncing sound waves off them, thus giving birth to sonar. He then transferred this experience to experiments with radio waves above water. In 1934 he astonished his naval command by thus detecting a ship seven miles distant and also a small aircraft that was flying by. Here a major example of radar was born in a nation whose young military experts zealously sought tactical breakthroughs in every service sector.[19]

Concurrently, as *Telefunken* (the German wireless combine) was experimenting with electronic navigational aids and the beginnings of television, the Luftwaffe was using similar principles to develop blind-landing capabilities for its aircraft. Into this active milieu came a very talented engineer, Ernst Breuning. Only twenty-seven years of age, he had risen by 1938 to supervise all civilian signals activity in the air ministry and had a sizable annual budget of twenty-million marks. German aviation at that time was using amplitude modulated (AM) ultra high frequency (UHF) for its ground-to-air communication and efforts were astir to adapt this system for plane-to-plane signals. Breuning knew that General Wolfgang Martini, chief of the Luftwaffe Air Signals Branch, was anxious to discover how far Germany's potential opponents had progressed in their own UHF development. For a time the Luftwaffe was using trimotor Junker transports equipped with UHF receivers, flying them along German frontiers to eavesdrop on Reich neighbors. The results, however, were frustrating because of excessive engine noise and short flight limitations. No doubt alerted by the Zeppelin centennial, Breuning suggested using the airship for these investigations. When contacted at Friedrichshafen, Dr. Dürr indicated that the airship could quickly be readied for flight and Eckener also gave his assent.[20]

From the very beginning, then, LZ 130—now named *Graf Zeppelin II*—flew in the service of electronic surveillance for the Luftwaffe. This was a unique, noncombatant military use of the airship, which had not figured in German-American arguments about helium or in the Ickes-Eckener exchange. Since LZ 130 had not yet been delivered to the DZR and was still the property of the Zeppelin Company, the Luftwaffe put Eckener in the awkward position of having to seek its patronage and then paying his company nicely for the services. Breuning moved in with dispatch. Twenty-four measurement consoles were built into the broad transverse dining room of the new ship, with equipment to monitor wavelengths over a broad frequency spectrum. Oscillographs were added to record the observed data. Several dozen Luftwaffe signalmen in mufti had the assistance of UHF technicians and whatever linguistic interpreters any given route required. Thus in preparation, LZ 130 first took to the skies on September 14, 1938, with Eckener in command, on a round trip to Nürnberg, a city still reverberating with echoes from the very recent (and last) Nazi *Parteitag*.

Breuning gave this account of subsequent operations:

> Occasionally we took along other people close to us, or whom we owed some favor. They were strictly committed to secrecy, while we explained away their presence with all sorts of possible or manufactured justifications. Our destinations and measurement tasks were always decided in prior consultation with Signals Chief Martini and the General Staff. I then determined the details of our flight routes. Since we could officially fly only within the frontiers of the Reich, or out over the open sea, we sometimes had the motors "fail" in order to excuse obvious violations of our neighbors' air space as we drifted across their borders. To camouflage our actual activity, we had the air ministry foster a series of weekend aviation meets [all over the Reich] in the summer of 1939. On those occasions we landed there and often exchanged philatelic mail.[21]

The third flight (of thirty in the series from mid-September 1938 to late August of 1939) occurred just before the Munich Crisis. Here the zeppelin flew to Vienna on September 22, 1938 for surveillance of the southern Czech frontier. Four Messerschmitt fighters, temporarily camouflaged in civilian police-green, accompanied LZ 130 to give the airship a "civilian" guard in case of interception by Czech aircraft. From the outset there would be no doubt about the military significance of these flights, and this was, ironically, Hugo Eckener's last command.[22]

Very soon Breuning's electronic experts aboard the airship found ample evidence of UHF traffic in their neighbors' aviation operations. Now General Martini wanted to know precisely which airfields and which air units were involved in this signals activity. Thereupon a new problem developed of locating these transmitters and taking bearings on them. It proved futile to use rotating directional antennas aboard LZ 130 because the huge metallic structure of the airship scattered the incoming UHF waves and made their reception impossible. Various efforts to amplify these waves were fruitless. Then an old device from the zeppelin raids on London in World War I came to the rescue. The chief electrostatic expert of the Zeppelin Company, Erich Hilligardt, who had worked there since 1917, resurrected an old "spy basket" from the Friedrichshafen museum. When the spy basket was lowered by a winch from the interior of the airship downward for a hundred to a thousand feet, it escaped all the frustrating interference. Operators inside LZ 130 identified foreign frequencies and fed these data to the operator below by way of a wireless voice link. Unhindered by any metallic diffusion, the lower operator could readily verify and improve the UHF reception, take his bearings, and thus identify the distant transmitter. Personnel aboard the airship avidly competed for the opportunity to serve in the spy basket. Service down there gave a unique experience of man's oneness with nature; even better, it was the only place to have a smoke. Thus the World War I relic fulfilled human and state needs twenty years later.[23]

Foremost among Germany's potential western opponents was England. As Breuning put it, "early on we heard the English 'coughing around' on UHF; General Martini and the whole General Staff promptly wanted to know the characteristics and points of origin of these transmissions."[24] Actually, the British were rather later on the proto-radar scene than the Germans. Stimulated by some earlier research and more recent random wireless observations of the British Post Office, Professor Henry Tizard began in early 1935 with a small group to examine the possibilities. They set up shop at the RAF experimental flight station on Martlesham Heath, with outlying units at Orfordness and Bawdsey Manor on the Suffolk coast, about seventy miles northeast of London. It was an era when official opinion was candidly pessimistic about successfully warding off enemy bomber attacks, and both regular service enthusiasm and financial support were hard to find for this kind of new fangled electronic defense. Tizard's chronicler wrote:

> Reactions were mixed when the Tizard Committee first reported that if money was not stinted a practical system for detecting and locating aircraft fifty miles away could be developed within two years. 'Why,' said one high officer, 'if that is possible, the whole plan of Air defense will be revolutionized!' 'Why not start the revolution now?' was Tizard's reply.[25]

Experimentation with the new process did accelerate somewhat, but it was not complete when the Munich Crisis of September 1938 emphasized the glaring gaps in British air defenses. Thereupon resources were more generously given to developing stationary and airborne radar. A chain of seventeen warning stations was constructed in a broad arc on the British coast, extending eastward from Southhampton, then curving northward toward upper Scotland. During the spring and summer of 1939, teams of experts from various British universities spent their vacations working at various of these interconnected stations. It was barely in the nick of time.[26]

The clusters of very tall antenna masts rising in the late spring of 1939 at Bawdsey Manor, and beginning to sprout elsewhere along the coast, attracted the curiosity of Lufthansa commercial pilots. Early in June Luftwaffe planes were increasingly reported on reconnaissance along the east coast and in the English Channel. *Graf Zeppelin II* was also caught up in this enterprise. Until the coordinates in all its logs are fully analyzed, it cannot be said exactly how many English flights it made; but there were probably just two: July 12–14 and August 2–4. The first was allegedly observed by a British farmer. His sighting, however, contradicts the later testimony by airship captain Heinrich Bauer—there were several officers with the rank of captain aboard the ship commanded by Albert Sammt—that LZ 130 flew as close to the English coast as possible while still avoiding any chance of visual observation there.[27]

The second British flight was a grandstand affair, with General Martini himself aboard. Apparently for security reasons the official log of the flight does not list his name among all the other Luftwaffe personnel there identified, but Bauer clearly indicated his presence and noted that he was addressed as "Herr Wolfgang."[28] In his account of 1981, Breuning reported only briefly on the flight itself:

> We were not only concerned about British radio traffic; we surmised that the British (like we with our 'Freya' and 'Würzburg A') already had search radar [for air space surveillance] and we wanted to verify that fact scientifically. We flew along the [eastern] English coast northward to the Shetland Islands. On the return flight we stopped our motors off Aberdeen, where we had seen a cluster of new antenna masts, and radioed our headquarters that we had motor trouble. So we let the east wind blow us like a free balloon toward the shore. Naval speedboats dashed out below us and for the first time we had a look at the brand new Spitfires that darted around our ship. Obviously it was too much for the British; we had drawn the bow too taut.[29]

A third of a century after the event, engineer Erich Hilligardt gave a very animated account:

> *Ach*, those were really very touchy flights. Only [Captain] Sammt and I had unimpeded access to the quarters where the tests were going on. Everybody else was strictly kept out, unless he had special permission. It got very hot at one point along the English coast. We were somewhere up around Aberdeen. The spy basket was way down and we also had a very large, broad-mesh, fine-wire antenna screen hanging a couple of hundred meters below the ship. Then

Artist's conception of LZ 130 on electronic surveillance, 1939. (© 1980 by Sanders Associates, Inc., Nashua, N.H. All rights reserved. Reproduced with permission. Illustration by Alfred "Chief" Johnson of Sanders Associates, Inc.)

suddenly the English were out after us with a couple of speedy new planes. It was pandemonium. Some of the crew were furiously getting the basket cranked up; others were slowly hauling in the cumbersome antenna screen. The English planes were so close we could see the pilots' faces. We were wildly gesticulating out of the control car windows to warn them away from the airship, because we were afraid they would fly underneath and get tangled up in the almost invisible wire mesh of the antenna screen. Upstairs the Luftwaffe people were dancing around from window to window to get pictures of the new planes. Such excitement![30]

The official log summarized the flight as follows:

> Ship moved out to mast at 19:45 [Aug 2] in light WSW wind. After arrival of all experiment personnel of Group R, ship left at 20:53 to reach work station in the North Sea by morning. Smooth departure from mast. Flight: in partially light clouding, ship flew at 700 m. height to Cuxhaven. In accordance with directives from Experiment Group R, requirements during this leg to fly frequently on specific courses and in circles for their experimental verification. On subsequent course to English Channel, encountered deteriorating weather with very low clouds and showers. Ascent to 1800 m. above lower cloud formation only partially effective on this course. After conference of captain with director of Experiment Group R, previously determined course towards English Channel abandoned to steer NW, to avoid extended influences of Low covering South England and to find more favorable weather for experiments at specific altitudes. Distance from shore so great that by subsequent clear visibility and height neither coastal lights nor land visible. North of Aberdeen, far from coast, interception by British reconnaissance plane and bomber that encircled airship several times. On sighting Orkney Islands, reversed course, flew southward, intermittently back and forth at 30 sea miles off English coast. After detour around several threatening storm fronts, sighted lightship at Norderney at 12:20 on Aug. 4; took course directly toward Frankfurt. Message from airfield commandant not to land before darkness. With danger of thunderstorm, captain sought immediate arrival. Further command from airfield—no landing before darkness. Subsequently clear landing without incident, as also movement into hangar.[31]

The terse wording of the official log was an uncomfortable compromise between the statutory requirements of peacetime flight reporting and secrecy demanded by the Luftwaffe. Breuning's account only hints at the realities affirmed by Bauer. The airship captain, in turn, was cautiously enlightened by the only officer of the crew to have direct political contact with "Experiment Group R"—Airship Chief Engineer Rudolf Sauter, who was a veteran of many earlier airship flights. Bauer thus learned more than most others knew about the passengers and their mission. With the exception of Sammt, Bauer, Sauter, and Hilligardt, all other crew members were strictly prohibited from entering the quarters where the Luftwaffe was monitoring electronic frequencies. Most of these four seldom used their opportunity. Instead, Breuning would come down to the control car to confer with Sammt or the navigating captain. Bauer later recalled, "I went up a few times and always got a critical and unfriendly reception. We were aware of Nazi secret service agents aboard, so we mostly avoided all those people and kept our mouths shut. We didn't want to attract any unfavorable attention.[32]

Political tensions aside, it was an atmosphere aboard LZ 130 much like that experienced about thirty years later by the crew of the U.S. Navy "oceanographic" ship *Pueblo*, conducting comparable electronic studies off the coast of North Korea.[33]

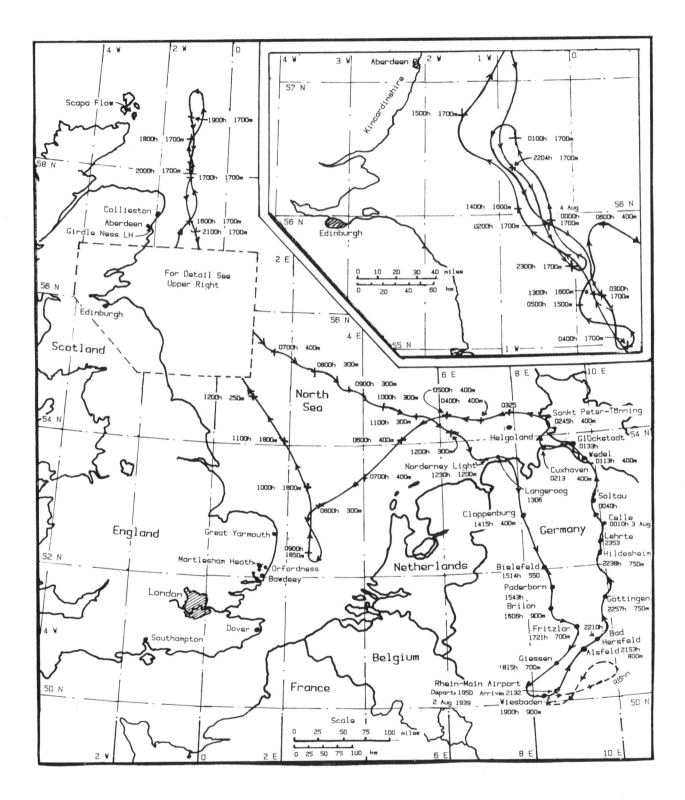

Scapa Flow

1900h 1700m
1800h 1700m
2000h 1700m
1700h 1700m
Collieston
Aberdeen
Girdle Ness LH
1600h 1700m
2100h 1700m

58 N
56 N
54 N
52 N
50 N

4 W
2 W
0

For Detail See
Upper Right

Edinburgh

Scotland

England

London

Southampton

Dover

Great Yarmouth
Martlesham Heath
Orfordness
Bawdsey

North
Sea

2 E
4 E

0700h 400m
0800h 300m
0900h 300m
1000h 300m
1100h 300m
1200h 250m
1100h 1800m
1000h 1800m
0800h 300m
0700h 400m
0600h 400m
1200h 300m
0900h
1850h

Norderney Light
1230h 1200m
Langeroog
1306

Netherlands

Belgium

France

Scale
0   25   50   75   100 miles
0 25 50 75 100 km

4 W
2 W
0

Aberdeen

57 N

Kincardinshire

1500h 1700m

0100h 1700m
2204h 1700m

1400h 1600m
0200h 1700m

2300h 1700m

1300h 1600m
0500h 1500m

0400h 1700m

4 Aug
0000h
1700m

0600h 400m

0300h
1700m

56 N
55 N

Edinburgh

0   10 20 30 40 miles
0   20   40   60 km

0500h 400m
0400h 400m
0325

Helgoland

Sankt Peter-Tönning
0245h 400m
Glückstadt
0133h
Wedel
0113h 400m
Cuxhaven
0213 400m

54 N

6 E
8 E
10 E

Soltau
0040h
Celle
0010h 3 Aug
Lehrte
2353
Hildesheim
2238h 750m

Cloppenburg
1415h 400m

Germany

Bielefeld
1514h 550
Paderborn
1543h
Brilon
1606h 900m

Göttingen
2257h 750m

Fritzlar
1721h 700m

2210h
Bad
Hersfeld
Alsfeld 2153h
800m

Giessen
1815h 700m

Röhn

Rhein-Main Airport
Depart: 1950 Arrive: 2132
2 Aug 1939

Wiesbaden
1900h 900m

50 N

As was indicated by the coordinated appearance of speedboats, Spitfires, and a twin-engine bomber, British eastern coastal defenses were sharply on alert. The RAF chain of stations had been in continuous operation since late April of 1939. The RAF Fighter Command already had authority to intercept and engage any suspicious aircraft crossing the international boundary three miles offshore. This aerial appearance, however, was not a new Nazi warplane. It was a zeppelin—about which British observers had few apprehensions since its defeats of 1917–18 and the airship disasters of the 1930s. As it was, quickened curiosity was the characteristic English response as LZ 130 slowly moved and maneuvered well off their shores. There is, in fact, little specific information at all in official British military aviation records about the flight of LZ 130 or of British reactions and responses thereto.[34] Some Britons may have actually sighted the airship as it was being "blown off course" to the east of their shores. The event was reported in five different English newspapers that included claims to actual sighting together with reports and denials from Germany.[35] A flight lieutenant on radar duty at Bentley Prior later recalled that the Germans had transmitted an erroneous position report back home. "We were sorely tempted," he said, "to radio a correction message to the airship; but this would have revealed that we were actually seeing her position on radar, so we kept silent."[36] Some reports have suggested that the British turned off their radar to frustrate German surveillance, but such action could also have alerted the Germans to the fact that the British had something to hide. Thus all around, the English attitude was mostly studied or actual laxness. Quite probably a full realization of the significance of the flight of LZ 130 did not sink in till several days or weeks later, when the flight path was reconstructed from those stations that recorded the airship sightings.[37]

As for events on the diplomatic front, there is hearsay that the Germans gave the English a harmless notice that LZ 130 would be cruising in the far western North Sea, allegedly to test its water-recovery apparatus—not a very convincing explanation, considering the fact that rain squalls could be found almost any day just off the north German coast. Once the airship had made its prolonged appearance so close to English shores, however, the British air attaché in Berlin was ordered to Frankfurt airport with a firm request to inspect LZ 130 upon its arrival there. Again we are indebted to Breuning for details:

When we approached Frankfurt in the late afternoon of the next day [August 4], and were checking with our controller for landing instructions, we got word that it was not possible. First we thought there had been some accident on the field, but on cruising high above the runways we could see no evidence of trouble. So we turned away, flew off eastward toward the Rhön [Mountains] for a while, and then radioed once again for landing confirmation. Again we got the answer: 'landing before nightfall impossible.' That struck us as very strange. I said to Capt. Sammt: 'Now, let's fly back to Frankfurt anyhow and get in touch with our landing crew by our own UHF radio. At that height of 400 meters no Frenchman can intercept us. Besides that, we'll talk in Swabian

Route of LZ 130 on electronic surveillance along English coast, Aug. 2–4, 1939. (Map by Prof. Robert G. Saunders, University of California, Irvine. © 1991)

dialect to the head of our airfield crew.' And that's what we did. There we heard from Chief Beuerle: 'You can't come down now. Things are mighty tense here. The English want to file a diplomatic protest against your flight. We have an English delegation here at the airport right now, which has German permission to board your ship for inspection as soon as you land. You are suspected of violating international law. We're still trying to figure out what to do.' So we flew off again. Soon we got an order: 'Clear the decks! Conceal all the equipment inside the ship [beyond the passenger quarters]. Do not land in the usual brightly lit arrival area, where (to be sure) a kind of landing crew is waiting for you. Go to the other, dark end of the airport, where your customary landing crew will identify itself with blinker signals. Immediately on landing, all the Breuning people are to disembark. A storm troop unit from Frankfurt will take their place as 'passengers.'

The airport director, Colonel Freiherr von Buttlar-Brandenfels—an experienced naval airship captain of the First World War—had organized everything superbly. [He told] the British they were in the wrong landing area. The airship had had to come in at another part of the airport for meteorological reasons. By the time the delegation had come trudging clear across the airport, our whole contingent was gone with kit and caboodle, already in the bus on the way to Frankfurt [city]. The English then examined the ship but found nothing to justify their suspicions and our storm-trooping 'passengers' were quite unhypocritically innocent.[38]

The *Graf Zeppelin II* made three further flights that August until its activities ceased with the imminence of war. By the tens of thousands, people trooped to the landing fields at Würzburg, Eger [eastern Germany], and Essen-Mülheim. The roundabout distances traversed en route to these events probably gave LZ 130 ample opportunity for further eavesdropping along the Polish and Franco-Belgian frontiers. In anticipation of the airship, bands played, flags waved, and paramilitary units displayed their talents. Just as it did thirty years before, *der Zeppelin* still mesmerized the masses, though now in officially sponsored and elaborately staged political theater. Again the philatelists were rewarded with handsome letters for their collections. As zeppelin fever rose anew, the results were also financial manna from heaven for the DZR. It handled the mail contracts for LZ 130, derived further income from the thousands who paid to visit the first *Graf Zeppelin* (now emptied of hydrogen and on display at Frankfurt), and profited from the sale of airship mementos at the site. DZR closed its books reasonably content in early 1940, as the "phony war" loitered on the Franco-German front.[39]

Whatever else the Luftwaffe may have learned from its electronic eavesdropping with LZ 130, the reconnaissance of nascent British radar was a failure. Quite simply, the Germans failed to monitor a wide enough frequency spectrum. The Luftwaffe worked with parabolic reflectors on wavelengths between 50 cm and 2.4 meters. Quite unbeknownst to Berlin, the British were working their chain of stations with echo-ranging equipment on shortwave bands around 11–12 meters. It was this mode of operation that required those sets of tall towers that had initially stimulated German investigation. As Breuning later indicated, however, the LZ 130 surveillance along the English

LZ 127, *Graf Zeppelin*, stripped away as museum exhibit, Frank-furt/M., 1939. (Luftschiffbau Zeppelin)

coast was doomed to failure by interference from another Luftwaffe signals activity concurrently in operation. They were continuously monitoring the intensity of European wireless traffic in order to discover optimum times and frequencies for their own transmissions. This effort required constant use of pulse transmitters to eject electromagnetic waves into the atmosphere in all kinds of frequencies and intensities. By measuring the reflection of these pulses from the Kennelly-Heaviside layer of the ionosphere, it seemed possible to determine optimum conditions for Luftwaffe wireless communication. As fate would have it, however, it was precisely in the 10–12 meter bands that these other transmissions produced massive interference for the receivers aboard LZ 130. Accordingly, the airship monitors avoided those wavelengths, and the British radar secrets remained undetected.[40]

For the builders and fliers of LZ 130 the flight season of 1939 was a source of pride and satisfaction. They put their airship through its paces; they tested sophisticated new equipment; they had some new trainees aboard for the future. In Friedrichshafen the builders sharpened their pencils and tools. Dies and jigs were set to construct girders and the first rings of LZ 131 were built. One wonders, though, if there was much more than the satisfaction and joy of the moment.[41]

When World War II broke out, LZ 130 joined her forebear as a deflated museum piece, hung high from the rafters of a neighboring Frankfurt hangar over a floor soon crowded with Me 109 fighters and equipment. Viewers of the scene must have thought of this hulk as a dinosaur of the aviation era. Unlike in 1914, no enemy bombers appeared in an attempt to destroy the German zeppelins. That action was decided upon, instead by the bureaucracy

227

in Berlin, the old enemy of the venerable Count and of Hugo Eckener—indeed, by the air minister himself. Initially there were several potential wartime tasks suggested by the zeppelin fliers. One involved using LZ 130 in night surveillance to determine the effectiveness of civilian blackout efforts in the Reich; another involved using the airship to fly rare metals from Manchuria across Russia to Germany. The Luftwaffe, however, fabricated a complaint that the airship hangars interfered with full wartime use of the airfield. On March 1, 1940, General Göring appeared there with a full retinue of high military aviation brass and civilian experts to survey the scene that he had already condemned to destruction. In vain the zeppeliners gave their detailed commentary to convince him of the possible future significance of airships. Climbing around in the stripped structure of LZ 130, the air minister responded to their efforts to inform him with the kind of folksy chatter that had long endeared him to the German public: "Na, that thing's for the birds! . . . One match and the whole contraption will go up in flames! . . . Go ahead, take a picture [of Göring in the airship]; it'll have real future scarcity value!" General Milch tried to soften the blow: "Look, fellows, be sensible. We need the space to regroup our squadrons. After the war we'll gear up again [with airships]. You can depend on it."[42]

The preparations for demolition continued. A third of a century later Bauer recalled a puzzling incident that echoed the flight of L 59 in 1917 to assist German forces in distress in East Africa:

> At one point—it was late April and I was then an air force officer—someone in the air ministry gave me orders to activate an airship crew in preparation for a flight to Narvik. Our forces there were then hard-pressed by the English. I was to load the ship with all kinds of supplies and equipment and crash-land LZ 130 there so she could also be cannibalized for any other useful materials. I flew to Frankfurt on these orders, but got there only to find both airships in the final stages of demolition.[43]

To the very end ideas were surfacing for the military use of LZ 130!

By the third anniversary of the burning of the *Hindenburg*, May 6, 1940, the last fragments of the demolished airships had been trucked away from the Frankfurt airfield. The airship hangars were then blown up to make way for the enlarged Luftwaffe fighter base. Count Zeppelin's great gift to the German nation was finally destroyed by the same god of war for whom it was originally created to enhance the political power and military superiority of the *Vaterland*.

Conclusion

The essays presented here about airshipmen, businessmen, and their varied interrelationships with the political forces of their times illuminate a half century of man's striving to navigate the skies in ships lighter than air. Other works analyze more thoroughly and professionally the design and construction details of these remarkable feats of engineering. The development of the arts of navigation and of general operation of these rigid sky giants is also capably examined elsewhere. The essays are spin-offs from a larger study of the political history of the airship and are primarily focused on the human drama. In that context history has a significant psychological dimension. It is concerned with emotional motivations and their conflict with rational resolution. It is an arena for the assertion of instinct and impulse. There is opportunity for conflict and behavior in a variety of contests: of men with each other, for human self-assertion, for financial rewards, and for political advantage. The half-century airship drama presents all these aspects in generous variety. The essays explore the motivations and other emotional dimensions of the designers and the fliers. They touch on those of the businessmen who presided financially—and with comparable emotion—over the construction and operation of the dirigibles. Clearly visible within the gigantic mazes of the airships abuilding and in flight, the personalities contend with each other in often high and usually honest passion. Ultimately each man is seen caught up positively, or enmeshed tragically, in the larger political forces of his time.

Much of airship history, particularly in Germany, has been excessively and understandably laudatory of its flying heroes, notably of Count Zeppelin and Dr. Hugo Eckener. Conversely, in Germany as elsewhere, the airship facilitators like Schütte, Colsman, Burney, Wallis, Thomson, Vissering, Litchfield, Arnstein, and von Meister have been overshadowed by the glamor of the pioneers or the spectacle of airship disasters. All of these individuals, either well-recognized or neglected, deserve more fully drawn portraits. They have all lived in a world of high-level artful management, either as one individual manipulated by another or as persons interacting with broader social and political forces. Airshipmen and businessmen were never above, or exempt from, participation in the inevitable interpersonal struggles of their careers at characteristic human levels. Nor were they ever immune from the larger political forces of their times. As these essays have opened out toward broader dimensions of airship history, they have sought to do so with full appreciation of the talent and sacrifice, of the accomplishments, and of the sometimes grim dilemmas that marked the careers of this remarkable generation of airshipmen.

Without a doubt the most significant airshipman of the rigid dirigible era was Count Ferdinand von Zeppelin. He was a pioneer in the conceptualization of airship design, construction, and flight. He led the way into mastering the art of moving his magnificent but ungainly contrivances under control through the skies against the wind. Whatever his motivations, whatever the immediate objectives in realizing his project, he, like every pioneer, trekked through largely unmapped territory. Quite independently he devised and improved upon his conception of a light metallic airship train. He had few precedents to consult here, no experimental data to draw upon, and much negative criticism from those whose assistance or acceptance he sought. Indeed, he had only a rudimentary knowledge of science and engineering, but withal he had the sound judgment initially to enlist expertise where he could obtain it in order to put it to use in his remarkable rule of thumb venture.

The same kinds of circumstances marked his pioneering efforts in airship flight. There were few accumulated data on problems of lift, stress, or propulsion. Scientific meteorology was in its infancy. He used what he could to his best ability. He was thwarted by the failures of engines lacking requisite power. Inexperienced with the natural physical phenomena involved in keeping his contraption afloat, stable, and forward moving, the Count rose and descended in a dogged process of learning essentially by trial and error. Thus he acquired experience and spurred others on to expand and build upon his efforts. In constructing a succession of cream-colored or light-grey ships, piloting them for the admiration of ever-growing crowds, and enduring a sequence of painful public pratfalls, the Count attracted the growing enthusiasm and ultimate financial support of the German nation. By 1908 his determined efforts had intersected with early twentieth-century enthusiasm for the air, with prevalent technological optimism, and with an exaggerated German admiration for *das Kolossale und Grossartige*. Count Zeppelin thus became a folk hero of the late German Empire, matching in admiration and popularity the personality of nation-builder Otto von Bismarck.

Where does the reality about Count Zeppelin's life and work lie? Hundreds of articles, pamphlets, and books sang extravagant praise in the last decade of his life. Today the imperial *Vaterland* that he worshipped and its dominant aristocratic social network that he so skillfully used are gone. Still, the semi-mythical echoes of that era linger on in various accounts of his struggle to build a rigid airship. Given this heritage, and given the lack of access to his voluminous personal archives, it is difficult to strike a fair balance in evaluating his motivations and modi operandi in the late German Empire. It does appear beyond dispute that he experienced a shattering trauma in 1890, when his detractors struck without warning to destroy the military career to which the Count was passionately devoted. His adjustments to that blow constitute a remarkable psychological case history in the phenomena of overcompensation and personality reorientation. In place of a relatively routine and untroubled service life amidst respected fellow professionals, the Count now set out with remarkable vigor and aggressive energy to achieve an alternative objective—doing so in provincial isolation amidst echoes of ridicule from the German capital, where he had recently held a significant diplomatic-political position. Yet, his personality retained its engaging external charm, though occasionally the new strength of his internal drives broke through the genial surface. The new circumstances of his life steeled his positive qualities but also permitted negative characteristics to become more apparent, especially as advancing age wrought its inevitable personality changes. He wisely employed the assistance of professional experts to convert the thrust of his original conceptions into technological reality. Still, he became increasingly stubborn and intolerant about improvements or innovations that were not his own intellectual creations. He had the inventor's characteristic suspicion of rivals, notably of the Prussian Airship Battalion, which he distrusted both for its expertise and its implied connection with his Berlin enemies. Zeppelin's much-admired dogged determination sometimes broke out in peevish recriminations against those who would not accompany him on his insistent ways. During the war his favorable public image was exploited on behalf of the German cause, but his image now obscured an unfortunate reality. Experts from the German navy rose to important production influence in the Zeppelin Company, pressed for constant technical improvement of the airships, and virtually barred the "interfering" old Count from his factory. His final turn to airplane building was probably less a disenchantment with airships than evidence of his struggle to have an enterprise he could still call his own. It was the same with his public appearances. When his bellicose speeches and writings called official censorship down upon him in early 1916, he retreated to privileged private gatherings and circulation of privately printed memoranda for his belligerent audiences. Toward the end, the less favorable characteristics of the wartime Count Zeppelin overshadowed his positive qualities and accomplishments.

The old aeronaut's turn to military vehemence in that era of superheated wartime emotions should come as no surprise. Count Zeppelin was always basically a militarist. When he reoriented himself to restore his affronted honor, to avenge himself nicely upon his enemies, and to give his beloved Germany a significant technological gift—he chose to build a military weapon to assure his nation's prestige, power, and potential domination of Europe. Neither the inscription on his Friedrichshafen memorial nor all the nostalgic memories of later transoceanic airship cruising can dispel that fact. It does him no dishonor to see him clearly as a child of his times and as a man psychologically redirected by his traumatic experience.

In contrast to the well-remembered Count Zeppelin, Professor Johann Schütte is almost completely unknown today. Just before World War I he was initially seen in some official circles as a welcome design and construction competitor to the testy aristocrat at Friedrichshafen. Though Schütte identified important shortcomings in zeppelin design and surmounted them with significant technical innovations, he was always in "the shadow of the titan." His most important contributions were made between 1908 and 1913, culminating in the new airship SL 2. He was an airshipman mostly in matters of design and construction. Though he was sometimes a passenger on SL flights, he had no qualifications as a pilot and left no record of his joy in "airship voyaging." The professor was an earthbound intellectual and ambitious businessman. Still, Schütte and his team were also pioneers with the crucial design innovations that were subsequently built into all rigid airships.

How different was the career and significance of Dr. Hugo Eckener! Between 1908 and 1911, at the very time that Schütte was at the peak of his design innovations, Eckener was moving from his interim career as a cultural newspaper commentator to public relations director at the DELAG and then to become a qualified airship flier himself. He brought three remarkable qualities to his new career: an almost intuitive effectiveness in dealing with weather conditions and other aspects of the art of aerial navigation; a great capacity to master the details of airship design and construction; and a broad cultural-philosophical dimension for his life's work. The last of these qualities was his refuge when he sought relief from the stresses of bureaucratic problems or from wrangling about airship matters with important but insensitive personalities outside of Friedrichshafen. Then he would escape to the concert hall, an art museum, or his writing desk. Above all, Eckener enjoyed the sense of accomplishment of flying zeppelins. Working with, or mastering, the physical challenges of the skies was a counterpart to his dealing with other forces on earth. He was the ideal airshipman, a commander without peer in the half century of rigid airship flight.

Although he directed Germany's most important airship training station during World War I, Eckener was no militarist. For all his admiration of the old Count, he devoted *his* life to realizing the peacetime commercial effectiveness of the airship. He pursued this objective at various levels. Basic was his unremitting struggle to keep the enterprise in Friedrichshafen economically viable by seeking government and popular support. Next was his practice of behavioral psychology in keeping the zeppelin in the public eye at home and abroad—serene, pleasurable, and dependable. Finally, the achievement of his objective was only possible by incessant attention to safe construction and, above all, safe operation of the airship. In that respect appearances were sometimes deceptive. The popular impression of the genial, avuncular Dr. Eckener flying his zeppelin with the greatest of ease, concealed a tough and demanding commander. His subordinates generally echoed the terse judgment of Capt. Bauer: "he was hard but just." ["*Er war hart aber gerecht*"].[1] He was unrelenting in the interest of passenger and airship safety. Capt. von Schiller recalled how, immediately after each South America trip with the *Graf Zeppelin*, he would have to spend several hours in Eckener's Friedrichshafen office going over the log of the just-completed flight, entry by entry. "There was one time when he judged that I had risked too dangerous a maneuver; then he really burned me! ["*Da gab er mir aber eine Zigarre!*"]. An hour later he came by and grudgingly apologized but then added, 'We just *have* to fly safely'"[2] Clearly with many others, Eckener understood that one cannot operate an airship by committee consensus.

These qualities of firmness and quick response to circumstances were evident in Eckener's other relationships. If he found laxness or incompetence on the factory floor, he could be rude and brutal in his commentary. Comparable strains appeared in his sardonic contributions to the press feud with Schütte or his amused ridicule of Capt. Bruns. A contemporary later recalled Eckener as *ein rauher Kämpe*, Schleswig dialect for a feisty fighter. He wrote himself about exploding against foreign minister Stresemann in 1925. Similarly he blew off his derogatory comment to journalist Shaffer about the niggardliness of the German people in failing fully to support his drive to build the *Graf Zeppelin*. Capt. Bauer recalled a characteristic snappy verbal comment, when Eckener would ask after 1933 about displaying the swastika flag as the airship began its flight: "Is the disgraceful rag already out?" ["*Habt Ihr den Schmachtlappen schon draussen?*"][3] His outburst to Capt. Lehmann on March 26, 1936, when the younger officer had damaged the lower fin of the *Hindenburg* on emerging hurriedly from the hangar for its notorious Nazi flight, brought him into direct confrontation with Propaganda Minister Joseph Goebbels, a crisis from which he barely escaped safely. "How dare you," he had bellowed, "risk the ship for this (excremental) purpose?"]"*Wie können Sie das Schiff für diese Scheissfahrt riskieren?*"][4] It does no discredit to Hugo Eckener to recall this colorful characteristic of his personality. And it illuminates the vigor of his contest with Schütte and the intensity of his internal company conflict with Alfred Colsman.

The common denominator of all Eckener's activities and reactions after 1909 was his devotion to the person and work of Count Zeppelin, and his conviction that development of the airship must be carried forward to its culmination in dependable commercial service. Whether on the factory floor or in airship flight, whether thrilling audiences with accounts of his experiences or writing his elegant biography of the old Count, whether fighting the Berlin bureaucrats or coaxing foreign governments: Eckener always focused on keeping the Zeppelin enterprise in flight and in business, thereby also serving to restore worldwide recognition for the German nation. Ultimately the Hitler regime frustrated him in both objectives, but to the last he kept the zeppelin flying.

Airships in ever-broader service: this objective was also in Eckener's mind as he dealt with the British and the Americans after 1919. Of course he sought advantage for his own projects as he kept contact with London and Cardington, as he negotiated directly with Akron and Washington. Still, the sense of these relationships expressed his conviction that the airship cause generally could only benefit from a generous sharing of experience between the three nations. Here his task was significantly facilitated in America by the enterprise of Willy von Meister, who in turn also quietly fostered airship interest in Britain. The talented young German-American blossomed in his business association with Friedrichshafen, while Eckener derived from him the psychological rewards of a virtual second son. While von Meister was neither a designer nor a flier, he was an enthusiastic airship voyager. His constant attention to a myriad of details turned the rigors of German pioneering flights with the *Graf Zeppelin* into the prestigious ambiance and impeccable passenger service of the *Hindenburg* and her planned successors.

There was an international bond of excitement and challenge that brought most of the airshipmen into a fraternity of mutual appreciation and friendship by 1930. It was there with the German designers from Count Zeppelin onward, to the British with Richmond and Wallis, to the Americans with Karl Arnstein and his staff. Novices like Harry Vissering and Lord Thomson got airship fever. The German captains and their crews had a joyous confidence about their profession. Sensing some disadvantage in their comparative lack of experience, and setting out with two bold new experimental ships, the British attitude was tempered with a touch of caution as they took to the skies. Finally, the Americans focused perforce on their naval service obligation and may have pressed the *Akron* and *Macon* too hard to gain their desired experience. In the background of the American naval airships, however, there was always the clear expectation of a commercial future. It was thus in the anticipations of Fulton, Rosendahl, and Settle and in the business planning at Akron by Litchfield, Hunsaker, and von Meister. Altogether in their various ways the airshipmen expressed their professional pleasure in a new consciousness of time and space.

From the very beginning, construction of the rigid airship was a matter for big business and required government financial support. Count Zeppelin was the first to discover these facts by grim personal experience. Whereas the first airplanes could emerge from backlot sheds, and subsequent prototypes even in the early 1930s cost but a few hundred thousand dollars, the rigid airship was an undertaking more like building a battleship—it required millions of marks or dollars. At the outset, pioneer Count Zeppelin himself personally financed most of his technological exploration. The German government only came to his rescue in 1907, when most of his family fortune was gone and he was heavily indebted to his suppliers. When the great national gift of 1908 occurred, it was not as a business transaction, but as a public appreciation of the Count's dream and of his steadfastness in seeking to realize it against heavy financial odds. Thus, curiously, the first airship construction business was substantially funded.

The old Count and his aristocratic board called an experienced, modern executive to develop and operate the new enterprise. To Alfred Colsman goes the credit for competent management and development of the Zeppelin Company conglomerate between 1909 and 1919. At the close of the war, his perception of a diversified future for the business enterprise increasingly clashed with Eckener's determination to realize only a commercial dimension of Count Zeppelin's dream. Internally more and more at loggerheads, the two men still presented a common front against external foes: postwar economic dislocation, efforts of the Allies to dismantle the Company, and the threat of Schütte's lawsuits. Between 1924 and 1929, as Eckener received and manipulated all the public attention, it was Colsman's business acumen that produced much of the funds for building the *Graf Zeppelin* which neither the German public nor its government would adequately fund. With worldwide attention focused on Eckener after the global flight of the *Graf Zeppelin* in 1929, Colsman left the Company for an uncertain future.

Eckener as a businessman, however, must not be underestimated. He had a clear understanding of economics and a practical business sagacity. He maintained the Company through the worst of the depression until, quite contrary to his personal inclinations, it thrived on the Nazi armaments orders of the later 1930s. In retrospect, and without nostalgia: building and flying airships was a glamorously deceptive blind alley, from which only Colsman's diversification would save the Friedrichshafen business community.

Johann Schütte, the fourth major German airship businessman, had an ill-starred business career. No doubt he was responsible for much of the Schütte-Lanz production mistakes. During the war he failed significantly to capitalize on the easy largesse of government construction contracts, the funds that enriched the Zeppelin Company. Immediately after the war he could not match Eckener's skill in putting new commercial airships into the skies, nor could he prevent the Allies from dismantling his factories. Unfavorable circumstances dogged his efforts to obtain a timely settlement for his somewhat justified patent and financial claims. In the venture to transfer his design and expertise to the United States, his staff produced several creditable projects for passenger and polar exploration airships. Here misfortune, and possibly some American skullduggery, condemned the effort to failure. One error or mishap compounded another after 1913, until Schütte was quite out of the running in the financially hazardous business of building airships.

Compared with the Germans, the British had a briefer experience in fabricating rigid dirigibles. From 1916 to 1921 the government alone determined designs and assigned them to private builders. Barnes Wallis's R 80 was the exception. He had almost a free hand in designing and building the ship at Vickers. Initially these were meant as airships of war, then as dual-purpose experiments either for commercial use or for naval scouting. The pioneering transatlantic flight of R 34 in 1919 had excited British plans for commercial airships. One after another, the late-arriving airships of war were readjusted by test and function to the possibilities of peacetime service—and one after another they failed either by flaws in design or operational accident. The crash of R 38, the naval scout for America, produced a four-year pause for reconsideration of technical plans and purpose. From that intermission emerged the final decision of the Imperial Airship Scheme to build two radically new craft designed to the latest airship research. It produced a strange contrast in both plan and financing. Cardington featured open opportunities, generously supplied with funds and talent, for experimentation and change during construction. Howden was held strictly to a private contract for a predetermined design and fixed costs. At the culmination, R 100 from Howden certainly had its teething problems; but R 101 from Cardington had expensive basic flaws in project and handling. The disaster of R 101 signaled the end of British airship building.

American rigid designs and construction were also originally derived from a German zeppelin. Assembled at Lakehurst, ZR 1 was a virtual copy of LZ 96 (L 49), captured in late 1917 after a forced landing in France. Harry Vissering got zeppelin fever from a trip on LZ 120 in 1919. By 1922 he was equally at home in Washington, Friedrichshafen, and Akron, promoting the naval and commercial prospects of the airship. Earlier, and again later, Zeppelin Company officials sought the support of Henry Ford, but the industrial magic of Detroit would only briefly touch the Metalclad ZMC2. Instead, intermediary Vissering would help to bring Eckener to favorable terms with Goodyear's Paul W. Litchfield in establishing the Goodyear-Zeppelin Corporation.

The German-built *Los Angeles* led the way toward building American airships. Designer Karl Arnstein and his "twelve apostles" came directly to Akron from building LZ 126 in Friedrichshafen. Zeppelin experience combined with American innovation to construct the *Akron* and the *Macon*. Litchfield invested heavily in the new plant and products at Akron; ultimately he lost more than three million dollars in the two decades of his airship venture. The Akronites confidently planned for the commercial derivative from their naval ships, enlisting for eight years the experienced consultation of Jerome C. Hunsaker, America's first and oldest airship expert. He and his staff were the uncompleted bridge from naval building to civilian airline operation.

Here Willy von Meister appears again, the consummate international business diplomat and facilitator. Under Eckener's tutelage he became a key figure. He maintained four-way communication between Akron, the German embassy in Washington, D.C., the U.S. Navy, and Friedrichshafen. His was the major influence in establishing the American Zeppelin Transport Company. The short-lived triumph of the commercial airship culminated in von Meister's impressive organization to fly the *Hindenburg* over the brilliant autumn colors of New England in 1936, with the cream of America's business world aboard. In subsequent planning for flight with helium, he secured inclusion of an elaborate color foldout of LZ 130 in the July 1938 *Fortune* magazine article about the imminent struggle for supremacy on the transatlantic air routes. This was "Germany's Bid" against the new generation of passenger flying boats, with Pan American Airways in the fore. Both airship and flying boat, however, would soon be under a new shadow. Just a month later the first four-engine landplane—a Focke-Wulf 200—arrived in New York, nonstop from Berlin, publicly almost unnoticed.

Businessmen like Colsman, Eckener, Burney, Vissering, Ford, Litchfield, and von Meister—yes, even the failed Schütte—played significant roles in the airship era. They took what began essentially as a ship of war and converted it to peaceful commerce among nations. They opened an era of conquering time and distance with ships that offered comfort and travel enjoyment—unfortunately interlaced with ever-present danger. Their airships are now gone, but not so the examples of their pioneering enterprise in constructing and operating the first twentieth-century airliners.

It requires both intellectual discretion and cautious phrasing to comment on the political interaction of the rigid airship with the personalities and related phenomena of its era. No doubt the airship was technologically an intriguing concept that evoked a strong emotional commitment from many of its designers, builders, and operators. Majestically aloft in the skies, it exerted a powerful influence upon the earthbound masses below—wonder in peacetime, horror in World War I. Recognizing its unusual psychological attractiveness, political groups and forces tried to manipulate this magical spell to causes and goals of their own, not necessarily part of the essential purpose or use of the airship itself. There appear to be three variations of these political circumstances:

(1) efforts of individual airshipmen to foster and use the rigid dirigible in their own immediate interest or as extensions of their own psychological drives;

(2) activities of competing personalities or groups to promote or reject the psychologically attractive airship in the context of their larger political or business ambitions;

(3) decisions of governments to manipulate the airship, together with the loyalties and influence it commanded, to their own ends.

Of course, the boundaries between these three areas of influence are sometimes indistinct and often fluid. Final determination about them awaits the completion of a more detailed study. Some tentative judgments and conclusions derived from the preceding essays, however, may be risked here.

The prime example in the first category of airship-political phenomena must be Count Ferdinand von Zeppelin himself. The trauma of the sudden, drastic, and humiliating termination of his military career converted his secondary interest for airships into a determined project for restoring his impugned honor and for fostering the military-political power of his *Vaterland*. That says it all.

Dr. Hugo Eckener also had a decisive personality relationship with the airship, though in a different way and toward a different objective. Until 1909, when Eckener was forty-two years of age, the years had given no definitive focus to his work. A doctorate in psychology, a book of social-economic analysis, various writings on technology and cultural-artistic criticism: none of these had turned his career in a fully satisfactory direction. Then in 1909, Alfred Colsman brought him to the emerging Zeppelin Company and soon Eckener found his life's work and goal clearly determined for him. Earlier circumstances had curbed his personality and no doubt frustrated him. Now he responded openly to the excitement of new technology and the venture into the skies. After the death of Count Zeppelin and Germany's defeat in the war, Eckener returned to Friedrichshafen, vigorously pressing forward to carry on the work of the Count, to restore his nation's good name, and to develop the zeppelin for peaceful communication between the peoples of the world. The airship was the vehicle of his self-realization, with evidence of his ambition and all its accompaniments of a will to dominate other personalities and circumstances. Nowhere are these elements more decisively evident than in the political origins of building the *Graf Zeppelin*. Here he skillfully and charmingly manipulated Sven Hedin and the Swedish situation. From that base he defied Berlin and the Allies in 1925–26 by mobilizing German popular nationalism on behalf of his zeppelin cause. Concurrently, and thereafter, he waged an uncompromising campaign to gain control of the Aeroarctic Society, using it as leverage with the German government to obtain a final million marks in order to complete the *Graf Zeppelin*. Thus Eckener became the zeppelin, and in the eyes of the world the zeppelin was Eckener. And so it would remain until he collided with the far more lethal opposition of national socialism.

The relationships of other airshipmen to their technology pale by comparison with the two pioneers at Friedrichshafen. Johann Schütte seized his moment and briefly starred, but then was felled by a succession of mistakes, unfavorable personality traits, and misfortune. The details of Harry Vissering's life are largely lost, but there is no doubt that he hitched his star to the zeppelin. Lord Thomson's fatal association with the airship is best discussed in another context below. Of all the American airshipmen (about whom these essays tell very little), Charles E. Rosendahl probably had the closest personal relationship with the rigid dirigible, struggling within the U.S. Navy to establish its important place there, and contesting outside for an American commitment to commercial airships.[5] For the rest—with exception of the low-spirited circumstance at Howden—most of the designers, builders, and fliers found something of a projection of their personalities into the construction and operation of the sky ships, though with few echoes in their own much smaller worlds of political participation.

In the second area of political relationships, the rigid airship experienced various fortunes at the hands of groups and interests affecting its fate in the three major industrial nations. Between 1907 and 1914, mostly in Germany, the airship prospered together with the growing public interest in flight. During the war, despite their developing poor combat record, the zeppelins continued to fly for Germany, while the country's enemies tried energetically to copy them. Peace came, the airplane developed rapidly, and airship critics multiplied. Still, the airship had undeniable advantages for long-distance flight. Initially the Germans were prohibited from participating in postwar dirigible development. The British rejected any future military role for the airship and focused instead upon its commercial potential. Only the Americans, with helium readily available, retained airships as naval scouts and as prototypes adaptable to later commercial development. Within these areas the groups and interests jockeyed for influence and success during the interwar years.

Despite the deep-rooted psychological sympathy for airships among the Germans, postwar official Berlin shied away from them. Possibly one wished to dodge postwar claims on the German treasury for unpaid aerial warships. Certainly one found the prospects of the rapidly developing airplane more attractive, both for open commerce and for secret rearmament. Eckener much more than Schütte represented a relatively small band of airship activists. He crucially influenced the decision to have LZ 126 built for America and as leverage for his own future zeppelin plans. In his strenuous push to seek public funds to build the *Graf Zeppelin*, he was opposed by every Berlin ministry except those for the mails and transportation. It must have galled him to know that, while he was trying to build an airship for peaceful commerce with donations of a few pennies and marks at a time, the navy ministry had secretly allocated five million marks to Dornier Aircraft for construction of a twelve-engine seaplane with distinct military potential.[6] At its heart the bureaucracy of the German foreign office was leery of Eckener's zeppelin. He seemingly carried on a foreign policy all his own. Single-handedly, it appeared, he was changing the image and enhancing the influence of Germans in South America, much to the dismay of France. Paris, in turn, complained to Berlin about every alleged or actual violation of frontiers or demilitarized zones, which sent the German foreign office scurrying after Eckener with its ineffective remonstrances. Concurrently the German socialists voted for commerce by zeppelin but against pocket battleships for war. In late 1931, when it appeared that President von Hindenburg might not stand for reelection against obvious candidate Adolf Hitler, some politicians of the center and moderate left seriously considered grooming zeppelin commander Eckener as their candidate for Germany's chief executive. All this zeppelin-spawned political controversy and notoriety would be a mixed blessing for Eckener's later years.

In immediate postwar Britain the cause of the airship suffered from the inner contradictions of a triple image. The public psyche was negatively attuned to memories of the wartime zeppelin raids. The navy and the new Royal Air Force rejected rigid dirigibles as militarily useless. Only the commercial interests considered the airship favorably, and these as operators, not as builders. For a while the services continued to fly their zeppelin copies— and intermittently to wreck them, with considerable press attention. The disaster of R 38 called a halt until radically new designs were developed. Comdr. Burney's commercial airship project waxed, waned, and underwent revision as various interests wanted to reap its potential benefits but not pay its massive costs. Ultimately the government met the bills for the Imperial Airship Scheme, constructing one ship itself and paying Vickers for the other. Despite all the publicity for the Cardington ship, despite the successful transatlantic flight of R 100 and its enthusiastic reception in Canada,[7] neither the British public nor the armed services ever warmed to the promise of the airship for the empire. The commercial groups and business interests alone could not have got as far as they temporarily did without the forceful intervention of the government by way of Lord Thomson's enthusiasm.

Nothing drew such public attention to the airship as its disasters. The United States had three of them within a decade, all related to service in the U.S. Navy. It was its alleged defense effectiveness that endeared the airship to various American groups. Initially there was a furious row between the navy and the army as to which should have exclusive use of the rigid airship in its service. Once won for the admirals, the airship soon faced an intraservice struggle for survival against the emerging carriers with their own squadrons of fighters and bombers. In the background, the developing seaplane laid claim to scouting advantages over the much slower, more vulnerable, and incredibly more expensive airship. Both naval commanders-in-chief Moffett and King pressed for full development of all three types of naval aviation in the best interests of the service and with admirable lack of prejudice in favor of any one. In the ranks below, however, it was all very competitive, with technological convictions, group loyalties, and emotional commitments often on edge—especially at naval maneuvers. Here the airshipmen, as a small and relatively expensive minority compared with the carrier fliers, were thrust somewhat on the defensive in their own service.

Inevitably the emotionalism of this technological and operational competition spread to, and was influenced by, the builders and purveyors of equipment in the American business world. It was an early example of the military-industrial complex at work. The concerns of the navy and the needs of business joined forces in the halls of congress. Here, too, the airship was on the defense. Its single builder stood against the various airplane makers. Its single potential operator—spawned by the same lone builder—faced rivalry with the first American international airline. By virtue of their inevitable interlocking interests as builders, purchasers, and fliers, the navy airshipmen had a common cause together with Goodyear-Zeppelin in the congressional struggles. The names of personalities are sometimes almost interchangeable between Washington, Akron, and the naval airship stations: Fulton, Hunsaker, Rosendahl, Litchfield, with von Meister ably facilitating in the background and Eckener just offstage to clinch the arguments.

The American public generally had a favorable impression of the airship. The battleship admirals responded to this enthusiasm, frequently showing their airships over land and reinforcing public awareness of the rigid dirigible in scouting service with the great grey line of the fleet—few seaplanes, just a few carriers. With the flight of LZ 126 and her naval baptism as ZR 3, several million German-Americans added their very positive ingredient to all-American airship optimism. In fact, America continually took strength from the German accomplishments, even after the swastika on zeppelin fins began to blur Eckener's popular image. An earlier reciprocity had been verified in the founding of Goodyear-Zeppelin. It had persisted in the presence of naval airshipmen and Goodyear engineers on almost every international zeppelin flight from 1928 onward.[8] It alone made possible the establishment of the American Zeppelin Transport Company in 1936. Most American rigid airship interests thus had something of a German cultural-technological component, and therefrom derived identifiable political interactions.

After the loss of the *Akron* in 1933, and the concurrent arrival of the Nazis on the German scene, the American airship cause encountered increasing difficulties within the navy, on Capitol Hill, and at the White House. Quite likely something of the young Roosevelt—who had experienced business failure with AIC, its Schütte airship plans, and Akron competition—lived on in the mature president, with his doubts reinforced by recent naval airship wrecks and a disdainful opinion of "that rubber company." The combined efforts of Goodyear, the navy, and other supporters of the airship to secure expensive legislation for a "merchant marine of the air" culminated in 1933, just to meet the bottom of the depression, an airship disaster, and the advent of the Nazis. As the American public's airship enthusiasm faltered, Pan American Airways became the "chosen instrument" of the state department to carry this nation's influence abroad by air. The wreck of the *Macon* in 1935 compounded the damage to the image of the airship in America. The carrier captains now seriously contested for supremacy and control of funds in the navy; the airshipmen were limited to flying their blimps. Goodyear had survived the depression, but no further major business initiative could be expected there. Now at Boeing Aircraft the new giant flying boats for Pan American Airways were taking shape, soon to dominate the transoceanic routes. Despite all the politicking about airships in America, here more than elsewhere, governmental influences did not intervene to save the rigid dirigible either from its later disasters or from competition with heavier-than-air machines.

Here one encounters the third area of airship-political phenomena. In contrast to America, the governments of Britain and national socialist Germany each exerted an unusually determining political influence on airship development at a specific stage of its development.

In the British case the government had, of course, been a party to years of discussion about various phases of Comdr. Burney's proposals to secure official sponsorship and subsidies for his commercial Imperial Airship Scheme. The unusual political intervention occurred with the arrival of socialist air minister Thomson in 1924. The Labour government of that year might have wished to nationalize airship building in opposition to private business contracting, but could not alienate the Liberal party support on which it depended. Thus emerged the political compromise for the government to build one airship in competition with another constructed by Vickers' Airship Guarantee Company. In this way the airship became an instrument of contest and conflict between socialism and free enterprise. Though the Labour government fell within a year, the building program continued as redirected. In 1929 Labour returned to power. Lord Thomson also returned as air minister just as both ships were being completed, as the depression began to take hold, and as funding for the airship program dwindled. Given his aviation enthusiasm, his commitment to greater empire cohesion by air, and his desire to see a Labour success for the program, Lord Thomson pressed the Cardington builders and fliers into a fatal risk. The R 101, rebuilt and partially untested, was flown off toward India in anticipation of an Imperial Conference, where Thomson hoped dramatically to prove his case and win wider support for his otherwise financially endangered program. Thus the airship became hostage to ideological ambition and bureaucratic self-preservation.

A much broader and deeper ideological and political manipulation of the zeppelin occurred in Nazi Germany. Much to Eckener's dismay and anger, the Weimar Republic had not effectively supported his airship revival—despite all its successes in winning friends abroad for Germany and humbling French aviation ambitions in South America. In 1933, after years of living almost from hand to mouth, the zeppelin cause received government subsidies for operation, funds to complete the *Hindenburg*, and promises of more money to come. What endeared the zeppelin to the Nazis was not nostalgia for the old Count, and even less, admiration and support for pioneer Eckener. Rather, they understood the unique impact of the zeppelin on the psyche of the German masses. They discerned the psychologically exciting attractiveness

LZ 127 (aloft) and LZ 129 at start of propaganda flight, Friedrichshafen, Mar. 26, 1936. Note hastily repaired lower fin of LZ 129. (Luftschiffbau Zeppelin)

of the airship, the silver mammoth moving serenely through the skies. They understood the impression it conveyed of superiority in technological accomplishment and the implied power moving from its massive dimensions. Therefore, early in their era they asserted control over the German airships and used them as flying billboards to demonstrate the alleged superiority and power of the new Germany under their control.

An essential part of their program was to remove the name and reputation of Hugo Eckener from its resonance with the zeppelin. This task was accomplished by March 1935, in separating the commercial operation of the airships from their construction. Eckener remained at Friedrichshafen as a builder. His DELAG, however, was abolished and reborn at Frankfurt as the Deutsche Zeppelin-Reederei under the direct control of Göring's air ministry. Eckener was needed for the initial *Hindenburg* flights to Brazil and Lakehurst as a propaganda asset, but the DZR was anxious to supplant him with other personalities.

A similar contest for control occurred in the factories at Friedrichshafen.[9] Here a majority of the workers were probably swept up in the same wave of enthusiasm and propaganda that engulfed all of Germany. The zeppelin crews apparently were less affected. On Germany's famous oceanliners the Nazis established patterns of political surveillance, but neither of the two commercial airships was penetrated by this type of control. The zeppeliners flew all their ships with the pride of their unique profession and the joy of its practice. Still, they were as vulnerable to Nazi slogans as the rest of the

LZ 127, *Graf Zeppelin*, on political demonstration flight at Nürnberg Nazi party rally, September 1933. (Verlag Volk und Reich)

German nation. Aware as one is today with hindsight about the progression of Nazi crimes, it would be a gross injustice to those airshipmen to suggest that they flew under the swastika in full awareness of what Hitler would ultimately do, or that they were willing accomplices to his sinister objectives. Like many other Germans, they were susceptible to initial Nazi pretensions that Hitler was basically merely removing the injustices of the Versailles Treaty—which had outlawed their airships in 1919—and that he was restoring the fine old values of conservative nationalism. Eckener was one of few conservatives to see through that sham. For two years the *Graf Zeppelin* carried swastikas on the port side of her horizontal fins, but on the starboard she displayed the colors of old imperial Germany. That was why Eckener flew the ship clockwise around the perimeter of Chicago in 1933, to show German-Americans there the proper symbol. With their professional commitment and national pride the crews, however, could passively accept the swastika as symbolic of a Berlin government that was at last giving unhesitating support to their enterprise.

Internationally the Nazis also juggled symbols for their purposes. All through the flight season of 1936 the *Hindenburg* displayed the interlocked rings of the Olympic Games on both sides amidship, though Eckener appeared less frequently as her genial host. With primary concern for their business and commercial interests, the Americans immediately involved could passively tolerate flying with the swastika. *You Can't Do Business with Hitler*, wrote Douglas Miller somewhat later;[10] but at the offices of Goodyear-Zeppelin and at AZT the German connection was now the only game in town and these Americans were not yet prepared to abandon it. The naval fliers faced the same dilemma. While they struggled within the service and in Washington, D.C., to revive their rigid airships, they also had to depend on the Germans to help maintain their professional skills. And, of course, the Germans they immediately worked with were not storm troopers or SS-men, but rather their respected professional coequals of fifteen years airship camaraderie and the congenial Willy von Meister, who was then himself a characteristic German-American, still somewhat taken in by the Nazi political dramaturgy.

At home in Germany the Nazi political exploitation of the airship reached its climax in the last two years before the war. All the zeppeliners keenly felt the disaster of the *Hindenburg* and warmed to Göring's publicly broadcast commitment to put their ships back into the skies. They chafed at the bit to get back into flying while the helium controversy raged. Like most Germans, they cheered the "return" of the nearby Austrians to the Reich; and they perceived the subsequent American denial of helium as generally anti–German and specifically aimed to destroy their advantage on the transatlantic routes. Eager to prove their competence and the prowess of their remaining new airship, they welcomed the opportunity to serve under the Luftwaffe and took LZ 130 into the skies with exuberant joy (according to Breuning) to put her through her paces. During the last year of escalating international tensions the airshipmen had to show more political obeisance in their flights. The rousing reception they received from the masses and bands and parades on their Sunday flights in the summer of 1939 diverted them from observing the gathering clouds of war. It would seem that primarily they were still so stimulated by the wondrous impact of their shining ship, so psychologically rewarded by the successful accomplishment of flying it, and still so intent

245

LZ 129, *Hindenburg*, propaganda flight over Olympic Stadium, Berlin, Aug. 1, 1936. (Strumann Archives)

upon projecting a valid future for the zeppelin that they were generally blinded to the improbity of the power that manipulated them and their venture.[11]

What, finally, shall be said about Dr. Hugo Eckener himself—the ultimate airshipman, the thorough business manager, the man of sensitive political perception? It is disquieting to see him in a photograph of 1940 with Albert Speer, almost lost in a sea of Nazi civilian and military officials.[12] In another picture of 1945 or 1946, he stands as an abject figure, amidst rows of cabbages

German-American airship cooperation, Olympic Stadium, Berlin, July 1938; left to right: Mrs. Charles E. Rosendahl, Mrs. F. W. von Meister, Comdr. Charles E. Rosendahl, Capt. Hans von Schiller, Reichssportsführer von Tschammer und Osten. (Von Meister Family Archives)

growing on the erstwhile Zeppelin Company airfield, present at the ruin of the converted zeppelin hangar where V-2 rockets had been built.[13] What would account for the fact that, with his clear record of anti–Nazi opposition, he stayed with the Zeppelin enterprise, active in its service for the German war machine to the bitter end?

Many important personalities in modern totalitarian nations have faced the grim dilemmas of expressing their resolute opposition to political tyranny either by emigration to another country or at least by withdrawal to domestic inactivity. Eckener was already potentially threatened by the Nazis at the time of the notorious Blood Purge of late June 1934. Momentarily he considered political asylum in America, then dropped it.[14] Much more dangerous was his conflict with Goebbels in the spring of 1936, from which he emerged unscathed only by the influence of Göring and some prominent German civilians. When he confronted Ickes about helium in May 1938, he could not foresee the use of an airship for military electronic reconnaissance. Yet, when that development occurred later in the year, he formally set the ball rolling for Luftwaffe use of the airship—and stayed on the job.

An understanding of his behavior in these critical circumstances is not difficult to find. First, he never deviated from the purpose to which he had devoted his later life: to carry on the work of Count Zeppelin into commercial service as far and as continually as possible. Second, he had a pervasive loyalty to his comrades in the air and to all his fellow airship builders at the factories of Friedrichshafen. Third, keeping alive the memory and achievement of Count Zeppelin also meant preserving the physical means—the design offices and the workshops—needed to realize the zeppelin mission, even if the factories were temporarily used for other purposes. The full strength of his commitments came clearly to the fore in 1947. When the Zeppelin Foundation turned to invoke Article 15 of the old Count's testament, which meant fully forsaking any future construction of airships or their operation, Eckener made a great demonstration of breaking all ties with the Company and returning to the city of Friedrichshafen the honorary citizenship and all other awards it had earlier bestowed upon him. He would not abandon the great cause, or the men who had worked with him for thirty years, or the physical plant essential to its development, even if it was in ruins. He remained at his post fearlessly through thick and thin, regardless of the personal revulsion he felt for his recent masters. He tried to survive them, thus saving his mission and its means for accomplishment for the future. At the end nothing was left for him but to turn even upon his colleagues and the city that he loved, when he felt that both had betrayed the noble heritage and promise of Count Zeppelin. Fundamentally, all this in context and sequence was behavior of signal integrity.

In some respects, the airships were paradigms of the men and nations that built and flew them. They seemed strong and were proud; yet, they were also at the constant mercy of winds no less shifting and unpredictable than those which buffeted their human counterparts. Forever vacillating between peace and war, they—like the world they traversed—never fully succeeded in either. Much like their creators, they were both political manipulators and victims of politics. Their temporary triumphs and ultimate descent into oblivion were mirrored in the lives of many of those who championed their cause. And rigidity, their very claim to superiority, failed to guarantee their survival—a fact well worth pondering.

Notes

CHAPTER 1: In Search of the Real Count Zeppelin

1. *Schwäbische Zeitung*, June 18, 1985.

2. Ibid., Sept. 3, 1985.

3. Hugh Eckener, *Graf Zeppelin. Sein Leben nach eigenen Aufzeichnungen und persönlichen Erinnerungen* [Count Zeppelin: An Account of His Life Based on his Own Notations and Personal Recollections of the Author] (Stuttgart: J. G. Cotta'sche Buchhandlung Nachfolger, 1938); hereafter cited as Eckener, *Zeppelin*. Rolf Italiaander, *Ferdinand Graf von Zeppelin. Reitergeneral-Diplomat-Luftschiffpionier. Bilder und Dokumente* [Ferdinand Count von Zeppelin: Cavalry General, Diplomat, Airship Pioneer. Pictures and Documents] (Konstanz: Verlag Friedr. Stadler, 1980); hereafter cited as Italiaander, *Zeppelin*.

4. Karl Brökelmann, ed., *Wir Luftschiffer. Die Entwicklung der modernen Luftschifftechnik in Einzeldarstellungen* [We Airshipmen: Individual Studies of the Development of Airship Technique] (Berlin and Vienna: Ullstein, 1909). Alfred Colsman, *Luftschiff Voraus! Arbeit und Erleben am Werke Zeppelins* [Airship Forward!: Work and Experience in the Zeppelin Enterprise] (Stuttgart and Berlin: Deutsche Verlags-Anstalt, 1933); hereafter cited as Colsman, *Luftschiff*. Germany. Luftwaffe. Militärgeschichtliches Forschungsamt, eds., *Die Militärluftfahrt bis zum Beginn des Weltkrieges 1914* [Military Aviation to the Beginning of the World War 1914] 2nd. ed., 3 vols. (Frankfurt: Mittler and Sohn, 1965–66); hereafter cited as *Militärluftfahrt*. Karl Clausberg, *Zeppelin. Die Geschichte eines unwahrscheinlichen Erfolges* [Zeppelin: The Story of an Improbable Success] (Munich: Schirmer-Mosel, 1979); hereafter cited as Clausberg, *Zeppelin*.

5. Eckener, *Zeppelin*, pp. 99–103.

6. Ibid., pp. 7–16; Colsman, *Luftschiff*, pp. 30–32.

7. Hugo Eckener, "Graf Zeppelin als Soldat" [Count Zeppelin as a Soldier], unpubl. ms., completed May 31, 1954 (ten weeks before Eckener's death), pp. 5–6. Uwe Eckener Archives, Konstanz.

8. Eckener, *Zeppelin*, pp. 32–39.

9. See the most recent account by Karl Schnell, *Zeppelins Fernpatrouille mit badischen Dragonern in das untere Elsass. Juli 1870* [Zeppelin's Cavalry Patrol with Baden Dragoons into Lower Alsace. July 1870] (Munich: Verlag für Wehrwissenschaften, 1984), pp. 116–23.

10. Quoted in Eckener, *Zeppelin*, pp. 80–81.

11. Eckener, "Zeppelin als Soldat," ms. unpubl., p. 9.

12. Eckener, *Zeppelin*, pp. 47–62.

13. Ibid., pp. 84–96.

14. See Ernst Rudolf Huber, *Deutsche Verfassungsgeschichte seit 1789*, vol. 3, *Bismarck und das Reich* [German Constitutional History Since 1789; Bismarck and the Empire] (Stuttgart: Kohlhammer, 1963), pp. 643–93, 701–64. For specific Württemberg attitudes, see Walther Wolz,

Württemberg im Bundesrat unter dem Ministerium Mittnacht [Württemberg in the Bundesrat during the Mittnacht Ministry] (Schramberg: Gatzer and Hahn, 1935), passim.

15. Text in Eckener, *Zeppelin*, p. 98. Translation by Douglas H. Robinson, *Giants in the Sky: A History of the Rigid Airship* (Seattle: University of Washington Press, 1973), p. 12; hereafter cited as Robinson, *Giants*.

16. Eckener, *Zeppelin*, p. 99.

17. Hans Philippi, *Das Königreich Württemberg im Spiegel der preussischen Gesandtschaftsberichte 1871–1914*) [The Kingdom of Württemberg as Mirrored in Reports of the Prussian Ambassadors from 1871 to 1914] (Stuttgart: Kohlhammer, 1972), pp. 60–81, 169–79.

18. Eckener, *Zeppelin*, pp. 99–103.

19. Quoted in ibid., pp. 100–01. On the role and concept of honor in the German army, see Karl Demeter. *The German Officer-Corps in Society and State, 1650–1945* (New York: Frederick A. Praeger, Inc., 1965), pp. 111–15.

20. Quoted in Eckener, *Zeppelin*, pp. 101–02.

21. Ibid., pp. 103–04.

22. Quoted in Luftschiffbau Zeppelin, *Das Werk Zeppelins. Eine Festgabe zu seinem 75. Geburtstag* [The Accomplishment of Count Zeppelin. In Honor of his 75th Birthday] (Friedrichshafen: Luftschiffbau, 1913), p. 2

23. Quoted in Eckener, *Zeppelin*, p. 108.

24. Hans G. Knäusel, *LZ 1. Der erste Zeppelin. Geschichte einer Idee, 1874–1908* [LZ 1. The First Zeppelin: The History of an Idea, 1874–1908] (Bonn: Kirschbaum Verlag, 1985), pp. 43–144; Robinson, *Giants*, pp. 15–25.

25. Quoted in Eckener, *Zeppelin*, p. 107.

26. Quoted in ibid., p. 133.

27. Quoted in ibid., p. 142.

28. Ibid., p. 152.

29. Alan Sillitoe, *Loneliness of the Long-distance Runner* (New York: Knopf, 1961), pp. 53–54.

30. *Militärluftfahrt*, vol. 2, doc. no. 26, p. 48.

31. Ibid., doc. no. 27, pp. 49–57.

32. Colsman, *Luftschiff*, p. 13.

33. Robinson, *Giants*, pp. 33–35.

34. Eckener, *Zeppelin*, pp. 158–59.

35. Ibid., pp. 159–61; Italiaander, *Zeppelin*, pp. 91–93; see personal reminiscence of the disaster by aviator Ernst Heinkel, *Stürmisches Leben* [A Stormy Life] (Stuttgart: Mundus-Verlag, 1953), pp. 13–14.

36. See illustrations in Italiaander, *Zeppelin*, pp. 118, 144–45.

37. Robinson, *Giants*, pp. 42–59, 330–31.

38. *Militärluftfahrt*, vol. 2, doc. no. 35, pp. 70–72.

39. See Thor Nielsen, *Eckener: Ein Leben für den Zeppelin* [Eckener: A Life Devoted to the Zeppelin] (Munich: Kindler and Schirmer, 1954), p. 210.

40. Colsman, *Luftschiff*, p. 112.

41. Italiaander, *Zeppelin*, p. 137. See Hugo Hergesell, *Mit Zeppelin nach Spitzbergen* [To Spitzbergen with Count Zeppelin] (Berlin: Deutsches Verlagshaus Bong and Co., 1911).

42. Georg von Tschudi, *Aus 34 Jahren Luftfahrt. Persönliche Erinnerungen* [Personal Recollections of 34 Years in Aviation] (Berlin: Reimar Hobbing, 1928), pp. 94–95.

43. Quoted in Clausberg, *Zeppelin*, p. 136.

44. *Militärluftfahrt*, vol. 1, 86–107; vol. 2, doc. nos. 36–52, pp. 72–103.

45. Colsman, *Luftschiff*, pp. 159–60.

46. *Militärluftfahrt*, vol. 1, 194–223; vol. 2, doc. nos. 87–99, pp. 192–229; Colsman, *Luftschiff*, pp. 152–61.

47. Ludwig Dehio, "Thoughts on Germany's Mission," *Germany and World Politics in the Twentieth Century*, D. Pevsner trans. (New York: Norton, 1967), pp. 72–108.

48. Telegram texts in Luftschiffbau Zeppelin Archives, Friedrichshafen.

49. Quoted in Hans Rosenkranz, *Ferdinand Graf von Zeppelin* (Berlin: Ullstein Verlag, 1931), pp. 189–90.

50. Quoted in Fritz Fischer, *Griff nach der Weltmacht. Die Kriegszielpolitik des kaiserlichen Deutschland 1914–18* [Grasp for World Power: The War Aims Policies of Imperial Germany, 1914–18] (Düsseldorf: Droste Verlag, 1962), pp. 354–55.

51. Full text in Italiaander, *Zeppelin*, p. 154.

52. Robinson, *Giants*, p. 90. In general see Robinson's authoritative *The Zeppelin in Combat* (London: G. T. Foulis and Co., 1962) for all airships during World War I.

53. Heinkel, *Stürmisches Leben*, pp. 89–92.

54. Karl von Einem, *Erinnerungen eines Soldaten, 1853–1933* [Recollections of a Soldier, 1853–1933] (Leipzig: K. F. Koehler, 1933), p. 164.

55. "Zeppelin und Reichskanzler" [Zeppelin and Imperial Chancellor], privately printed and distributed as manuscript [1916?], p. 15.

56. Quoted in Clausberg, *Zeppelin*, pp. 139–40.

57. See George W. Haddow and Peter M. Grosz, *The German Giants: The Story of the R-planes, 1914–1919* (London: Putnam, 1962).

58. The cartoon is reproduced in Italiaander, *Zeppelin*, p. 172.

59. Colsman, *Luftschiff*, pp. 131–32.

60. Clausberg, *Zeppelin*, p. 140.

61. Quoted in Italiaander, *Zeppelin*, p. 158.

62. Robinson, *Giants*, pp. 40–113.

63. Knäusel, *LZ 1*, pp. 14–17.

CHAPTER 2: In the Shadow of the Titan

1. "USA Professor Folgt den Spuren Schüttes" [USA Professor Tracking Down Schütte], *Nordwest Zeitung* (Oldenburg), Aug. 1, 1979; Klaus Wiborg, "Im Schatten des Titanen. Johann Schütte und der Luftschiffbau. Was Wird aus dem Nachlass?" [In the Shadow of the Titan. Johann Schütte and Airship Construction. What Will Become of his Papers?], *Frankfurter Allgemeine Zeitung*, May 23, 1984.

2. Johann Friedrich Jahn, *Technischer Nachlass Johann Schütte. Ein Bericht* [The Technical Papers of Johann Schütte: A Report] (Oldenburg: priv. publ., 1978). These papers are temporarily located at the *Landesmuseum für Technik und Arbeit* in Mannheim, once the main branch of the Schütte-Lanz airship construction business from 1909 to 1920. Next to the presently inaccessible archives of the Brandenstein-Zeppelin family, these papers are the best record anywhere in the world of private initiative in the airship business. Hereafter cited as Schütte Papers. These materials underlie the business history analysis of Schütte-Lanz by Dorothea Haaland, *Der Luftschiffbau Schütte-Lanz, Mannheim-Rheinau, (1909–1925)* . . . [The Airship Construction Works of Schütte-Lanz at Mannheim-Rheinau] (Mannheim: Institut f. Landeskunde und Regionalforschung der Universität Mannheim, 1987); hereafter cited as Haaland, *S-L*.

3. Gotthold Baatz, Johann Schütte. "Vortrag anlässlich der Ehrung von Geh. Rat Prof. Dr.-Ing. Johann Schütte am 26. 3. 1938 in Oldenburg" [Address on the Occasion of Honoring Dr. Schütte in Oldenburg on March 26, 1938]. Text in author's collection of Schütte documents.

4. See Frederick S. Hardesty, *Key to the Development of the Super-Airship, Luftfahrzeugbau Schuette-Lanz, Mannheim-Rheinau, Germany, 1909–1930: A Succinct Statement of Facts, Authorities, and Supporting Data. Patent Status, History, Legal and Technical Opinions* (New York: priv. publ., 1930), pp. 2–3; hereafter cited as Hardesty, *Key*.

5. See Johann Schütte, *Der Luftschiffbau Schütte-Lanz, 1909–1925* [The Airship Construction Works Schütte-Lanz] (Munich and Berlin: R. Oldenbourg, 1926), p. 126; hereafter cited as Schütte, *Luftschiffbau*. Baatz, Schütte Vortrag, passim; Eugen Zabel, *Deutsche Luftfahrt. Rückblicke und Ausblicke* [German Aviation in Retrospect and Prospect] (Berlin: Verlag Braunbeck, 1918), pp. 118–19; eulogies of Schütte, March-April 1940, by Georg Christians, Johannes Moeller, and Georg Schnadel; ms. texts in author's collection of Schütte documents.

6. See account and correspondence in Schütte, *Luftschiffbau*, pp. 1–10; Haaland, *S-L*, pp. 49–68.

7. The very best account of the pros and cons of the Schütte airships is in Robinson, *Giants*, pp. 68–76, 90–91, 140–41. See also his *The Zeppelin in Combat* (London: Foulis and Co., 1971),

passim; Haaland, *S-L*, pp. 30–32. Note that Robinson adjusted his evaluation of Schütte in reviewing Haaland's book; see *Bouyant Flight. The Bulletin of the Lighter-Than-Air Society*, 35, no. 4, (May-June, 1988), 2–7.

8. Robinson, *Giants*, p. 75. Haaland indicates that much subsequent innovation was introduced by various members of Schütte construction engineers, notably F. Kruckenberg. See *S-L*, pp. 58–61.

9. Robinson, *Giants*, pp. 70–76. See also the best British general airship study. Guy Hartcup, *The Achievement of the Airship* (London: David and Charles, 1974), pp. 79–85.

10. See Georg W. Haddow and Peter M. Gross, *The German Giants: The Story of the R-planes, 1914–1919* (London: Putnam, 1962); also Raymond H. Fredette, *The Sky on Fire: The First Battle of Britain 1917–1918 and the Birth of the Royal Air Force* (New York: Holt, Rinehart and Winston, 1966); hereafter cited as Fredette, *Sky on Fire*.

11. Schütte, *Luftschiffbau*, pp. 114–18; Wilhelm Hillmann, *Der Flugzeugbau Schütte-Lanz* [The Aircraft Construction Firm Schütte-Lanz] (Berlin: Deutsche Verlagswerke, 1928), pp. 7–28.

12. Haaland, *S-L*, pp. 95–128; Robinson, *Giants*, pp. 69, 71; Schütte, *Luftschiffbau*, pp. 132–35; Hardesty, *Key*, pp. 18–24; Hans von Schiller, *Zeppelin. Wegbereiter des Weltluftverkehrs* [Zeppelin, The Pioneer of Worldwide Air Travel] (Bad Godesberg: Kirschbaum Verlag, 1967), p. 67.

13. Robinson, *Giants*, pp. 163–66; idem., *Zeppelin in Combat*, pp. 284–96; Schiller, *Zeppelin*, pp. 70–72.

14. Robinson, *Giants*, pp. 256–59.

15. Schütte Reisebericht [Report of Schütte trip to America, 1920], Schütte Papers, A Box 103, T-BVG 019.

16. Memorandum: To the German Group of the International Chamber of Commerce at Berlin, Concerning American Investigation Corporation in New York, from the Schütte-Lanz Company, Berlin-Wilmersdorf, March 28, 1928; Schütte Papers, 106/S-ama 021. Haaland, *S-L*, pp. 154–59. See also "Reiseschilderung des Herrn Kommerzienrat Colsman nach Amerika, 1 Mai [19] 20–21 Juli [19] 20" [Travel Journal of Commercial Councillor Alfred Colsman to America] with appended copies of letters to the Zeppelin Company offices. Mss. In Luftschiffbau Zeppelin Archives, Friedrichshafen.

17. Antony G. Sutton, *Wall Street and FDR* (New Rochelle, N.Y.: Arlington House, 1975), p. 53; hereafter cited as Sutton, *Wall Street*. This curious book is written to affirm the strange proposition that the New Deal of 1932–39 was yet another example of "the interest of the Wall Street financial establishment to attain a socialist society." (p. 9). Still, the author gives evidence of extensive research in the Franklin D. Roosevelt Archives at Hyde Park, N.Y. The materials he uses therefrom in discussion of Schütte and AIC intersect reasonably with data in the Schütte Papers.

18. Quoted in Frank Freidel, *Franklin D. Roosevelt*. vol. 2: *The Ordeal* (Boston: Little, Brown, and Co., 1954), p. 149.

19. For list of Schütte patents in America from 1911 onward, see Hardesty, *Key*, pp. 29–34, 71–93.

20. Quoted in Sutton, *Wall Street*, p. 62.

21. Ibid., pp. 61–62.

22. Ibid., pp. 55–56. A full list of AIC participants is published in F. Chandler, "Advent of the American Air Liner," *Current History*, vol. 16 (Apr.-Sept. 1922), pp. 410–14.

23. Sutton, *Wall Street*, p. 62.

24. "Advent," p. 413. These airship plans had also been very briefly noted three months before in the first issue of a new experiment in weekly journalism called *Time* magazine, vol. 1 (Mar. 3, 1923), p. 21.

25. Baatz, Schütte Vortrag, passim.

26. Memorandum: Concerning AIC New York, Schütte Papers, passim; Schütte Organization, Fahrtechnische Grundlagen des Luftschiffverkehrs [Technical Principles of Commercial Airship Operation], ms. text in Schütte collection of the author; Schütte, *Luftschiffbau*, pp. 72–74; Sutton, *Wall Street*, pp. 56–57; 62–63; Haaland, *S-L*, pp. 160–67.

27. Sutton, *Wall Street*, pp. 60–61.

28. *New York Times*, "Big Airship Line Planned for U.S.," Feb. 10, 1923, p. 9; ibid., Feb. 12, 1923, p. 12.

29. *Literary Digest*, vol. 76 (Mar. 24, 1923), pp. 60–62.

30. Letter, Edward Schildhauer to Johann Schütte, June 1, 1923. Schütte Papers, 99/D-c 08.

31. Vissering expressed his enthusiasm in a somewhat factually flawed but nicely illustrated book, *Zeppelin: The Story of a Great Achievement* (Chicago: priv. publ., 1922). His nephew, Hallett Cole (who left a large but rather disorganized collection of airship data and memorabilia to the library of the University of Oregon) stated that the book had a printing of five hundred copies, of which many were lost in a hurricane in Florida, where Vissering had retired. That event would also account for the disappearance of Vissering's other documentation.

32. Letter of Harry Vissering to Luftschiffbau Zeppelin, Feb. 17, 1922. Copy in Papers of Garland Fulton, Naval Historical Foundation, Washington Navy Yard, Washington, D.C. On Schütte's part, see Hardesty, *Key*, pp. 66–71.

33. Letter of Oct. 13, 1923, Goodyear Archives, File 4. Aviation A-101A.

34. Letter of Nov. 15, 1923, Goodyear Archives, File 4. Aviation A-101A.

35. Letter of Nov. 19, 1923, Goodyear Archives, File 4. Aviation A-101A.

36. "Bericht über Reise Bleistein nach Amerika" [Report of Bleistein's Trip to America]. Schütte Papers, 99/D-c 08.

37. Letter of July 11, 1924. Goodyear Archives, File 4. Aviation A-122.

38. Concerning American Investigation Corporation, New York, Mar. 28, 1928. Copy in Papers of Garland Fulton, Naval Historical Foundation, Washington Navy Yard, Washington, D.C. From its appearance, this is probably the copy of a report of the U.S. naval attaché in Berlin.

39. See Hardesty, *Key*, pp. 105–11.

40. Various folders, boxes, and binders in the Schütte Papers and in the Luftschiffbau Zeppelin Archives.

41. The Luftschiffbau Zeppelin Archives has several shelves of data about the confrontation of the Zeppelin Company and Schütte-Lanz, from which this summary is taken. Terms of the final out-of-court settlement are reproduced in Hardesty, *Key*, pp. 112–18. Obviously lawyer Hardesty's book is a completely one-sided presentation on his and Schütte's behalf, but it does reproduce important testimony praising Schütte's work. Further data, in much greater volume, survive in the Schütte Papers.

42. Hans Hildebrandt, ed., *Zeppelin-Denkmal für das deutsche Volk* [Zeppelin Memorial for the German People] (Stuttgart: Germania Verlag, [1925]); Schütte, *Luftschiffbau*, passim. An almost complete collection of the articles from a "scientific" point of view survives in the Luftschiffbau Zeppelin Archives. See also Haaland, *S-L*, pp. 138–40, 167–77, 260–65.

43. Letter, Paul Halling to Johann Schütte, Dec. 3, 1927. Schütte collection of the author.

44. Letter, Wilhelm Hillman to H. C. Meyer, Mar. 30, 1977. The second bracketed paraphrase in the quotation masks potentially libelous material; indeed, the entire fifteen-page letter is a model of restrained character assassination.

45. Letters: Colsman to the Aviation Science Society, Sept. 9, 1927; Capt. G. Krupp (of that society) to Colsman, Sept. 12, 1927; Colsman to Krupp, Sept. 14, 1927; Schütte to Colsman, Sept. 12, 1927. Luftschiffbau Zeppelin Archives.

46. Various letters in Luftschiffbau Zeppelin Archives, including Colsman to Schütte, Oct. 21, 1927.

47. Robinson, *Giants*, pp. 226–27.

48. See Thor Nielsen, *The Zeppelin Story: The Life of Hugo Eckener*, trans. P. Chambers (London: Allan Wingate, 1955), pp. 182–84. Nielsen based his book on several weeks of interviews with Eckener in the last year of the airshipman's life. His account of the incident has Eckener alone solving the problem for the allegedly nonplussed naval base commandant—possibly a last reflex on Eckener's part of the old feud with Schütte.

49. Baatz, Johann Schütte Vortrag, passim; Wilhelm Dursthoff, "Zum Gedächtnis an Prof. Dr. Ing. E. h. Johann Schütte" [In Memory of Professor Dr. Ing. E. h. Johann Schütte, *Oldenburger Jahrburch* 73 (1973), 35–40.

50. Walter Brockmann, "Luftschiffe. Leistungen in der Vergangenheit und Möglichkeiten in der Zukunft" [Airships: Accomplishments in the Past and Possibilities in the Future], *Oldenburger Jahrbuch*, ibid., pp. 41–67. See also Haaland's evaluation, *S-L*, pp. 207–13.

51. Dursthoff, "Zum Gedächtnis," ibid., p. 39.

52. See *Begegnungen mit der Technik in der Industriegesellschaft* [Encounters with Technology in Industrial Society] (1983) and other attractive pamphlets published by the *Landesmuseum für Technik und Arbeit* in Mannheim, Germany.

CHAPTER 3: Building Rigid Airships

1. On airship history in general, see Robinson, *Giants* and Schiller, *Zeppelin*. Also Guy Hartcup, *The Achievement of the Airship* . . . (London: David and Charles, 1974). Specifically with focus on Britain and the United States, see Robin Higham, *The British Rigid Airship, 1908–1931* (London: G. T. Foulis, 1961); Richard K. Smith, *The Airships Akron and Macon* . . . (Annapolis, Md.: U.S. Naval Institute, 1965); and Douglas H. Robinson and Charles L. Keller, *"Up Ship!" U.S. Navy Rigid Airships 1919–1935* (Annapolis, Md.: U.S. Naval Institute Press, 1982); hereafter cited as Robinson and Keller, *"Up Ship!".*

2. Karl G. Grismer, *Akron and Summit County* (Akron, Ohio: Summit County Historical Society, 1952), pp. 437–48.

3. Elmar L. Kuhn, *Geschichte am See.* 24 1. *Industrialisierung in Oberschwaben und am Bodensee* [History at the Lake: Industrialization in Upper Swabia and at the Lake of Constance] (Friedrichshafen: Kreisarchiv Bodenseekreis, 1984), pp. 372–73; hereafter cited as Kuhn, *Geschichte.*

4. Fredette, *Sky on Fire*, pp. 11, 26.

5. Kuhn, *Geschichte*, pp. 315–68. I am indebted to Mr. Rolf Striedacher of Tettnang (near Friedrichshafen) for permission to study his unpublished ms. on the history of the Luftschiffbau Zeppelin, 1918–1925. I also received much benefit in interviews and correspondence with Capt. Hans von Schiller, Capt. Albert Sammt, Erich Hilligardt (one of the Zeppelin Company experts who spent some time with the contingent in Akron), and German Zettel (zeppelin machinist on all major flights from 1928 to 1937) during visits in 1972, 1973, 1975, and 1979. See also Oswald Burger, "Zeppelin und die Rüstungsindustrie am Bodensee," ["Zeppelin and the Armanents Industry at the Lake of Constance"], *1999. Zeitschrift für Sozialgeschichte des 20. und 21. Jahrhunderts,* Heft 1, 1987, pp. 6–49.

6. See Colsman, *Luftschiff*, passim.

7. Sir Peter G. Masefield, *To Ride the Storm: The Story of Airship R 101* (London: William Kimber, 1982); Geoffrey Chamberlain, *Airships-Cardington: A History of Cardington Airship Station and Its Role in World Airship Development* (Lavenham, Suffolk: Terence Dalton, Ltd., 1984); J. E. Morpurgo, *Barnes Wallis: A Biography* (London: Longman, 1972); Nevil Shute Norway, *Slide Rule: The Autobiography of an Engineer* (New York: Morrow, 1954). I am indebted for interviews and correspondence to Sir Barnes Wallis, Sir Peter G. Masefield, Lord Kings Norton, Lord Baker of Windrush, Prof. J. E. Morpurgo, Crispin Rope, and Guy Hartcup.

8. Quoted in Barry Countryman, *R 100 in Canada* (Erin, Ont.: Boston Mills Press, 1982), p. 11.

9. Countryman's excellent study of R 100 in Canada gives a detailed analysis of the social and psychological impact of the visit of a rigid airship to a country and people that had never viewed such a sky giant before.

10. Hugh Allen, *The House of Goodyear* (Cleveland, Ohio: Corday and Gross Co., 1943), passim. See also successive annual editions of Hugh Allen, *The Story of the Airship* (Akron, Ohio: Goodyear Tire and Rubber Co., 1925 ff.); Smith, *Akron and Macon*, pp. 319.

11. Akron *Beacon-Journal*, Oct. 1, 9, 14, 26–30, 1929. Akron Chamber of Commerce, "What Has the Chamber of Commerce Done? . . . , 1928–1929." [1929].

12. Some of this material about Akron and Goodyear-Zeppelin comes from Clifton C. Slusser's draft for an official history of Goodyear, from the Goodyear Archives, notably Part 3, "Reorganization and Recovery, 1919–1928," and Part 4, "Versatility and Vitality, 1928–1938." Similar information appears in Paul W. Litchfield, *Industrial Voyage: My Life as an Industrial Lieutenant* (Garden City, N.Y., Doubleday and Co., 1954), passim. I am indebted for interviews or correspondence with Thomas A. Knowles of the Goodyear Company, Vice Admiral T. G. W. Settle (U.S. Navy Inspector at Akron, 1928–34), Kurt Bauch (one of the original "twelve apostles" who came to Akron from Germany with Dr. Karl Arnstein in 1925), George Lewis

(who also represented Goodyear in Friedrichshafen from 1934 to 1936), Prof. George W. Knepper (urban historian at the University of Akron), and historian Dr. Richard K. Smith.

13. See discussion on competition between airship and flying boat in "Tomorrow's Airplane," *Fortune*, vol. 18, no. 1 (July 1938), 53–65.

14. Kuhn, *Geschichte*, pp. 341–69.

15. Eckener, *Zeppelin*, pp. 42–45.

16. Kuhn, *Geschichte*, pp. 369–73; "Die Zeppelin-Wohlfahrt G.m.b.H., Friedrichshafen," *Werkzeitschrift der Zeppelinbetriebe*, vol. 3 (1938), 50–52, 66–70; Burger, "Rüstungsindustrie," pp. 14–17; John Provan, Zeppelindorf Friedrichshafen. Privately compiled documentation of descriptions, statistics, plans, and illustrations, 1983; "Vor 70 Jahren zogen die ersten Siedler im Friedrichshafener Zeppelindorf ein," *Schwäbische Zeitung* (Friedrichshafen), Mar. 29, 1986.

17. Kuhn, *Geschichte*, pp. 387–421; Burger, "Rüstungsindustrie," pp. 29–33.

18. Reference again here to Striedacher's admirable unpublished history of the Luftschiffbau Zeppelin, 1919–1925.

19. See Harold G. Dick, with Douglas H. Robinson, *The Golden Age of the Great Passenger Airships: Graf Zeppelin and Hindenburg* (Washington, D.C.: Smithsonian Institution Press, 1986), pp. 12–24, 161–71. Hereafter cited as Dick and Robinson, *Golden Age*.

20. Chamberlain, *Airships-Cardington*, pp. 111–33; Morpurgo, *Barnes Wallis*, pp. 126–52; Norway, *Slide Rule*, pp. 52–143.

21. Smith, Akron *and* Macon, pp. 31–45. Note W. J. Gonder, "Experiences of an Airship Worker," *Bouyant Flight*, vol. 19 (March-April 1972), 9–10. Correspondence with Mr. D. W. Brown, Goodyear airship worker, 1929–72, during summer 1987.

22. Litchfield, *Industrial Voyage*, passim. See also his *The President Talks to His Men: A Group of Radio Addresses* (Akron, Ohio: The Goodyear Tire and Rubber Co., 1935) and *The Industrial Republic: Reflections of an Industrial Lieutenant* (Cleveland, Ohio: Corday and Gross Co., 1946).

23. Slusser, History Draft, Goodyear Archives, Part 4. See also Zenon Hansen, "When the Zeppelin Took to the Rails . . . ," *The Railroad Capital*. [Official Publication of the Railroad Club of Chicago], Apr. 1985, pp. 1–10.

24. See the vividly written and illustrated book of the Goodyear-Zeppelin representative in Friedrichshafen, 1936–38, Dick and Robinson, *Golden Age*, pp. 20–24, 48–64, 111–37, 172–84.

25. Interview with Erich Hilligardt, Friedrichshafen, July 9, 1973. Note his "Bericht über den Verbleib der Luftschiffunterlagen," Mar. 9, 1956 [Report on the Survival of Airship Technical Documentation], Luftschiffbau Zeppelin Archives, Friedrichshafen.

26. Hilligardt and Sperger, Bericht über den Stand der Studien zur Wiederaufnahme eines Luftschiffverkehrs, Feb. 25, 1957 [Report on Status of Studies on Resumption of Airship Service], Luftschiffbau Zeppelin Archives, Friedrichshafen.

27. Interviews with various Zeppelin individuals already indicated above; *Schwäbische Zeitung*, Friedrichshafen, 1972–87, passim.

28. Chamberlain, *Airships-Cardington*, pp. 196–207. The author visited Cardington on June 30, 1985 and is indebted for escort and interviews there with Cardington Museum head, Frank Kiernan, and Mr. Geoff Keep. The Friends of Cardington Airship Station, a new society, alone hold the thin threads to keep its memory alive.

29. Paul W. Litchfield and Hugh Allen, *Why Has America No Rigid Airships?* (Cleveland, Ohio: Corday and Gross Co., 1945).

30. Visits and interviews with Dr. A. D. Topping in Akron, Ohio in 1973, 1974, 1978, and 1981. Dr. Topping has been editor of the society's bimonthly publication since 1959. The publication has been called *Bouyant Flight* since 1971. Dr. Topping is currently writing a major work on the career of Dr. Karl Arnstein.

CHAPTER 4: Eckener's Struggle to Save the Airship for Germany

1. The best biography of Eckener is Rolf Italiaander, *Ein Deutscher namens Eckener . . .* [A German Named Eckener] (Konstanz: Verlag Friedrich Stadler, 1981). See also Italiaander's beautifully illustrated *Hugo Eckener. Ein moderner Columbus. Die Weltgeltung der Zeppelin-Luftschiffahrt in Bildern und Dokumenten* [Hugo Eckener: A Modern Columbus. The Worldwide Impact of the Airship in Pictures and Documents] (Konstanz: Verlag Friedrich Stadler, 1979); hereafter

cited as Italiaander, *Eckener*. The only biography in English is Thor Nielsen, *The Zeppelin Story*, trans. P. Chambers (London: Allen Wingate, 1955), but it is badly flawed with inaccuracies and evidences of Eckener's failing memory. Eckener's own memoirs, *Im Zeppelin über Länder und Meere. Erlebnisse und Erinnerungen* [By Zeppelin over Lands and Seas: Experiences and Memories] (Flensburg: Verlagshaus Christian Wolff, 1949) are available in a scarce abridged English edition by Douglas H. Robinson entitled *My Zeppelins* (London: G. T. Foulis and Co., 1958).

2. See Douglas H. Robinson, *The Zeppelin in Combat* (London: G. T. Foulis and Co., Ltd., 1962).

3. Various files in the Political Archives. German Foreign Office, Bonn; fragments of documentation in the archives of Luftschiffbau Zeppelin in Friedrichshafen.

4. See copies of various reports and letters in the Papers of Garland Fulton, Naval Historical Foundation, Washington Navy Yard, Washington, D.C.; hereafter Fulton Papers.

5. Securing reliable data about Harry Vissering is a continuing, elusive paper chase. The voluminous and beautifully indexed Harding Papers in the Manuscript Division of the Library of Congress have not a single reference to Vissering. There are fragments of correspondence in the Goodyear Archives and that of the Luftschiffbau Zeppelin. A few other fragments reside in the Hallett Cole Airship Collection at the library of the University of Oregon, Eugene, Oreg. Inquiries with his son, Maj. Gen. Vissering, indicated that no documentation has survived in the family. What *does* remain is Vissering's own enthusiastic book about the airship future, enhanced with data from Eckener. See Vissering's *Zeppelin: The Story of a Great Achievement* (Chicago: privately printed, 1922).

6. Letter, Garland Fulton to Jerome C. Hunsaker, Oct. 20, 1922. Fulton Papers. Naval Historical Center, Washington Navy Yard, Washington, D.C.

7. See chapter 2 on Johann Schütte.

8. Letter, Ingeborg Colsman to Werner Strumann, Feb. 6, 1987. Strumann Archives, Münster/Westf. Schütte wrote a long critical memorandum: "Stellungnahme Schütte's zu dem Buch LUFTSCHIFF VORAUS! von Alfred Colsman," Stuttgart, 1933. [Schütte's Response to Colsman's Book] File labeled "Schütte-Lanz gegen Fiskus und Zeppelin" 09/26, Schütte Papers.

9. Letter, Bruno Pochhammer to Georg Blasweiler, Oct. 10, 1923. Douglas H. Robinson Collection.

10. "LZ Monatsberichte" [LZ Monthly Reports], March 1924. Luftschiffbau Zeppelin Archives.

11. Eckener, *Im Zeppelin*, p. 95

12. Germany. Bundesarchiv Koblenz. Reichskanzlei, R 43 I, vol. 737, no. 5802.

13. Letter, Hugo Eckener to Chancellor Hans Luther, Aug. 15, 1925. Ibid., no. 5907.

14. Hildebrandt, ed., *Zeppelin-Denkmal für das deutsche Volk*.

15. Telegram, Gustav Stresemann to Hugo Eckener, Aug. 24, 1925. Political Archives. German Foreign Office, Bonn, Folder IIF-Luft 65/2. Note Stresemann's precautionary tardiness in transmitting his greetings—so that they might not be read at the jubilee!

16. Postcard reproduction of painting of LZ 126 in flight, by Otto Amtsberg. Text by staff of *Zeppelin-Eckener-Spende*, Feb. 20, 1926.

17. Documentary sequence, Bundesarchiv, Reichskanzlei, R 43 I, vol. 737, passim.

18. Interview with Ernst N. Shaffer, Bonn-Röttgen, July 20, 1974. Schaffer indicated that he had told Eckener that he would not incorporate this exchange in his article.

19. See chapter 4 on various aspects of Colsman's activities at the Zeppelin Company. Full details are recorded in the unpublished business history of the Zeppelin Company between 1919 and 1925 by Rolf Striedacher.

20. Heinz Steude, Alfred Colsman. Unpublished ms. of 1964 in the Luftschiffbau Zeppelin Archives.

CHAPTER 5: Zeppelin Intermezzos in Detroit

1. See Robinson, *Giants*, pp. 206–13; Hans G. Knäusel, *Zeppelin and the United States of America . . .* (Friedrichshafen: Zeppelin-Druckerei, 1981), pp. 33–43; A. Wittemann, *Die Amerikafahrt des Z.R. III* [The America Flight of Z.R. III] (Wiesbaden: Amsel-Verlag, 1925); Italiaander, *Eckener*, pp. 52–59 for excellent illustrations.

2. Alfred Colsman, "Reiseschilderungen des Kommerzienrat Alfred Colsman nach Amerika, 1 Mai 1920–21 Juli 1920" [Travel Journals of Commercial Councilor Alfred Colsman to America]. Ms. In Luftschiffbau Zeppelin Archives. See also the brief account of Colsman's trip in his *Luftschiff*, pp. 235–40.

3. Quoted in Anne Jardim, *The First Henry Ford: A Study of Personality and Business Leadership* (Cambridge, Mass.: MIT Press, 1970), p. 34.

4. Ibid., p. 34

5. Peter Collier and David Horowitz, *The Fords. An American Epic* (New York: Summit Books, 1987), pp. 69–90; Robert Lacey, *Ford: The Man and the Machine* (Boston: Little, Brown, and Co., 1986), pp. 183–84.

6. Allan Nevins and Frank Ernest Hill, *Ford*. vol. 2, *Expansion and Challenge, 1915–1933* (New York: Charles Scribner's Sons, 1957), pp. 63–82.

7. Robinson, *Giants*, pp. 162–66.

8. Ford Motor Company Archives, Dearborn, Mich., Accession No. 902. Chronological History of Ford Motor Co., Subsection 1—Aviation, pt. 5. Dirigibles. Also comments to the author by Garland Fulton, Bala Cynwd, Pa., Aug. 8, 1974.

9. Colsman, *Reiseschilderungen*.

10. Ibid., appendix 11, June 20, 1920.

11. Quoted in *Automotive Industries*, July 22, 1920, p. 189.

12. David Ansell Weiss, *The Saga of the Tin Goose* (New York: Crown Publishers, Inc., 1971), pp. 63–64.

13. Sutton, *Wall Street*, pp. 55, 62–63.

14. Harry Vissering to Edward G. Wilmer, July 11, 1924. Goodyear Archives. 4. Aviation. A-122.

15. Richard K. Smith, "Ralph H. Upson: A Career Sketch and Bibliography," *American Aviation Historical Society Journal*, vol. 13 (Winter 1968) 282–84.

16. Henry Ford, *Today and Tomorrow* (London: Wm. Heinemann, Ltd., 1926), p. 206.

17. William Bushell Stout, *So Away I Went!* (New York: Bobbs-Merrill, 1951), pp. 133–85; Weiss, *Tin Goose*, pp. 64–71.

18. Ibid., pp. 73–74.

19. Nevins and Hill, *Ford*, vol. 2, p. 240; Lacey, *Ford*, p. 244.

20. Ernst A. Lehmann, *Auf Luftpatrouille und Weltfahrt. Erlebnisse eines Zeppelinführers in Krieg und Frieden* [On Air Reconnaissance and Worldwide Flights: Experiences of a Zeppelin Captain in War and Peace] (Leipzig: Schmidt and Günther, 1936), pp. 269–70.

21. Ibid., pp. 271–72.

22. For full details on committee members and program, see *Detroit Free Press*, Oct. 29 and 30, 1924.

23. Robinson, *Giants*, pp. 223–26.

24. Quoted in Jardim, *First Henry Ford*, p. 128.

25. *Detroit Free Press*, Oct. 31, 1924.

26. Weiss, *Tin Goose*, pp. 81–82; Stout, *So Away I Went!*, pp. 198–99.

27. Admiral Count Erich von Zeppelin to Henry Ford, Jan. 6, 1925, and C. A. Zahnow, Office of Henry Ford, to Admiral von Zeppelin, Jan. 31, 1925, Ford Motor Company Archives.

28. Ford Motor Co. Chronological History, accession no. 902, Chronological History, Aviation.

29. Weiss, *Tin Goose*, p. 80.

30. Writers' Program Michigan, *A Guide to the Wolverine State* (New York: Oxford University Press, 1941), p. 225.

31. Robinson and Keller, *"Up Ship!"*, pp. 105–09.

32. Reminiscences of Ernest G. Liebold, Oral History Section, vol. 9, ch. 15, p. 754. Ford Motor Company Archives.

33. Letter, Hepburn Walker, Jr. to H. C. Meyer, June 16, 1987.

34. *Ford News*, Dearborn, Mich., Oct. 23, 1926.

35. Ibid., Nov. 1, 1926.

36. Michigan, *Guide*, p. 225.

37. Letter, Lehmann to Litchfield, Nov. 28, 1925. Goodyear Archives, 4. Aviation A-122.

38. Robinson, *Giants*, pp. 223–26.

39. *New York Times*, Oct. 13, 1928, p. 2.

40. *Detroit News*, Oct. 19, 1928.

CHAPTER 6: The Political Origins of the Airship *Graf Zeppelin*

1. *New York Times*, Oct. 13–16, 1924, passim. The quotation is from ibid., Oct. 18, 1924.

2. Germany. Auswärtiges Amt. Politisches Archiv.; hereafter cited as AA: Büro Reichsminister 135/7. Akten betreffend Luftschiffahrt, 31/10/23-22/5/26 [Documents Relating to Airship Aviation], No. 561, Oct. 16, 1924.

3. AA. IIF-Luft 64/1. Luftschiffexpeditionen allgemein, mit Zeppelin-Eckener-Spende. [Airship Expeditions Generally, with Data on Zeppelin-Fund-Campaign] U.S. National Archives, microfilm T120, roll 4037, frame L022659/60, Blücher to Nord, Oct. 18, 1924. Hereafter cited as AA, T120, roll 4037 and frame number.

4. Archives of the Royal Swedish Academy of Sciences, Ur Konl. Vetenskapsakademiens Protokoll 1924:2, pp. 179–82. Hereafter cited as Archives, Swedish Academy. On Sven Hedin, see Eric Wennerholm, *Sven Hedin*, trans. by W. Müller (Wiesbaden: F. A. Brockhaus, 1978), passim; George Kish, *To the Heart of Asia: The Life of Sven Hedin* (Ann Arbor: University of Michigan Press, 1984).

5. AA, T120, roll 4037, no. L022655/6 to 67/70, Oct. 31, 1924, and Nov. 11, 1924.

6. Archives, Swedish Academy, Protokoll 1924:2, pp. 254–61.

7. AA, T120, roll 4037, nos. L022655-57, Rosenberg to Berlin, Nov. 13, 1924.

8. Ibid., nos. L022658-71, Nord to Rosenberg, Nov. 14 and 16, 1924.

9. Ibid., no. L022672/5, Blücher to Nord, Nov. 20, 1924.

10. Ibid., nos. L022677-82, Berlin to Stockholm Embassy, Nov. 27 to Dec. 1, 1924.

11. Archives, Swedish Academy, Protokoll 1925:1, pp. 191–201.

12. On Nansen and Aeroarctic, see W. L. G. Joerg, ed., *Problems of Polar Research* (New York: American Geographical Society, 1928), pp. 2, 418–25; E. E. Reynolds, *Nansen* (London: Penguin Books, 1949), passim.

13. AA, File IIF Luft. Aeroarktis. Rosenberg to foreign office, Berlin, Nov. 29, 1924. Hereafter cited as IIF Luft.

14. *8 Uhr Abendblatt* [Berlin], Dec. 5, 1924.

15. AA, IIF Luft. Eckener to Foreign Office, Dec. 8, 1924; Berlin to Rosenberg, Dec. 15, 1924.

16. Ibid., Rosenberg to Berlin, Dec. 31, 1924.

17. AA, T120, roll 4037, nos. L0226859-90. Blücher to Berlin, Dec. 30, 1924; Schulz-Sponholz notation to files, Jan. 3, 1925, on phone conversation with Eckener; Eckener to Berlin, Jan. 3, 1925.

18. On Eckener's visit to Stockholm, see Sven Hedin, *50 Jahre Deutschland* [Fifty Years of Association with Germany] (Leipzig: F. A. Brockhaus, 1938), pp. 214–216. Much of the following account is based on fourteen letters of Hugo Eckener to Sven Hedin, Apr. 1, 1925 to July 23, 1926. Copies provided by Library of the Royal Swedish Academy of Sciences.

19. AA, IIF Luft, protocol submitted by Prof. Kohlschütter (Aeroarctic) to foreign office, Berlin, Feb. 25, 1925.

20. AA, IIF Luft, documents between Mar. 11 and July 17, 1925, culminating in text of agreement reached at Berlin ministry of transport. See also AA, T120, roll 4037, nos. L022697-731, Jan. 20 to Aug. 12, 1925.

21. Eckener to Hedin, June 16, 1925.

22. Eckener to Hedin, July 6, 1925.

23. *Vossische Zeitung* [Berlin], Aug. 22, 1925. The three quotations are from a report by the U.S. naval attaché in Berlin from the *Münchener-Augsburger-Abendzeitung* [sic], Aug. 22, 1925. Report of Attaché dated Berlin, Oct. 21, 1925. National Archives, ONI Serial no. 362, file no. 401/900.

24. AA, IIF Luft, Kohlschütter to German ministry of transport, July 31 and Aug. 3, 1925.

25. Ibid., copy of letter, Hedin to Eckener, Aug. 5, 1925.

26. Ibid., Blücher to Berlin, Aug. 12, 1925.

27. Ibid., Blücher to Berlin, on conference with Hedin, Sept. 10, 1925.

28. Ibid., memoranda, Kohlschütter to foreign office, Dec. 28, 1925.

29. Ibid., Embassy Stockholm to Berlin, Nov. 26, 1926, report on article in *Svenska Morgon-bladet*, Nov. 24, 1926.

30. Ibid., Nansen's recapitulation to Foreign Minister Stresemann, Apr. 14, 1928.

31. Ibid., Apr. 14, 1928.

32. Ibid., memoranda to file by Schulz-Sponholz, Apr. 25 and Aug. 17, 1928.

33. Ibid., conference report and agreement, Nov. 30, 1928.

34. Ibid., copy of letter, Eckener to Bruns, Sept. 2, 1930.

35. L. Kohl-Larsen, *Die Arktisfahrt des "Graf Zeppelin"* [The Arctic Flight of the *Graf Zeppelin*] (Berlin: Union Deutsche Verlagsgesellschaft, 1931). See also J. Gordon Vaeth, "Exploring the Arctic," in C. V. Glines, *Polar Aviation* (New York: Franklin Watts, Inc., 1969), pp. 77–87.

CHAPTER 7: France Perceives the Zeppelins

1. In general see Eckener, *Im Zeppelin*; von Schiller, *Zeppelin*; Robinson, *Giants*; and Peter W. Brooks, *Historic Airships* (London: Hugh Evelyn, 1973).

2. Henry Cord Meyer, "Popular Perceptions of Modern Technology: The Case of the Airship, 1919–1939," ms. article. After 1934 the intermediate range seaplane became a serious competitor to the airship; see "Tomorrow's Airplane," *Fortune* vol. 18 (1938–39), p. 53 ff.

3. Jean Du Plessis de Grenédan, *Les grands dirigeables dans la paix et dans la guerre* (Paris: Plon-Nourrit, 1925); Commandant de Brossard, *Lachez tout!* (Paris: 1956); *Icare* 46 (Été-automne 1968), pp. 44–47; Robinson, *Giants*, pp. 329, 344–49.

4. Foreign Ministry to sixteen French embassies and legations, Mar. 10, 1925, Ministère des Affaires Étrangères. Série Allemagne, 1923–26 (Aviation), fasc. 554. Hereafter cited as Archives, with dates.

5. Telegram, Tirard to Foreign Office, Oct. 3, 1928, Archives, 1928. fasc. 555.

6. Dispatch, Saugon (Consul at Hamburg), Oct. 16, 1928 and reports from Stockholm, Bern, and Stuttgart, Archives, 1928, fasc. 555.

7. De Margerie to Paris, Nov. 26, 1928, Archives, 1928. fasc. 555. Concurrently French companies and German Lufthansa were cooperating effectively in a continental air service pool. Heinz M. Wronsky (Lufthansa general agent in Paris, 1926–30), 15 Jahre Luftfahrt, ms. 1938, pp. 19–28.

8. Minister of War to Foreign Ministry, Mar. 2, 1929; Sous-Secrétaire des Postes to Foreign Minister, Mar. 22, 1929; Morain (Consul at Patras), Mar. 27, 1929; all in Ministère des Affaires Étrangères, Série Allemagne: Graf Zeppelin, 1921–29. Fasc. 559. Hereafter cited as Archives-Zeppelin.

9. German Ambassador, Paris, to Foreign Ministry, Apr. 16, 1929, plus enclosures; Consul-General at Tangiers to Foreign Minister, Apr. 24, 1929; Pralon to Foreign Ministry, May 2, 1929; M. Schneider to Foreign Minister, Apr. 25, 1929; notes, Service Technique d'Aéronautique to Foreign Minister, Apr. 30; May 8, 1929. All in Archives-Zeppelin.

10. Minister of War to Foreign Minister, May 10, 11, 1929, Archives-Zeppelin.

11. Foreign Minister to Minister of War, May 13, 1929; Minister of War to Foreign Minister, May 14, 1929, Archives-Zeppelin.

12. *Ostpreussische Zeitung* of May 16, 1929, as quoted in report from Sous-Direction des Unions Internationales, May 27, 1929, Archives-Zeppelin.

13. Letter, H. M. Wronsky to H. C. Meyer, Aug. 8, 1974.

14. Foreign Minister's report to ministers of war, navy, and air on German press reactions, May 23, 1929, Archives-Zeppelin.

15. Telegram to Foreign Minister, May 18, 1929, Archives-Zeppelin.

16. Dispatch to Foreign Minister, Aug. 31, 1929; dispatch to Foreign Ministry, Sept. 7, 1929, Archives-Zeppelin.

17. *L'Action Française*, Apr. 27, 1930; *Le Temps*, Apr. 28, 1930; *L'Humanité*, Apr. 27, 1930.

18. Jean Gérard Fleury, *La ligne de Mermoz, Guillamet, Saint Exupéry et de leurs compagnons de l'épopée* (Paris, Gallimard, 1939), p. 219. Note also: Joseph Kessel, *Mermoz* (Paris, Gallimard, 1938); Geroges Clerc, *L'Aéropostale* (Paris, Éditions de Minuit, 1955).

19. The French Ministry Archives from 1930 onward are in process of reorganization and reclassification; references are thus restricted to identification of senders, recipients, and dates of transmission. Dispatch to Foreign Minister, June 1, 1930 and Dec. 5, 1930, Archives.

20. Fleury, *La ligne de Mermoz*, pp. 241–43.

21. Campana (Sous-Directeur des Unions) on conversations with German Ambassador Clodius, Apr. 28, 1931; Politisches Archiv des Auswärtigen Amts, Bonn, II-F Luft, Band 100/4, Ambassador Hoesch to German Foreign Minister, May 1, 1931; ibid., report on attack by Bouilloux Lafont, Director of Aéropostale by "Open Letter" to Dr. Hugo Eckener, May 26, 1931; letter, Kammerer (Brazil) to Président du Conseil, Oct. 13, 1932; French Commercial Attaché, Rio, to Minister of Commerce, June 24, 1933. All in Archives.

22. Gentile (Ambassador at Montevideo) to Foreign Ministry, June 29, 1934; also, Gaussen (Consul at Valparaiso) to Foreign Ministry, June 26, 1930; Ambassador to Argentina to Foreign Ministry, Jan. 10, 1931; Saulnier de Saint Jouan (Ambassador to Peru) to Foreign Ministry, June 25, 1934. All in Archives.

23. Foreign Minister to Minister of Air, Apr. 20, 1933; and response, May 10, 1933; report of Saint Léger to Foreign Minister, June 30, 1933; Kammerer (Ambassador to Brazil) to Foreign Minister, Jan, 21, 1933 and June 3, 1933; letter to Foreign Minister, June 17, 1933; letter to Minister of Interior, Oct. 18, 1933; report, Minister of Interior to Foreign Minister, Nov. 22, 1933. All in Archives.

24. Procès-Verbale, Réunion de Décembre 6, 1933; Survol de France du Graf Zeppelin, Archives.

25. Air Attaché Poincaré, Berlin, to Minister of Air, Dec. 12, 1933, Archives; note photographs of *Graf* at German-Brazilian May Day rallies, 1936 and 1937 in Kurt Peter Karfeld, ed., *Kapitän Hans von Schiller's Zeppelinbuch* (Leipzig, Bibliographisches Institut, 1938), p. 193.

26. See *50 Jahre Dornier* (Mainz, Krauskopf-Flugwelt-Verlag, 1965), pp. 45–76.

27. Wronsky ms., p. 33.

28. French Foreign Minister to German Ambassador, Paris, Aug. 16, 1934, Archives.

29. Notation for Secretary General of Foreign Office, Feb. 14, 1936; Minister of Navy to Minister of Air, July 11, 1936, Archives.

30. Notes on interministerial meeting of Feb. 27, 1936; dispatch to Minister of Air, Mar. 23, 1937, Archives.

31. Germany tried to maintain her bid for transatlantic air supremacy; but American refusal to supply helium for the sistership of the *Hindenburg* ended the airship era, except for continuing training flights in Germany during the summer of 1939.

32. Interview, H. C. Meyer with V. H. Pavlecka (Metalclad airship designer), Irvine, Calif., Jan. 8, 1975. On Eckener's identification with German nationalism, note the lavish volume published by the Luftschiffbau Zeppelin, Hans Hildebrandt, ed., *Zeppelin-Denkmal für das deutsche Volk* (Stuttgart: Germania, 1925).

CHAPTER 8: Politics, Personality, and Technology

1. Dr. Hugo Eckener was lionized by the German and international press in innumerable accounts and articles. Thor Nielsen, *The Zeppelin Story* (London: Allan Wingate, 1955) draws an Eckener portrait of unrelieved adulation. Eckener's memoirs, *Im Zeppelin*, place him comfortably in resolution of circumstances. The most recent studies are Italiaander's beautifully illustrated book, *Eckener*, and his biography of the famous captain, *Ein Deutscher*. Lord Thomson's reputation for ambition and recklessness comes largely from Janes Leasor, *The Millionth Chance* (New York: Reynal, 1957), and N. S. Norway, *Slide Rule . . .* (New York: Morrow, 1954). The design and engineering vicissitudes of the government airship *R 101* appear in unfavorably bold relief in J. E. Morpurgo, *Barnes Wallis* (London: Longman Group, 1972). Wallis was the designer of the Vickers-built competing airship *R 100*. Robin Higham, *The British Rigid Airship, 1908–1931* (London: G. T. Foulis and Co., 1961), pp. 260–324, places Thomson and the airship program in more judicious perspective. For the most recent and authoritative account of Thomson, see Sir Peter G. Masefield, *To Ride the Storm. The Story of the Airship R 101* (London: William Kimber, 1982).

2. On airship history in general, see the standard work of Robinson, *Giants*. Note Patrick Abbot, *Airship: The Story of R-34* (New York: Scribner, 1973).

3. See Paul Ditzel, "The Day Los Angeles Had Zeppelin Fever," *Westways*, vol. 61 Mar. 1969, pp. 2–5; Apr. 1969, pp. 24–26.

4. Eckener, *Im Zeppelin*, pp. 5–23; data from family letters in possession of Mrs. Lotte Simon (née Eckener); interviews with Mrs. Lotte Simon, Capt. Hans von Schiller (airship commander under Eckener), and Mr. F. W. von Meister, U.S. representative of the German Zeppelin interests, 1929–38. On the British see C. B. Thomson, *Smaranda*, (New York: George H. Doran Co., 1926)—a thinly veiled novelized rendition of his journals and notes between 1912 and 1921; Liddell Hart, "Lord Thomson," *Fortnightly Review* 134 (1930), pp. 577–83; Masefield, *Storm*, pp. 14–15; letter P. G. Masefield to H. C. Meyer, Feb. 8, 1977.

5. Robinson, *Giants*, passim; Eckener, *Im Zeppelin*, pp. 25–79.

6. Higham, *British Rigid Airship*, pp. 124–300, passim; Masefield, *Storm*, pp. 15–38.

7. Thomson address in House of Lords, May 21, 1924.

8. Eckener, *Im Zeppelin*, pp. 80–94. Under sponsorship of his firm was published a sumptuous commemorative volume, *Zeppelin Denkmal für das deutsche Volk* (Stuttgart: Germania, 1925).

9. Eckener, *Im Zeppelin*, p. 95.

10. Conclusions based on perusal of 134 documents in Bundesarchiv, Koblenz, R431/737.

11. Various items of correspondence in possession of Mrs. Lotte Simon; Eckener, *Im Zeppelin*, pp. 98–105.

12. Higham, *British Rigid Airship*, pp. 267–279.

13. C. B. Thomson, *Air Facts and Problems* (London: J. Murray, 1927).

14. My conclusions from three documents in the Public Record Office: AIR 5, 984, No. 9091, memo from DAD to S.9, 28/3/30; AIR 5, 984, No. 9091, minutes of staff conference in air ministry, 2/9/30; AIR 5, 984, No. 2914, Bullock to Dowding, 13/8/1930. These materials were not available to Higham in 1959–60. See also Masefield, *Storm*, pp. 47–296, passim.

15. PRO, AIR 2, 364, No. 3034, AMSR to SoS Air, 14/7/30. Marginal reply by Lord Thomson. Full details are in Masefield, *Storm*, pp. 297–430.

16. Thomson, *Air Facts*, pp. 15, 59, 192.

17. Quoted in Leasor, *Millionth Chance*, p. 2.

CHAPTER 9: F. W. (Willy) von Meister

1. Possibly von Meister rearranged, and may have embellished, the details of his comments in order to make the stories more dramatic. On family background see the memoirs of his mother, Leila von Meister, *Gathered Yesterdays* (London: Geoffrey Bles, 1963), pp. 13–43; on the imperial godfathers, pp. 86–87.

2. See Paul Ditzel, "The Day Los Angeles Had Zeppelin Fever," *Westways*, vol. 61 (Mar. 1969), pp. 2–5; (Apr. 1969), pp. 24–26.

3. See *New York Times*, Apr. 1 and 3, 1936; editorial, Apr. 4, 1936.

4. See H. C. Meyer, "How Philatelists Kept the Zeppelin Flying," *American Philatelist*, Sept. 1979, pp. 796–98.

CHAPTER 10: Problems of Helium and Spy Flights

1. On helium and airships in general, see Garland Fulton, "Helium Through W. W.'s I and II," *Naval Engineers Journal* (Oct. 1965) pp. 733–38.

2. For examples, see Ferdinand C. W. Käsmann, "Die Dinosaurier der Luftfahrt," [The Dinosaurs of Aviation], *Damals. Zeitschrift für Geschichtliches Wissen* vol. 16 (1984), p. 114; Peter Kleinhans, ed., *Die grossen Zeppeline. Die Geschichte des Luftschiffbaus* [The Great Zeppelins: The History of Airship Construction] (Düsseldorf: VDI Verlag, 1985), p. 222; Italiaander, *Ein Deutscher*, p. 351. The author often heard such views in Germany, even in discussions with otherwise expert airship enthusiasts.

3. Dick and Robinson, *Golden Age*, pp. 98–100.

4. "Vierjahresplan zur Entwicklung der deutschen Luftschiffahrt" [Four-year Plan for Development of German Airship Service], DZR Study, Oct. 1936. Author's collection, originally from archives of Max Schorn, Friedrichshafen.

5. Addendum to above document: Ausbau-Möglichkeiten der Welt-Luftschiffahrt [Expansion Possibilities for Worldwide Airship Service], ibid.

6. Sitzung vom 20. November 1936 betreffend Luftschiffragen [Meeting of November 20, 1936 on Airship Matters], Reichsminister der Luftfahrt, LB 1, 2 Nr. 6046/36, Confidential. To the Foreign Office, Dec. 14, 1936. Political Archives, Foreign Office, Bonn.

7. Letter to Mrs. Eckener, May 12, 1937. Eckener Papers, Mrs. Lotte Simon, Konstanz.

8. *New York Times*, May 13, 1937.

9. Italiaander, *Ein Deutscher*, p. 354

10. Reich Interior Ministry *Schnellbrief*, May 13, 1937. Bundesarchiv, Koblenz. R 43 II, no. 697b.

11. [The Future of] American Commercial Airships. Memorandum prepared by Staff of American Zeppelin Transport, Inc., New York, Aug. 1, 1937. From von Meister files. Author's collection. Pp. 11–12.

12. For a full account of the various shades of opinion and steps in making helium available to Germany and others, see Michael D. Reagan, "The Helium Controversy," in Harold Stein, ed., *American Civil-Military Decisions* (Birmingham, Ala.: University of Alabama Press, 1963), pp. 45–48.

13. AZT memorandum, Aug. 1. 1937, pp. 11–19.

14. Reagan, "Helium Controversy," pp. 48–52.

15. Hugh Wilson to State Department, National Archives. State Department File CA 811.659. Helium 120.

16. Thomas A. Knowles to Joseph C. Green, State Department, May 17, 1938. National Archives. State Department File CA 811.659. Helium Confidential.

17. Harold L. Ickes, *The Secret Diary . . .* , 3 vols., vol. 2, *The Inside Struggle, 1936–1939* (New York: Simon and Schuster, 1954), p. 399.

18. Minutes, DZR Board of Directors meeting, Berlin, June 17, 1938; memorandum, Issel and von Schiller to Air Minister Göring, July 9, 1938, on behalf of DZR. Copies of both documents in von Schiller Archives.

19. For a detailed account, see Sean S. Swords, *Technical History of the Beginnings of Radar* (London: Peter Peregrinus, 1986), pp. 91–101.

20. "Mit *Graf Zeppelin II* auf Funkhorch—und Funkortungsfahrt," [With *Graf Zeppelin II* On Signals Research and Bearings Flights] in Albert Sammt, *Mein Leben für den Zeppelin* [My Life for the Zeppelin] (Kinderdorf Wahlwies: Verlag Pestalozzi, 1981), pp. 157–58.

21. Ibid., p. 158.

22. Ibid., p. 167.

23. Breuning, "Mit Graf Zeppelin II," pp. 158–63.

24. Ibid., p. 159.

25. Ronald W. Clark, *Tizard* (Cambridge, Mass.: M.I.T. Press, 1965), p. 129.

26. Swords, *Technical History*, pp. 82–91; Clark, *Tizard*, pp. 128–92.

27. British Air Ministry History. The Second World War, 1939–1945. Royal Air Force. *Signals*. vol. 4. Radar in Raid Reporting (1950), pp. 58–59. Public Record Office, Kew London, Air 41/12, 9114. Farmer sighting reported in Aleyn R. Jordan, *LZ 130-The Last of the Great Zeppelins* (Gorleston-on-Sea: McClellan Printing, 1977), p. 86. Letter, Capt. Heinrich Bauer to H. C. Meyer, Nov. 14, 1975.

28. Personnel roster in official log of the flight, Aug. 2-4, 1939. Luftschiffbau Zeppelin Archives. Interview with Heinrich Bauer, Immenstaad, July 11, 1975; letter, Nov. 14, 1975.

29. Breuning, "Mit Graf Zeppelin II," pp. 167–68.

30. Interview with Erich Hillgardt, Friedrichshafen, July 9, 1973.

31. Official log. Luftschiff "Graf Zeppelin" LZ 130. 18. Versicherungsfahrt. 24. Fahrt. 2–4 8. 1939, pp. 15–16. Luftschiffbau Zeppelin Archives, Friedrichshafen.

32. Interview with Heinrich Bauer, Immenstaad, July 11, 1975.

33. See Trevor Armbrister, *A Matter of Accountability. The True Story of the Pueblo Affair* (New York: Coward-McCann, Inc., 1970), pp. 20–21.

34. Letter, Air Commodore H. A. Probert [Ministry of Defense. Air Historical Branch (RAF)] to H. C. Meyer, Sept. 9, 1980. Interview with Air Commodore Probert and J. P. McDonald [Air Historical Branch] at Lacon House, London, May 13, 1981.

35. For facsimile reproductions and other data about these accounts, see Jordan, *LZ 130*, pp. 81–84.

36. Air Marshal Sir Walter Pretty, quoted in Derek Wood and Derek Dempster, *The Narrow Margin* . . . (New York: McGraw-Hill, 1961), p. 18. Both the Jordan and Wood-Dempster accounts were published before Breuning's article and thus contain some fancies and inaccuracies.

37. The author is indebted to correspondence with Luftwaffe Col. Günter Baum (ret.), Prof. R. V. Jones, Mr. Brian Johnson [author of *The Secret War* (London: BBC, 1978)], Dr. Alfred Price, Dr. E. G. Bowen, Mr. R. Hanbury Brown, Mr. Sidney Jefferson, and Mrs. Nancy Wilkins.

38. Breuning, "Mit Graf Zeppelin II," p. 168–69.

39. Sammt, *Ein Leben*, pp. 171–73. DZR Directors' Report, July 31, 1939; authenticated typed copy studied in the airship history archive of the late Alfred F. Weber, Karlsruhe.

40. Breuning, "Mit Graf Zeppelin II," p. 169.

41. DZR, Annual Report of Flight Operations, 1939; authenticated typed copy studied in the airship history archives of the late Alfred F. Weber.

42. Authenticated typed copies of correspondence about the future of the airship and of the protocol of Göring's visit, studied in the airship archives of the late Alfred F. Weber.

43. Interview with Heinrich Bauer, Immenstaad, July 11, 1975.

CONCLUSION

1. Interview with Heinrich Bauer, Immenstaad, July 11, 1975.

2. Interview with Hans von Schiller, Tübingen, July 14, 1975.

3. Bauer interview, Immenstaad, July 11, 1975.

4. Von Schiller interview as above. He was not actually present at the moment of the incident, being already aloft with the *Graf Zeppelin*; but he relayed this comment from accounts of several other Zeppelin personnel then present at the scene.

5. For a full account, see Robinson and Keller, *"Up Ship!"*, passim.

6. See D. Jung, B. Wenzel, A. Abendroth, *Die Schiffe und Boote der deutschen Seeflieger, 1912–1972* [The Airships and Flying Boats of German Naval Aviators] (Stuttgart: Motorbuch Verlag, 1977), p. 45.

7. See Countryman, *R 100 in Canada*, passim.

8. Dick and Robinson, *Golden Age*, pp. 48–78, 111–37.

9. Ibid., pp. 161–71.

10. Douglas Miller, *You Can't Do Business with Hitler* (Boston: Little, Brown, and Co., 1941).

11. On the role of concentration camp inmates and slave labor in Friedrichshafen during World War II, see Burger, "Rüstungsindustrie," part 2, Heft 2, pp. 52–87.

12. Italiaander, *Eckener*, p. 126.

13. Italiaander, *Ein Deutscher*, plate 23.

14. Interview with Rear Adm. Scott E. Peck (ret.), San Diego, Calif., May 20, 1973.

Selected Annotated Bibliography

This list indicates the major works consulted in preparation of the preceding essays. They constitute an indispensable continuation to the archival sources and other scattered documentation. Otherwise the other documentary sources, records of interviews with airship survivors, magazine articles, and lesser works are cited in the appropriate footnotes. Brief annotations indicate the significance of each work and note important collections of illustrations.

Allen, Hugh. *The House of Goodyear*. Cleveland, Ohio: Corday and Gross Co., 1943. A court history of the famous tire and rubber company.

Allen, Hugh. *The Story of the Airship*. Akron, Ohio: Goodyear Tire and Rubber Co., 1931. Published and updated annually from 1925 to the mid-1930s in furtherance of Goodyear's lighter-than-air products.

Beaubois, Henry. *Airships: An Illustrated History*. M. and A. Kelly, trans. London: Macdonald and Jane's, 1974. A spectacularly beautiful work on every aspect of lighter-than-air craft. Authoritative.

Brooks, Peter W. *Historic Airships*. London: Hugh Evelyn, 1973. Fifteen gorgeous color plates together with some other illustrations and much expert statistical and historical detail.

Chamberlain, Geoffrey. *Airships-Cardington. A History of Cardington Airship Station and Its Role in World Airship Development*. Lavenham, Suffolk: Terrence Dalton, Ltd., 1984. A standard work profusely illustrated.

Clausberg, Karl. *Zeppelin. Die Geschichte eines unwahrscheinlichen Erfolges* [Zeppelin. The Story of an Improbable Success]. Munich: Schirmer-Mosel, 1979. The most important work to date on Count Zeppelin and his airships in the sociopsychological context of their times, 1900–17. Hundreds of illustrations from the Luftschiffbau Zeppelin Archives.

Collier, Basil. *The Airship: A History*. London: Hart-Davis McGibbon, 1974. Useful.

Colsman, Alfred. *Luftschiff Voraus! Arbeit und Erleben am Werke Zeppelins* [Airship Forward! Work and Experience in the Zeppelin Enterprise]. Stuttgart: Deutsche Verlags-Anstalt, 1933. Indispensable record of Count Zeppelin's business manager and a general director of the Zeppelin Company until 1929.

Countryman, Barry. *R 100 in Canada*. Erin, Ont.: Boston Mills Press, 1982. Authoritative work on the building of R 100 at Howden, together with full account of the airship's trip to Canada in July 1930. Profusely illustrated.

Cuneo, John R. *Winged Mars*. I. *The German Air Weapon, 1870–1914*. Harrisburg, Pa.: Military Service Publ. Co., 1942. Written before publication of the authoritative German Luftwaffe study of 1943, but still very competent in light of sources then available.

Dehio, Ludwig. *Germany and World Politics in the Twentieth Century*. D. Pevsner trans. New York: Norton, 1967. Thoughtful essays on imperial German militarism and power politics.

Deighton, Len. *Airshipwreck*. London: J. Cape, 1978. Informed commentary and spectacular photographs of airship smash-ups.

Dick, Harold G., and Robinson, Douglas H. *The Golden Age of the Great Passenger Airships* Graf Zeppelin *and* Hindenburg. Washington, D.C. and London: Smithsonian Institution Press, 1985. Dick was Goodyear representative in Friedrichshafen in 1936–38; Robinson is dean of American airship historians. Together they make this the standard work on the subject. Many illustrations and expert technical drawings. Translated crew manual of the German Zeppelin Transport Company, 1935–40.

Eckener, Hugo. *Graf Zeppelin. Sein Leben nach eigenen Aufzeichnungen und persönlichen Erinnerungen* [Count Zeppelin: An Account of His Life Based on His Own Notations and Personal Recollections of the Author]. Stuttgart: J. G. Cotta'sche Buchhandlung Nachfolger, 1938. A sound, adulatory study. There is a scarce English translation by Leigh Farrell, *Count Zeppelin: The Man and His Work*. London: Massie Publ. Co., Ltd., 1938.

Eckener, Hugo. *Im Zeppelin über Länder und Meere. Erlebnisse und Erinnerungen* [By Zeppelin over Lands and Seas: Experiences and Memories]. Flensburg: Verlagshaus Christian Wolff, 1949. Douglas H. Robinson's excellent translation, *My Zeppelins*. London: Putnam, 1958, is almost unobtainable.

Fischer, Fritz. *Germany's Aims in the First World War*. New York: W. W. Norton, 1967. Standard, very critical analysis of German militarism and grasp for world political power in 1914–18.

Germany. Luftwaffe. Militärgeschichtliches Forschungsamt, eds., *Die Militärluftfahrt bis zum Beginn des Weltkrieges 1914*. [Military Aviation to the Beginning of the World War 1914], 2d ed., 3 vols. Frankfurt: Mittler and Sohn, 1965–66.

Haaland, Dorothea. *Der Luftschiffbau Schütte-Lanz Mannheim-Rheinau (1909–1925)* [The Airship Construction Works of Schütte-Lanz at Mannheim-Rheinau]. Mannheim: Institut für Landeskunde und Regionalforschung, 1987. Excellent business history of the Schütte-Lanz company.

Haddow, George W., and Gross, Peter M. *The German Giants; The Story of the R-planes, 1914–1919*. London: Putnam, 1962. Illustrated account of Count Zeppelin's foray into airplane building.

Hardesty, Frederick S. *Key to the Development of the Super-Airship, Schütte-Lanz, Mannheim-Rheinau, Germany, 1909–1930*. New York: priv. publ., 1930. A one-sided compilation of documents and data by Johann Schütte's American lawyer.

Hartcup, Guy. *The Achievement of the Airship: A History of the Development of Rigid, Semi-rigid, and Non-rigid Airships*. London: David and Charles, 1974. Scholarly, detailed, readable. Illustrations and diagrams. The best of all the general books from England.

Heiss, Friedrich. *Das Zeppelinbuch*. Berlin: Volk und Reich Verlag, 1936. Now a rare book, but a superb example of airship technological history (profuse illustrations and plaintive commentary) warped to Nazi political purposes.

Higham, Robin. *The British Rigid Airship, 1908–1931: A Study in Weapons Policy.* London: G. T. Foulis and Co., Ltd., 1961. Detailed, scholarly, authoritative.

Hildebrandt, Hans. *Zeppelin-Denkmal für das deutsche Volk* [Zeppelin Memorial for the German People]. Stuttgart: Germania, 1925. Technologically authoritative, profusely illustrated, sumptuously published volume issued by Luftschiffbau Zeppelin to commemorate the old Count and help lay a foundation for fundraising to build LZ 127, the later *Graf Zeppelin.*

Italiaander, Rolf. *Ein Deutscher namens Eckener. Luftschiffpionier und Friedenspolitiker. Vom Kaiserreich bis in die Bundesrepublik* [A German Named Eckener: Airship Pioneer and Peace Politician. From the Imperial Reich to the Federal Republic]. Konstanz: Verlag Friedr. Stadler, 1981. Admiring biography, the best to date.

Italiaander, Rolf. *Ferdinand Graf von Zeppelin. Reitergeneral-Diplomat-Luftschiffpionier. Bilder und Dokumente* [Count Zeppelin: Cavalry General, Diplomat, Airship Pioneer. Pictures and Documents]. Konstanz: Verlag Friedr. Stadler, 1980. Superb illustrations, excellent documents; both can be studied for more than the captions reveal.

Italiaander, Rolf. *Hugo Eckener. Ein moderner Columbus. Die Weltgeltung der Zeppelin-Luftschiffahrt in Bildern und Dokumenten* [A Modern Columbus: The Worldwide Impact of the Airship in Pictures and Documents]. Konstanz: Verlag Friedr. Stadler, 1979. Superb illustrations of German airships and various personalities worldwide. Unabashedly admiring of both the airship and its commander.

Jackson, Robert. *Airships in Peace and War.* London: Cassell, 1971. Useful.

Jordan, Aleyn R. *LZ 130—The Last of the Great Zeppelins.* Gorleston-on-Sea, McClellan Printing, 1977. Primarily devoted to stamp collecting, but some data on the notorious spy flight of Aug. 2–4, 1939. Many illustrations, mostly philatelic.

Kitchen, Martin. *The German Officer Corps, 1890–1914.* Oxford: Clarendon Press, 1968. Good for understanding the military world in which Count Zeppelin operated.

Kleinhans, Peter, ed. *Die Grossen Zeppeline. Die Geschichte des Luftschiffbaus* [The Great Zeppelins: A History of Rigid Airship Construction]. Düsseldorf: VDI Verlag, 1985. A thorough engineering approach with excellent illustrations and diagrams.

Knäusel, Hans G. *LZ 1. Der erste Zeppelin. Geschichte einer Idee 1874–1908* [The First Zeppelin: The History of an Idea, 1874–1908]. Bonn: Kirschbaum Verlag, 1985. An absolutely superb book of scholarly text, documentation, illustrations, and diagrams.

Knäusel, Hans G. *Zeppelin and the United States of America: An Important Episode in German-American Relations.* Friedrichshafen: Luftschiffbau Zeppelin, 1981. Very readable, useful compilation of text, documents, and illustrations.

Kohl-Larsen, L. *Die Arktisfahrt des "Graf Zeppelin."* [The Arctic Flight of the *Graf Zeppelin*]. Berlin: Union Deutsche Verlagsgesellschaft, 1931. The official account of the zeppelin polar flight. Illustrations.

Leasor, James. *The Millionth Chance.* New York: Reynal, 1957. Journalistic exaggeration of British politics and technology concerning R 101.

Lehmann, Ernst A. *Auf Luftpatrouille und Weltfahrt. Erlebnisse eines Zeppelinführers in Krieg und Frieden* [On Air Reconnaissance and World Flights: Experiences of a Zeppelin Captain in War and Peace]. Leipzig: Schmidt and Günther, 1936. Significant account from one of the four zeppelin captains who have left memoirs.

Litchfield, Paul W. and Allen, Hugh. *Why Has America No Rigid Airships?* Cleveland, Ohio: Corday and Gross Co., 1945. The last effort of Goodyear to capitalize on its construction experience to resurrect the rigid airship as a viable transport competitor with the flying boat or airplane.

Masefield, Sir Peter G. *To Ride the Storm: The Story of Airship R 101*. London: William Kimber, 1982. The standard work, nicely illustrated.

Morpurgo, J. E. *Barnes Wallis: A Biography*. London: Longman, 1972. Readable account of Sir Barnes's entire life and work, based on family papers and on materials from the Vickers archives subsequently destroyed. Basic for R 100. Some illustrations.

Morrow, John Howard, Jr. *Building German Airpower, 1909–1914*. Knoxville: University of Tennessee Press, 1976. Nicely illustrated, basic study derived from German sources.

Neilsen, Thor. *The Zeppelin Story: The Life of Hugo Eckener*. P. Chambers trans. London: Allen Wingate, 1955. Journalist interacting with aged Eckener's somewhat flawed memory.

Norway, Nevil Shute. *Slide Rule: The Autobiography of an Engineer*. New York: Morrow, 1959. Superb account of this engineer-novelist's life up to 1939. With Morpurgo and Countryman, the best source on building R 100 though very critical of R 101.

Payne, Lee. *Lighter Than Air: An Illustrated History of the Airship*. South Brunswick, N.J.: A. S. Barnes, 1977. Carefully researched with many illustrations.

Robinson, Douglas H. *Giants in the Sky: A History of the Rigid Airship*. Seattle: University of Washington Press, 1973. The standard work on the subject by America's best rigid airship historian. Readable and well-illustrated. Indispensable statistical tables.

Robinson, Douglas H. *LZ 129 The Hindenburg: Famous Aircraft Series*. New York: Arco Publishing Co. Inc., 1964. Authoritative account, fully illustrated. Translation of Hugo Eckener's LZ 120 *Bodensee* flight manual appended.

Robinson, Douglas H. *The Zeppelin in Combat: A History of the German Naval Airship Division, 1912–1918*. Henley-on-Thames: G. T. Foulis and Co., 1971. The standard book.

Robinson, Douglas H., and Keller, Charles L. *"Up Ship!": U.S. Navy Rigid Airships, 1919–1935*. Annapolis, Md.: Naval Institute Press, 1982. Another standard work, fully illustrated.

Rosendahl, Charles E. *"Up Ship!"*. New York: Dodd, Mead, and Co., 1931. America's best known airshipman writes enthusiastically about his profession.

Rosendahl, Charles E. *What About the Airship? The Challenge to the United States*. New York: Charles Scribner's Sons, 1938. A fervent plea to revive the airship for defense and commerce in America.

Sammt, Albert. *Mein Leben für den Zeppelin* [My Life for the Zeppelin]. Kinderdorf Wahlwies: Verlag Pestalozzi, 1981. Enthusiastic reminiscences, nicely illustrated, by the last zeppelin captain. Basic chapter on LZ 130 spy flight.

Schiller, Hans von. *Zeppelin. Wegbereiter des Weltluftverkehrs* [Zeppelin: The Pioneer of Worldwide Air Travel]. Bad Godesberg: Kirschbaum Verlag, 1967. More scholarly reminiscences and research of another zeppelin captain. Illustrations and statistical appendices. Revised, enlarged edition by Hans G. Knäusel, ed. Hans von Schiller. *Zeppelin-Aufbruch ins 20. Jahrhundert* [Zeppelin-Take-off into the 20th Century]. Bonn: Kirschbaum Verlag, 1988. Many new illustrations added.

Smith, Richard K. *The Airships* Akron *and* Macon: *Flying Aircraft Carriers of the U.S. Navy*. Annapolis, Md.: U.S. Naval Institute, 1965. The standard work, fully illustrated.

Toland, John. *Ships in the Sky: The Story of the Great Dirigibles*. New York: Henry Holt and Co., 1957. Reads like a novel. For the disaster buff. Inevitable inaccuracies.

Vaeth, J. Gordon. *Graf Zeppelin: The Adventures of an Aerial Globetrotter*. New York: Harpers, 1958. Written with assistance by F. W. (Willy) von Meister. Interesting and reliable, with appealing travel illustrations.

Lord Ventry and Kolesnik, Eugene M. *Airship Saga: The History of the Airship Seen Through the Eyes of the Men Who Developed and Built Them*. Poole, Dorset: Blandford Press, 1982. Nice documentary and reprint collection by one of Britain's venerable men of lighter-than-air enthusiasm.

Vissering, Harry. *Zeppelin: The Story of a Great Achievement*. Chicago: priv. publ., 1922. Rare book by the man who initiated German-American airship cooperation.

Zeppelin Metallwerke GmbH, ed. *Zeppelin. Ein bedeutendes Kapitel aus der Geschichte der Luftfahrt* [Zeppelin: A Significant Chapter in the History of Aviation]. Friedrichshafen: Zeppelin-Druckerei, 1983. The fifth edition of this company history, lavishly illustrated; also account of industrial development since 1945.

Index

Note: Page numbers in italics indicate references to captions.